Monarchy to **Republic**

George Winterton

Monarchy to Republic

Australian

Republican

Government

With a new Introduction

Melbourne

OXFORD UNIVERSITY PRESS

Oxford Auckland New York

OXFORD UNIVERSITY PRESS AUSTRALIA

Oxford New York Toronto
Delhi Bombay Calcutta Madras Karachi
Kuala Lumpur Singapore Hong Kong Tokyo
Nairobi Dar es Salaam Cape Town
Melbourne Auckland Madrid
and associated companies in
Berlin Ibadan

OXFORD is a trade mark of Oxford University Press

National Library of Australia
Cataloguing-in-Publication data:

Winterton, George, 1946–
  Monarchy to Republic

  New ed.
  Bibliography
  Includes index

  ISBN 0 19 554562 1.

  1. Australia. Constitution. 2. Republicanism -
  Australia. 3. Australia - Politics and government -
  1990– . I. Title.

321.860994

Printed by Kyodo Printing, Singapore.
Published by Oxford University Press,
253 Normanby Road, South Melbourne, Australia

Contents

Preface

Since this book first appeared in 1986, Australian republicanism has moved from the periphery to the centre of our national agenda. With the report of the Republic Advisory Committee in October 1993, public debate has at last begun on the constitutional and governmental implications of abolishing the monarchy and establishing an Australian republic. Those issues are the subject of this book.

The opportunity has been taken to update the original work, reproduced here in its original form, including pagination, by adding a substantial new Introduction outlining developments since 1986, including public opinion polls on the monarchy vs republic issue published since those included in Table 1.1 (page 13), and substantially updating the discussion of constitutional amendment. The Introduction generally addresses topics in the order in which they appear in the book. A new consolidated Bibliography has also been substituted for the original. (The new Introduction has not been indexed.)

With the exception of the 'legal' chapter dealing with constitutional amendment (chapter 8 — see below), the seven years since the book was published have seen few developments which would warrant substantial revision. The evolution of the republican debate over that time has reflected the principal arguments 'for' and 'against' outlined in chapters 2 and 9, and the chapters examining the role of the Crown in Australian government and comparing various forms of republican government require relatively little revision. However, were the book to be written now, reference would, of course, be made to recent literature.

The book concentrates upon the practical constitutional and governmental issues involved in establishing an Australian republic. Discussion of the nature of republican government, and the reasons why Australians might choose it, is followed by a comparison of the principal competing models: essentially an American or French-style executive presidency, or a parliamentary republic along the lines adopted in India, Ireland, Italy and Germany. These models of republican government — especially the American — are compared with the present operation of Australian government, a topic which includes a detailed review of the functions and powers, including the 'reserve powers', of the Governor-General and State governors. Consideration is also given to the implementation of republican government at the State level, and to some practical questions arising upon conversion to a republic, such as retention of the erstwhile prerogative powers, privileges and immunities of the Crown, and a future president's powers, tenure, appointment and removal. After discussing the constitutional issues involved in amending the Commonwealth and State constitutions to achieve a republic, a concluding chapter reviews some of the arguments adopted by those favouring retention of the monarchy.

Chapter 8 (Constitutional amendment') was written before the enactment of the Australia Act 1986 (U.K. and C'th) on 3 March 1986, which severed residual imperial constitutional links (excluding the monarchy). However, with one exception, its principal elements had long been known, and were foreshadowed in the text. The Act empowered the Australian States to enact legislation repugnant to imperial legislation applying therein by paramount force, Privy Council appeals were terminated, and the British Government may no longer advise the Queen on State matters. The Queen now acts in State matters on the advice of the State Government tendered to her directly by its Premier. Consequently, the obsolete devices for effecting imperial control of colonial legislation — disallowance of State laws, and mandatory reservation of State Bills — have been abolished. State governors are now empowered to exercise all the Queen's powers in respect of the States, except the appointment and removal of the governors themselves.

The one provision previously unreported and, hence, not foreshadowed in the original text was section 1 of the Australia Acts 1986, which provides that henceforth 'No Act of the Parliament of the United Kingdom ... shall extend ... to the Commonwealth, to a State or to a Territory' as part of its law. Chapter 8 reviews the position as at the end of 1985 and, therefore, examines the possible role of the British Parliament in amending the Commonwealth and State constitutions. This discussion no longer has practical relevance but may remain of interest to constitutional historians.

I wish to express my gratitude to those who have assisted in the completion of both the original work and this revised edition. For assistance in the original work: to Keven Booker, who read portions of the original manuscript and made helpful suggestions for improvement; to James Thomson, George P. Smith and Geoffrey Lindell, who assisted in various ways; to the ever-helpful staff of the Law Library of the University of New South Wales, especially Cheryl White, for their assistance in obtaining material; and to Paddy Baldwin, Coralie Lowe and Kerrie Stone for typing the manuscript.

I owe a special debt of gratitude to my parents for assistance in translating the cantonal/*Land* constitutions of Switzerland, West Germany and Austria for the original work; to Coralie Lowe and Carol Mallos for their devoted secretarial assistance over many years; and last, but certainly not least, to my wife, Ros, and my family, for their constant encouragement and support.

George Winterton
December 1993

Introduction

The seven years since this book was published have seen a transformation in the republic debate — not that the two are causally related. In 1986, public opinion polls were showing republican support at around 30% (and monarchical support at about 60%), essentially unchanged for at least a decade. Although republican parties and groups existed in most State capitals, they were disunited, with small membership, and appeared condemned to the periphery of Australian politics for the foreseeable future.

Seven years later, the prospect of an Australian republic appears much rosier. As was seen in the opinion polls up to 1986 (chapter 1, p.14), while republican support appeared to fluctuate quite widely between contemporaneous polls, the pro-monarchy vote has been more stable, although considerably less so than in the earlier period. In other words, the pro-republic vote has varied among contemporaneous polls mainly in relation to the 'undecideds', rather than the monarchists.

Table I-1 (page I-2) suggests present republican support at around 45% to 50%, with monarchical support varying between 35% and 40%. Thus the past seven years have seen an apparent shift from monarchical to republican support of between 15% and 20%.

However, the history of Australian republicanism cautions against republican euphoria that their time has finally come. Republican support has risen and fallen before, and an allegedly 'inevitable' event seems never to arrive. The republican efflorescence of the early 1990s may yet prove to be just another swing of the monarchical pendulum, although there are reasons to doubt it. After all, never before has republicanism been espoused as a high priority by the Commonwealth government, especially the Prime Minister personally.

The Australian events which appear to have contributed significantly to the transformation in republican support are the resolution of the Australian Labor Party National Conference in June 1991 that Australia should become a republic by 2001; the formation of the Australian Republican Movement the following month; and Prime Minister Keating's adoption of the republican cause, especially in his election policy speech of 24 February 1993, followed by the establishment of a Republic Advisory Committee on 28 April 1993 to outline 'the minimum constitutional changes necessary' to achieve a viable federal republic of Australia.

Table I.1 National Opinion Polls on Monarchy v. Republic 1985–93[1]

Date	Pro-Monarchy (%)	Pro-Republic (%)	Undecided (%)
1984–85 (National Social Science Survey)[a]	59	41	–
April 1985 (Quadrant)[b]	62	30	8
March 1986 (Frank Small & Associates)[f]	45	39	16
1986–87 (National Social Science Survey)[a]	59	40	–
October 1987 (Newspoll)[b]	64	21	15
1987–88 (National Social Science Survey)[a]	59	41	–
1990 (National Social Science Survey)[a]	58	41	–
June 1991 (Newspoll)[b]	52	34	14
February 1992 (Saulwick)[c]	39	57	4
February-March 1992 (Newspoll)[b]	40	44	16
April 1992 (Saulwick)[c]	42	56	3
May 1992 (Newspoll)[b]	45	41	14
March 1993 (Saulwick)[c]	30	66	4
April 1993 (Newspoll)[b]	35	46	19
April 1993 (AGB McNair)[b]	36	45	19
April 1993 (Morgan)[d]	38	52	10
April 1993 (Morgan)[e]	35	56	9
July 1993 (Newspoll)[b]	36	46	18
July1993 (Saulwick)[c]	34	62	4
September 1993 (Newspoll)[b]	44	39	17
October 1993 (AGB McNair)[b]	42	48	10
November 1993 (Newspoll)[b]	44	39	17
December 1993 (Morgan)[d]	48	44	8

Question asked:

a   Should Australia retain the Queen as head of state or become a republic? ('Definitely' and 'probably' figures combined in table.)

b   Should Australia become a republic?

c   Should Australia remain a monarchy within the (British) Commonwealth, become a republic within the Commonwealth, or a republic outside the Commonwealth? (Republic figure in table is a composite of the latter two answers.)

d   Should Australia remain a monarchy or become a republic with an elected president?

e   Should Australia remain a monarchy or become a republic by the year 2001?

f   Question not specified.

(That Committee presented its report on 5 October 1993.) No doubt also significant were the personal difficulties of the Royal Family in 1992.

By early 1993, republican momentum briefly appeared almost unstoppable, with several State Liberal Party leaders and even the New South Wales Legislative Assembly declaring that an Australian republic was 'inevitable'.[2]

However, the republic's opponents were far from conceding defeat, and the establishment of Australians for Constitutional Monarchy in June

1992 ensured that the campaign to establish an Australian republic would be long and hard-fought. That struggle, essentially for the minds, if not hearts, of Liberal Party supporters, may well falter and even fail more than once before a republic is finally achieved. But, although it may not occur by 2001, there remains little doubt that Australia will eventually become a republic.

ARGUMENTS FOR AND AGAINST

The principal argument of Australian republicans remains the 'national identity' argument discussed in chapter 2 (pp.18–22). Australia is undoubtedly as independent of foreign control as any other country, but it is not constitutionally free-standing. Our head of state is primarily the head of state of another nation, a fact brought into sharper focus by the prospect of the monarch opening the 2000 Olympic Games in Sydney. The monarch is, of course, legally monarch of Australia, and has been since 1931[3] (recognized in the Royal Style and Title since 1953), but will the world not find it curious that, as they will perceive it, the Queen of the United Kingdom will be opening the Olympics in Australia, even though Australia has long ceased to be a British dependency?

Monarchists will respond: so what if foreign athletes and television viewers are confused about Australia's constitutional arrangements? Does it matter that we may be perplexed by the details of the American electoral college, Indian presidential elections or Swiss referenda?

Of course not. But such analogies miss the point, which is not whether domestic constitutional intricacies are understood by foreigners (indeed locals rarely understand them), or whether Asians prefer republics or monarchies (another monarchist red-herring), but rather whether we are perceived as a grown-up, free-standing, self-assured nation comfortable with its place in the world, culturally and geographically, as well as economically.

In an influential article published in *Quadrant* in September 1991, John Hirst focussed on the internal aspects of 'national identity', arguing that the present system's 'chief failing is that the Queen in Australia has lost her civic personality'[4] In a subsequent comment, Hirst tied together the constitutional and cultural consequences of our continuing dependence on the United Kingdom to supply our head of state:

What angers [republicans] are assertions that Australia must continue to rely on another country to operate one part of its constitution. This confession of incapacity works against the development in this country of a strong civic culture . . . . The monarchist claim that Australia is now completely independent of Britain is not true — we depend on Britain maintaining its monarchy. If Britain became a republic, our constitution would be unworkable once the Governor-General retired or died.[5]

Interestingly, the negative aspects of the institution of monarchy itself continue to exert little influence in the republican debate. Thus, surprisingly few commentators appear to object to the notion of hereditary succession to public office or to the religious and sexual discrimination inherent in the rules of succession to the throne,[6]notwithstanding its incompatibility with modern domestic and international civil rights notions. It is, for example, difficult to reconcile the requirement that the monarch 'shall join in communion with the Church of England'[7] with the prohibition of any religious test 'as a qualification for any office or public trust under the Commonwealth' in section 116 of the Constitution.[8] (However, section 116 is not contravened as a matter of law because it presumably must be read compatibly with covering clause 2 of the Constitution which effectively incorporates the British law on succession to the throne.)

The fact that one hears so few echoes of Paine or Jefferson (see chapter 2, pp.22–23) in the current republican debate probably reflects the general irrelevance of the monarchy in Australia. Even the monarchists focus their attention on the supposedly desirable features of the office of Governor-General, rather than the monarch herself; the principal monarchist arguments purport to be constitutional, rather than sentimental.[9] There appear to be few true 'royalists' among the ranks of the leading 'monarchist' defenders of the status quo. Thus, even the Executive Director of Australians for Constitutional Monarchy recently remarked that

[b]ecause the monarch actually lives 20,000 km away we are spared some of [the monarchy's] less desirable trappings such as Grenadier Guards and the class system.[10]

As foreshadowed in this work, the principal monarchist argument has been: Why change an institution which works well?; 'If it ain't broke, don't fix it' (chapter 9, pp.143–144). Defenders of the current system maintain that the present balance of power between the Governor-General and the government works well and cannot possibly be duplicated in a republic because it depends upon factors which would inevitably be absent there: appointment and removal of the Governor-General by the Prime Minister, nominally via the monarch, who supposedly acts as a filter; legally undefined reserve powers constrained by convention; and behind it all the supposed 'moral authority of the Crown' which the Governor-General must not injure by rash or controversial action. A leading defender of the present system recently remarked:

I rather like the existing system where the prime minister and the governor-general can each sack each other in the event of misconduct on the part of either. That's the genius of the existing system.[11]

Yet Governors-General, such as Sir Zelman Cowen and Sir John Kerr, have criticised the Governor-General's present insecurity of tenure, noting that the Governor-General could be a more effective constitutional guardian if tenure of office were more secure.[12]

Since the essential features of the present relationship between the Governor-General and the government could be preserved in a republic by careful constitutional engineering (as the experience of nations like Ireland, Israel and Germany attests), monarchists are effectively forced to argue that the present balance between Governor-General and government represents perfection incarnate and could not possibly be improved upon, making the slightest change unacceptable. Thus they attack the republic for increasing Prime Ministerial power one moment, and for increasing the head of state's powers the next.

Their position was admirably expressed recently by Lloyd Waddy, the Convenor of Australians for Constitutional Monarchy:

Any change means giving *more or less* power to the executive (and Prime Minister) and *either* change is wholly undesirable.[13]

One of the difficulties with this position is that it implies that Australia must retain the present system *forever*, since the argument would be just as plausible in two hundred years' time as it is now.

Since our present system is not really a monarchy but a 'Governor-Generalate' (chapter 2, p.28), it is difficult to defend the present system on the ground that constitutional monarchy is a desirable system of government. So the beneficial effects of monarchy in Belgium, Spain and Thailand, for instance, are strictly irrelevant.

The most plausible argument for retaining the monarchy is its sentimental role as a living, personal symbol of Australia's links with Britain. A leading republican recently asked rhetorically:

When [the Queen] visits Perth and proceeds down the Terrace, do the people lining the route say 'there goes Australia'?[14]

No, perhaps not. But for many admirers of the Queen and lovers of the monarchy that is the essential point. Legally, she may be Queen of *Australia*, but to them she represents our link with Britain, the land of their forebears, the land from which our laws and institutions largely derive and, above all, a nation and people of which they still desire to feel part. This sentiment will no doubt diminish over time in view of the changing composition of the Australian community and the diverging geo-political and economic interests of the two countries.

Finally, there are echoes in the current debate of the *in terrorem* arguments of O'Connell and Hailsham (chapter 1, p.4; chapter 9, pp.143, 144), threatening instability and dictatorship if Australia cuts its links with the monarchy. The former Chief Justice of Australia, Sir Harry Gibbs, has been the principal exponent of this spectre. He warns that a republican head of state would inevitably be politically partial and, since the current constitutional conventions would not apply if the monarchy were abolished, dictatorship could result:

If we had a president who was given the present powers of the governor-general, the strength of the president and the prime minister in conjunction could well enable them, if they were minded to do so, to proceed on the road to dictatorship.[15]

With respect, this is a curious argument. Why on earth would the President and the Prime Minister collaborate — especially to establish a dictatorship? When popular election of the President is proposed, monarchists usually express concern at possible dissension between President and Prime Minister, which is far more likely than subversive collaboration. Moreover, the republican Constitution is likely to provide for the continued application of the constitutional conventions formerly constraining the exercise of power by the Governor-General, as South Africa's did when it became a republic in 1961.[16] Ultimately, however, Sir Harry's warning is a somewhat overstated argument for caution in framing a republican Constitution, rather than an argument for retaining the monarchy. The experience of many successful democratic republics with responsible government, such as Germany, Ireland, Israel and Austria, demonstrates that the threat of dictatorship is a mirage, which insults the Australian people by pretending that our democracy and liberty depend upon the Crown, instead of the tolerance and good sense of the Australian people. As one commentator has aptly noted, '[f]orecasting that a republic could usher in a dictatorship . . . is substituting paranoia for common sense.'[17]

THE CROWN'S RESERVE POWERS[18]

Two State Governors have recently averted constitutional crises by threatening to exercise reserve powers.

When Queensland Premier Sir Joh Bjelke-Petersen, who had apparently lost the support of his parliamentary colleagues, proposed to resign in order to reconstitute his government in November 1987, Governor Sir Walter Campbell warned that he would not necessarily re-commission him, and requested the Premier to discuss the proposed reconstitution with his entire Ministry before any Ministers were dismissed. This vice-regal action helped to defuse a tense political stalemate, ultimately leading to the Premier's resignation six days later.[19]

Likewise, in June 1989, when Tasmanian Premier Robin Gray, who had lost a (constructive) vote of no-confidence in the House at its first meeting after a general election, informally sounded-out Governor Sir Phillip Bennett on the possibility of obtaining another dissolution, the Governor rightly made it clear that if such advice were to be formally tendered, it would be refused.[20]

In each case, the threatened exercise of a reserve power restrained improper behaviour by a headstrong chief Minister, giving the reserve powers something of a fillip. Moreover, both Premiers were from the Conservative side of politics, which should help to reassure Labor that the reserve powers are not stacked against it, as many thought after the Whitlam dismissal of 1975. Rather, they protect constitutional democracy against improper behaviour by either side of politics. Labor's acceptance of reserve powers could have an important effect on its attitude towards the powers and method of selection of a republican head of state.

SYSTEM OF GOVERNMENT

The essential contours of an Australian republic are already reasonably foreseeable, even at this early stage of the debate. Although, of course, a theoretical possibility, there is no real prospect of our present parliamentary executive — 'Washminster'[21] — system of government being abandoned in favour of one based upon a constitutional separation of the legislative and executive branches of government along American lines. This is for reasons both of principle and pragmatism.

The principled reason is that, whatever the virtues in abstract of the American system, and however attractive it might appear if we were starting from scratch, the critical point is that we are *not* starting from scratch. Australia has had almost a century and a half of experience in operating a 'Westminster' system and adapting it to changing needs. Our political culture, shaped by that system, is very different from America's, especially in its strong party system. Transplanting a different system of government into an alien political and cultural environment could not only prove extremely disruptive, but experience elsewhere suggests that if we imported the American system into Australia, the result would not be the *American* system, but instead some hybrid mutant which might well combine the worst features of both systems (chapter 5, pp.101–102).

The difficulty the Keating government faced in securing passage of its 1993–94 budget Bills in the Senate illustrates how disruptive the American system could prove if it were transplanted to Australia.

Like the Carter Administration sixteen years earlier, the Clinton Administration demonstrated yet again that deadlock and stalemate in the passage of vital legislation in Congress is a serious defect of the American system, even when the same party controls the White House and both houses of Congress. What prevents the system breaking down is the weakness of party discipline. The very characteristic which frustrates a President, like Clinton, whose party nominally controls Congress, enables Presidents like Reagan and Bush, whose party never controlled both houses and usually controlled neither, to secure the passage of legislation with the support of Opposition party legislators.

But such flexibility is foreclosed by the rigid discipline of Australian political parties. There is little prospect of a Labor government enticing Liberal or National Party senators to support its Bills unless those parties as a whole agree to support the legislation. If the American system were introduced here, party discipline could prevent the passage of Bills in *both* houses, making government extremely difficult, since the deadlock could not be broken by early parliamentary or presidential elections. Party discipline would probably soften in time under such a system, as it did in the United States where it was considerably stronger in the past, but the system could prove difficult to operate in the meantime.

Moreover, one feature of the American system, often overlooked by those advocating its transplantation elsewhere, is that the legal separation of legislative and executive powers and functions means that there is a sphere of executive action immune from legislative control.[22] Do we really want such executive independence in Australia, especially since we lack a constitutional Bill of Rights, which is at least able to control the exercise of executive power in the United States?[23]

In this respect it is interesting to note that Sir Owen Dixon, whose logical mind made him a somewhat extreme proponent of the separation of powers,[24] believed that the structure of the Commonwealth Constitution, modelled as it was on the American, logically supported a similarly strict separation of powers doctrine. In a speech delivered in New York in December 1942, while he was Australian Minister to the United States, he remarked:

I can . . . discover no reason in the form or text of the Australian constitution why the legal implications of the separation of powers should not have been as full as they have been in [the United States]. That is to say, on the face of the constitution there is nothing to displace the inference to which its form gives rise, I mean the inference that the judicature shall receive nothing but judicial power, the executive nothing but executive power, and the parliament nothing but legislative power, and the further inference that no organ other than the judiciary might exercise judicial power, none but the parliament, legislative power and none but the executive, executive power.'[25]

Dixon was, of course, well aware that responsible government operated in Australia, but thought that system 'not incompatible with a strict legal separation of powers between the three organs of government'.[26] The reason, as he aptly put it, was that 'Power . . . is one thing. The political means of controlling its exercise is another'.[27]

That may theoretically be so, but what Dixon apparently overlooked was the pervasive influence in our system of the British doctrine of parliamentary supremacy over the executive, of which responsible government is an application and means for enforcement. As Justice Jacobs of the High Court noted in 1975:

The Parliament is sovereign over the Executive and whatever is within the competence of the Executive under s.61 [of the Constitution] . . . may be the subject of legislation of the Australian Parliament.[28]

This vital principle is an essential attribute of the rule of law in Australia and should not lightly be abandoned. Indeed, a republican Constitution ought to entrench it more firmly by expressly subjecting the exercise of executive power to the over-riding control of Parliament, not only politically through ministerial accountability to Parliament, but *legally* as well, through subjection to legislation.[29]

The pragmatic reason for retaining our present system of government is that public opinion polls show general satisfaction with it,[30] and preference in the order of about 75% for retaining it, as compared with 25% for moving to a presidential executive.[31] Even if one may be sceptical regarding public understanding of the American system, let alone our own, these figures suggest that a fundamental change to our system of government would encounter stiff resistance.

Nor is there the slightest evidence that the French system — a hybrid presidential/parliamentary executive combination — holds any appeal for Australians. Apart from the serious detraction from parliamentary democracy inherent in articles 34 and 37 of the French Constitution (chapter 4, p.65), the threat of a President of one party having to govern with a Prime Minister of another (foreshadowed in chapter 4, pp.63–65), has come to pass. On two occasions, Conservative victory in National Assembly elections during the presidency of François Mitterrand has forced a 'cohabitation' between a Socialist President and a Gaullist (RPR) Premier: Jacques Chirac (March 1986–May 1988) and Edouard Balladur (from March 1993). This 'collaboration' was admittedly less traumatic than had been feared,[32] but was certainly not a feature one would wish to emulate in Australia.

Hence, it is virtually certain that the present system of government will be retained. Though, of course, far from perfect, little of the necessary reform requires constitutional alteration. Mostly it requires political will-power.

THE PRESIDENT: SELECTION AND POWERS

Presidential selection, removal and power are all clearly interrelated, for the greater the President's claim to popular legitimacy and the more secure his or her tenure, the greater is the risk of intervention in government, whether by the exercise of power or through public comment on governmental affairs.[33] So, if our present system of government is to be retained, and not drift into some presidential/parliamentary hybrid, in general the stronger the President's independent power base, the more necessary will it be to define and limit the powers vested in that office.

The present Constitution vests power in the Governor-General in general terms, on the understanding that its exercise will be governed by constitutional conventions.[34] As Sir Harry Gibbs noted recently:

The Constitution gives to the governor-general powers which, on their face, are the powers of a dictator . . . . The exercise of these powers is controlled not by laws, but by constitutional conventions.[35]

Since those conventions developed under the monarchy, and constrain the exercise of power by the monarch and her representatives, they might lose their raison d'être and cease to apply if the monarchy were abolished.[36] So a republican Constitution could not simply continue the present position of conferring power upon the head of state in general terms and rely upon convention to confine it. It would be necessary either to provide expressly that the conventions should continue to apply, preferably as non-justiciable, evolving, conventions[37] or to codify the present conventions, wholly or partially, and convert them into law.[38] Power could also be conferred upon Parliament to regulate the exercise of presidential power, the passage of such legislation preferably requiring a two-thirds majority in each house to ensure bipartisan support. It would also be wise to provide expressly that 'ordinary' executive powers (i.e., those on which ministerial advice *must* ultimately be followed) are exercisable only in accordance with ministerial advice, thereby making clear on the face of the Constitution which powers are reserve powers (i.e., those on which ministerial advice can be departed from) and which are not.

The most appropriate method of presidential selection is election by a two-thirds majority of each house of the Commonwealth Parliament, or perhaps a two-thirds majority of a joint sitting of both houses. However, recent public opinion polls reveal strong public support (about 80%) for popular election of a republican head of state, as compared with election by Parliament or appointment by the government.[39] This presumably reflects a widespread popular desire to take the choice of head of state out of the hands of politicians and exercise it themselves, making it one of the features of a republic for which people express considerable enthusiasm. This is understandable, but the practicalities of popular election suggest that the public has not really thought the matter through, for there are also strong indications that many people would prefer a non-politician as head of state. Yet, unless strong counter-measures were adopted, popular election would almost guarantee the election of a politician. Nevertheless, if public opinion remains steadfast, popular election may have to be conceded, perhaps with careful provision being made to minimise the role of political parties in presidential election campaigns and for the public funding of campaigns by nominees selected by an independent and impartial presidential nominating commission.

Political neutrality is one of the concerns expressed regarding a popularly-elected head of state. More important, perhaps, are fears that such a head of state will feel empowered by a 'popular mandate' to exercise reserve powers, unconstrained by the conventions hitherto governing the monarch and her appointive representatives. The experience of the popularly-elected presidencies of Ireland and Austria belies such notions, but they are nevertheless likely to be influential in the republican debate, and to lead to demands that the reserve powers be codified, and thereby narrowly confined.[40]

Although the boundaries of the reserve powers are contentious, bipartisan agreement on most issues should not prove impossible. The exception, however, is resolution of the appropriate consequence of Senate blockage of Supply, on which the political parties seem as divided today as they were in 1975.

If it is necessary to resolve the controversy over the appropriate consequence of the Senate blocking Supply before a republic can be achieved, the advent of a republic will be long delayed. This is a serious dilemma for republicans, but a solution of sorts may lie in leaving the present uncertainty unresolved and introducing carefully tailored constitutional checks and balances to discourage the exercise of the reserve powers to force a dissolution of Parliament and to dismiss the government in the event that the Senate blocks Supply.[41]

THE STATES

As noted in chapter 8 (pp.141–142), the monarchy can be abolished at both Commonwealth and State level pursuant to section 128 of the Constitution. Such a referendum would require approval by the normal referendum majorities specified in that section — a national majority and a majority of electors in four States. Contrary to the argument of some monarchists,[42] the penultimate paragraph of section 128 would not apply to such an amendment.[43] As Quick and Garran made clear in 1901, the word 'thereto' in that paragraph refers not to all proposed amendments affecting a State, but only to those affecting the provisions of the Constitution in relation to one or more of the three matters specifically mentioned in that paragraph.[44] Abolition of the monarchy is not one of these.

Consequently, a referendum could be carried even though the electors in two States were strongly opposed to it. Such opposition is little cause for concern insofar as abolition of the monarchy at the national level is concerned — indeed it is a result clearly envisaged by section 128, which did not require the approval of electors in all States — but there is greater cause for concern regarding abolition of the monarchy at State level. Why, it might be asked, should the electors of other States be able to dictate the form of a State's government against the wishes of the electors of that State?

This is, of course, a political, not a legal issue, and if it be considered politically appropriate that the monarchy be abolished at the State level of government only when the people of that State wish to do so, two alternatives arise.

The referendum to abolish the monarchy and establish an Australian republic could be deferred until approval in all States was considered certain. But even that would not be foolproof, for what if the public opinion polls proved incorrect, and the electors in one or more States voted against the proposal? The only recourse would be for the government to advise the Governor-General not to consent to the Constitution Alteration Bill approved by the electors pursuant to section 128.[45] That would hardly be a satisfactory basis for the continuation of the monarchy, and would place the monarch in the embarrassing position of continuing as head of state of a nation whose people had rejected her by substantial majorities.

So if it be considered politically inappropriate for the monarchy to be abolished in a State over the objection of its people, the only alternative is to allow the electors of each State to determine when the monarchy should be removed from that State's government. The Bill put to a national referendum could provide that the monarch should cease to be head of state in those States where a majority of electors had approved the Bill, but remain in those States where they had not.[46]

The result could be an Australian republican Commonwealth which included one or two States in which the Governor continued to represent the Queen (see chapter 6, pp.103–105). Many commentators have condemned such a polity as a bizarre monstrosity;[47] Sir Zelman Cowen, for example, considers the concept 'absurd'.[48]

However, although undoubtedly incongruous, a federation combining monarchical and republican governments would not be unprecedented: apart from Imperial Germany, a monarchical federation which included three city republics, the thirteen States of Malaysia (a federation headed by an elected hereditary State ruler) include nine sultanates and four 'republican' States headed by a Governor.[49]

Moreover, it would not be the first time Australia's federal system had demonstrated somewhat bizarre features, with far greater practical consequences than a Commonwealth republic/State monarchy combination. For example, from 1931 to 1986 Australia was an independent nation comprising six British colonies,[50] and from 1975 to 1986 Australia effectively had two highest courts in matters of State law; whether a case ended in the High Court or the Privy Council depended upon the appellant's whim — or assessment of the prospect of success.[51]

Indeed, these incongruities arguably included the very anomaly raised by State retention of the monarchy, namely a different head of state at the Commonwealth and State levels, for while the same person has always been head of state throughout Australia, some (not including the present writer) would argue that the monarch of the United Kingdom remained head of the States until 1986, whereas there has been a legally separate monarch of Australia since 1953, if not 1931,[52] which would mean that the Commonwealth and the States had legally different heads of state for 33, if not 55, years. And yet, somehow, life went on, and the country prospered.

In any case, in the unlikely event that the Queen would be willing to serve as head of state of only one or two States, this anomaly would probably be only temporary, and would be unlikely to persist as long as some of the earlier absurdities. Whether it is seen as a colossal monstrosity or merely a relatively inconsequential anomaly really depends upon one's view of the Crown's role. If one perceives it in quasi-mystical terms, the incongruity of simultaneous allegiance to Commonwealth republic and State Crown appears gross and prohibitive, but if it be viewed more prosaically as simply a form of government, it would seem to make little practical difference whether a State Governor formally represents the State's absentee monarch or its people — as Sir Ninian Stephen has remarked, the Governor-General presently 'represent[s] . . . the Australian nation to the people of Australia'.[53]

As already noted, in view of section 128's requirement of approval by the electors in only four States, it would not prove feasible to defer the advent of a republic until the electors in all States had approved it. Hence, although the subsistence of State monarchies under a Commonwealth republic would certainly be far from ideal, ultimately it may be the only realistic alternative to compelling an unwilling State to abandon its link with the Crown, which could make the advent of a republic a source of serious contention.

Of course, monarchists would respond that there is another realistic alternative, namely to retain the status quo. Indeed the report of the Republic Advisory Committee outlining the various options relating to the selection and powers of a republican head of state and the alternatives regarding abolition of the monarchy at State level has led to the argument that the republic should be abandoned on the ground that the issue is too complex. Moreover, the beauty of this argument is that it would apply in perpetuity, for the task will not become any easier in the future.

Thus, as soon as the report appeared, the Convenor of Australians for Constitutional Monarchy claimed that it demonstrated that a republic would be a 'revolutionary change' of great complexity, which 'could destroy the Australian federation'.[54] That organisation's Executive Director went even further, alleging that:

becoming a republic could threaten the whole basis of our Federation and mean tearing up the whole Constitution.[55]

This dramatic assertion was amplified in an opinion issued some weeks later. Written by Sir Harry Gibbs and endorsed by the Legal Committee of 'Australians for Constitutional Monarchy', it argued that the existence of the monarchy was a fundamental term of the 'federal compact', so that abolition of the monarchy without the consent of all parties to the compact (i.e., the people or Parliaments of all the States) would constitute a fundamental breach of that compact, supposedly severing the federation:

The peoples of the Australian colonies agreed to unite under the Crown. It was the *basis of the union* that Australia should be a constitutional monarchy. The Crown was the *tie that bound* the peoples of the various colonies in the union. If that bond is severed, a new basis of union must be found, or in other words, there must be *a new agreement to unite.*[56]

With respect, there is no justification for the notion that the existence of the monarchy is a fundamental term of federation or the 'federal compact'. It was the Commonwealth of Australia Constitution Act 1900 (U.K.) which bound the people of the various colonies together, not the Crown. Indeed, as has already been noted,[57] it is arguable that the Commonwealth and the States did not share the same Crown from 1953 to 1986, and perhaps even from 1931 to 1986,[58] so did the 'federal compact' dissolve without anyone noticing it in 1931?

The preamble to the Commonwealth of Australia Constitution Act 1900 (U.K.) recites that the people of the various colonies had agreed to unite in 'one indissoluble Federal Commonwealth under the Crown of the United Kingdom of Great Britain and Ireland' (which, technically, no longer exists[59] and, in any event, no longer reigns over Australia, whose monarch has long been the 'Queen of Australia'). But the preamble is not a prescriptive part of the statute, and it is legally and politically significant that the prescriptive provision, covering clause 3 (section 3 of the Commonwealth of Australia Constitution Act) merely authorises the Queen to declare that the people of the various colonies 'shall be united in a Federal Commonwealth under the name of the Commonwealth of Australia'. No further reference is made to the Crown. The monarchy was indeed an important feature in the Constitution but, like all other elements thereof, it was inherently subject to alteration pursuant to section 128. Moreover, it was not one of the matters especially entrenched in what was originally the final paragraph of that section.[60]

In other words, the existence of the monarchy was merely an ordinary provision of the federal compact, inherently subject to alteration pursuant to section 128, not a fundamental term.

CONSTITUTIONAL AMENDMENT

The most significant event since chapter 8 of this book was written was the enactment of the Australia Acts, which came into effect on 3 March 1986. The Act was enacted in virtually identical terms by both the Commonwealth Parliament, acting at the request of all States pursuant to section 51(xxxviii) of the Constitution, and the British Parliament, acting at the request and with the consent of the Commonwealth Parliament (itself acting at the request and with the consent of all States), pursuant to section 4 of the Statute of Westminster 1931 (U.K.).

The Australia Act has had considerable impact on the constitutional issues involved in becoming a republic, in some respects facilitating that development, in others making it more difficult.

The relevant effects of the Australia Act can be stated briefly:

1. The authority of the British Parliament to legislate for Australia, even with the latter's request and consent, was terminated,[61] thereby eliminating British legislation as one means of amending the Constitution's covering clauses. The discussion of British legislation in chapter 8 of this work (pp.127–132, 138–140) is, therefore, obsolete, and is of interest only as a matter of constitutional history.

2. State Parliaments were empowered to enact legislation repugnant to British legislation applying in the State by paramount force.[62] Accordingly, British legislation which before 1986 may have entrenched the monarchy at State level[63] can now be amended or repealed by State Parliaments. The Act itself repealed all legislation requiring a State Governor to reserve Bills for the Queen's assent.[64]

3. It might be argued that the monarchy is entrenched at State level by section 7(1) of the Australia Act, which provides that 'Her Majesty's representative in each State shall be the Governor'. However, this provision is too unspecific to be regarded as entrenching the monarchy. It clearly is predicated on the Queen remaining head of state, providing, in effect, that while there is a Queen of Australia, her representative shall be the Governor.[65] But it does not entrench the position of the Queen. The other provisions of section 7 are expressed even more allusively: when read carefully, they are seen not to ensure that the Queen has any 'powers and functions in respect of the State', not even the power to appoint and dismiss the Governor which is not, itself, conferred by section 7(3).

So if the monarchy were abolished pursuant to section 128, the factual basis on which section 7 is predicated would vanish and the provision would effectively cease to operate, though it would be appropriate to repeal it for essentially cosmetic reasons. This could be accomplished pursuant to either section 15(1) or section 15(3) of the Australia Act.

However, section 7 probably presents a greater barrier to unilateral abolition of the monarchy (at State level) by a State because such State legislation would be inconsistent with section 7(1) of the Australia Act while it still operated, the monarchy not having already been abolished pursuant to section 128.[66] Hence, State abolition of the monarchy (at State level) would require the amendment or repeal of section 7 of the Australia Act, which is beyond its legislative capacity.[67]

4. The Australia Act 1986 (U.K.) has removed some of the uncertainty regarding amendment or repeal of the covering clauses.

This work argues that the preamble and covering clauses do not entrench the monarchy (chapter 8, pp.123–124) and that, even if they do, they can be amended or repealed pursuant to section 128 of the Constitution (pp.124–126),[68] and presumably would be, at least for cosmetic reasons.

However, although the latter opinion was very much a minority viewpoint,[69] the Australia Act 1986 (U.K.) has opened two further avenues for amendment or repeal of the preamble and covering clauses because, as British legislation applying in Australia by paramount force, they have the same constitutional status as the Statute of Westminster 1931 (U.K.) and the Australia Act 1986 (U.K.). Accordingly, such provisions can now be amended in the same way as the Australia Act 1986 (U.K.) and the Statute of Westminster 1931 (U.K.), namely by Commonwealth legislation enacted at the request, or with the concurrence, of all State Parliaments pursuant to section 15(1) of the Australia Act 1986 (U.K.)[70] or (which is effectively much the same, except that, like all section 51 powers, it is subject to the Constitution) pursuant to section 51(xxxviii) of the Constitution.[71]

Alternatively, and of greater value to the Commonwealth, since it does not require the concurrence of the States, the preamble and covering clauses could be amended or repealed pursuant to section 15(3) of the Australia

Act 1986 (U.K.), which enables the Australia Act and the Statute of Westminster 1931 (U.K.) to be amended or repealed by Commonwealth legislation enacted pursuant to power conferred by a constitutional amendment under section 128 of the Commonwealth Constitution.[72]

The focus in these comments on the Australia Act should not distract attention from the principal issue involved in constitutional amendment to achieve a republic, namely whether it can be accomplished pursuant to section 128 of the Constitution.

This work argued that the monarchy could be abolished at both Commonwealth and State level pursuant to section 128 (chapter 8, pp. 122–126, 135, 140–142), and there is no reason to revise that opinion,[73] which was recently confirmed by the Acting Solicitor-General's advice to the Republic Advisory Committee.[74]

The view that the advent of a republic faces no insuperable constitutional hurdle has recently been challenged by Greg Craven, a leading constitutional lawyer, who asserted that:

[t]he legal complexities involved can scarcely be overestimated; there are virtually no questions in Australian constitutional law and theory more complicated and perplexing than those that surround the process by which the monarchy might be abolished. . . .[It] may well prove a constitutional quagmire.[75]

Craven queries whether the monarchy can be abolished under section 128 on three grounds:

1. The verb 'alter' in section 128 may not extend to the supposedly radical change involved in becoming a republic.[76]

2. The constitutional amendment power in section 128 may be subject to an implied limitation, as it is in India, which prevents alteration of the Constitution's 'fundamental', 'basic' or 'essential' features, and the monarchy may be one of these.[77]

3. Finally, the High Court might not accept the argument that the State Constitutions are incorporated into the Commonwealth Constitution via section 106, thereby enabling them to be amended pursuant to section 128.[78]

With respect, these arguments are unconvincing, and even Craven himself concedes that they are merely 'plausible', not necessarily correct.[79]

The High Court has not had occasion to determine the ambit of section 128, but there is no justification for a restrictive interpretation of the word 'alter' in that provision. Such an interpretation was opposed, for example, by Quick and Garran, who concluded that 'there is no limit to the power to amend the Constitution'.[80] As they noted, since section 128 expressly restricts the constitutional amendment power in certain respects, the maxim *expressio unius exclusio alterius* suggests that that is the limit of the restriction.[81]

Nor is there any reason for importing the Indian 'basic features' doctrine into the Australian Constitution. The Indian doctrine would appear to be a consequence of the ease with which that Constitution can be amended. With some exceptions, all that is required is approval by an absolute majority of the members of each House of Parliament and two-thirds of the members present and voting.[82] No-one could accuse the Commonwealth Constitution of being too easy to amend, and the principles both of popular sovereignty and federalism are embodied in the requirement of approval by a double majority at a referendum — an overall majority of electors and a majority of electors in a majority of States.

As Chief Justice Mason recently acknowledged, 'ultimate sovereignty reside[s] in the Australian people'.[83] Imposing implied limitations on the already restrictive constitutional amendment power would be a gross infringement on that sovereignty. Were Craven's arguments to be upheld, an Australian republic would be constitutionally barred in perpetuity, which suggests that his interpretation is implausible. Moreover, permanently to deny a people the opportunity to realize their aspirations is not only undemocratic, but dangerous. If peaceful constitutional change is foreclosed, change will surely be effected in the streets.

In any event, leading authorities not reputed to be radical republicans have expressly recognized that the monarchy could be abolished pursuant to section 128.[84]

Finally, regarding amendment of State Constitutions pursuant to section 128, the writer can only reiterate the comments in chapter 8 (pp.140–142), noting that they are supported by the weighty authority of Quick and Garran.[85]

So, in sum, the position regarding constitutional amendment can be stated briefly as follows:

1. The monarchy can be abolished at both Commonwealth and State level by a constitutional amendment enacted pursuant to section 128 of the Commonwealth Constitution.

2. The preamble and covering clauses contain nothing which entrenches the monarchy, but the advent of a republic would make (at least) amendment of the preamble and repeal of covering clause 2 appropriate.

3. That amendment and repeal could probably be effected by a constitutional amendment enacted pursuant to section 128 but, since that view is widely disputed, it would be constitutionally more prudent to employ the legislative procedures in section 15(1) of the Australia Act 1986 (U.K.), if the States were willing participants, or section 15(3) if they were not.

4. If the monarchy is to be abolished at both Commonwealth and State levels, it may not be strictly necessary to repeal section 7 of the Australia Act. But that provision should be repealed, if only for cosmetic purposes, and such repeal could be effected through either of the procedures for amending the Australia Act specified in section 15 of that Act.[86]

Notes

[1]   *Sources:* 'Should Australia Become a Republic?' (1991) 2 *National Social Science Survey Report* 20 (November 1991); I.W. McNair (ed.), *Australian Public Opinion Polls (The Gallup Method) 1973–1987* (Sydney, undated), 1; *Sun-Herald* (Sydney), 11 May 1986, p.36; *Sydney Morning Herald,* 29 February 1992, p.2; *Australian,* 4 March 1992, p.1; *Sydney Morning Herald,* 11 May 1992, p.4; *Australian,* 5 May 1992, p.2; *Weekend Australian,* 10–11 April 1993, p.2; *Bulletin,* 11 May 1993, p.14; *Time* (Australia), 26 April 1993, p.8; *Australian,* 19 July 1993, p.2; *Age,* 9 August 1993, p.2; *Australian,* 29 September 1993, p.2; *Bulletin,* 19 October 1993, p.13; *Australian,* 18 November 1993, p.2; *Time* (Australia), 3 January 1994, p.7. For further opinion polls and discussion regarding the statistics, see M. Goot, 'Contingent Inevitability: Reflections on the Prognosis for Republicanism', in G. Winterton (ed.), *We, the People: Australian Republican Government* (Sydney, 1994), ch. 4; M. Goot, 'The Queen in the Polls', in J. Arnold, P. Spearritt and D. Walker (eds.), *Out of Empire: The British Dominion of Australia* (Melbourne, 1993), 295; M. Goot, 'Monarchy or Republic?: An Analysis of the Questions and Answers in Surveys of Australian Public Opinion, 1953–1986', in (Australian) Constitutional Commission, *Report of the Advisory Committee on Executive Government* (Canberra, June 1987), 85.

[2]   See A. Darby and G. Roberts, 'March to Republic Gains Pace', *Sydney Morning Herald,* 30 March 1993, p.1; *New South Wales Parliamentary Debates,* 30 March 1993, 948–51, 958–61.

[3]   G. Winterton, 'The Evolution of a Separate Australian Crown' (1993) 19 *Monash University Law Review* 1, 16–21.

[4]   J. Hirst, 'The Conservative Case for an Australian Republic' (1991) 35 *Quadrant,* No.9, 9,9.

[5]   J. Hirst, 'What if Britain Became a Republic?' (1991) 35 *Quadrant,* No.11, 7. Accord J. Hirst, 'The Time has Come to Manage On Our Own', *Weekend Australian,* 9–10 October, 1993, p.34: 'If for any reason there ceased to be a monarch of Britain, our Constitution would seize up. When the present Governor-General retired or died, there would be no mechanism to replace him. Without a governor-general, ministers could not be appointed, Bills could not be passed into law, Parliament could not be summoned and elections could not be held. Australia does not have a self-sufficient Constitution'. As Malcolm Turnbull has noted, a literal interpretation of covering clause 2 would make the President of a republican Britain 'Queen' under the Constitution: see M. Turnbull, 'Why We Need the Republic' (National Press Club Speech, 18 March 1992) (1992) 1 *Verbatim Report* 103,103.

[6]   See the Act of Settlement 1701 (Engl.), 12 & 13 Wm.III, c.2.

[7]   Ibid, s.3.

[8]   See Constitutional Commission, *Report of the Advisory Committee on Executive Government* (June 1987), 8; P. Derriman, 'Royalty: The Equal Opportunity Argument', *Sydney Morning Herald,* 19 November 1992, p.14.

[9]   But see G. Winterton, 'The Constitutional Implications of a Republic', in Australia — Republic or Monarchy (M. A. Stephenson and C. Turner eds., Brisbane, 1994).

[10]   T. Abbott, 'Political Impossibility of a Vision Not So Splendid', *Weekend Australian,* 9-10 October 1993, p. 32.

[11]   Tony Abbott, in debate with Malcolm Turnbull, *Weekend Australian,* 9–10

October 1993, p.31. See also the similar remarks of Governor McGarvie, quoted *infra*, note 12.

[12] Z. Cowen, 'The Office of Governor-General' (1985) 114 *Daedalus*, No.1, 127, 140; J. Kerr, 'Kerr Rejects "Ambush" Myth: "PM Knew I Could Sack Him"', *Bulletin*, 10 September 1985, pp.72, 79. On the other hand, the Governor of Victoria does not favour secure tenure because 'the present system creates a sophisticated and flexible balance between Premier and Governor which a guaranteed term for the Governor would upset': R.E. McGarvie, 'Governorship in Australia Today' (unpublished Address to Senior Executive Chapter Luncheon of the Australian Institute of Management, Melbourne, 8 September 1993), 8.

[13] L. Waddy, 'Inevitable? Not at All' (1993) 28 *Australian Lawyer*, No.5, 16, 18. Emphasis added.

[14] Malcolm Turnbull, in debate with Geoffrey Blainey, *Age*, 26 June 1993, p.13.

[15] Sir Harry Gibbs, 'Remove the Queen and the Whole Structure Could Fall', *Australian*, 7 June 1993, p.11. See also Sir Harry Gibbs, 'Changes Would Bring Country No Material Benefit', *Weekend Australian*, 9–10 October 1993, pp.34,30.

[16] South African Constitution 1961, section 7(5). See, likewise, G. Winterton, 'A Constitution for an Australian Republic', *Independent Monthly*, March 1992, section 60A.

[17] M. Turnbull, 'Real Substance of Constitution is Unwritten', *Australian*, 9 June 1993, p.11.

[18] For a recent discussion of the reserve powers of the Governor-General, see Republic Advisory Committee, *An Australian Republic: The Options — The Appendices* (Canberra, 1993), Appendix 6.

[19] On these events, see B. Galligan, 'Australia', in *Sovereigns and Surrogates* (D. Butler and D.A. Low eds., London, 1991), 61, 85–92.

[20] For an analysis of these events, see G. Winterton, 'The Constitutional Position of Australian State Governors', in *Australian Constitutional Perspectives* (H.P. Lee and G. Winterton eds., Sydney, 1992), 274, 304 *ff*; G. Winterton, 'Tasmania's Hung Parliament, 1989' [1992] *Public Law* 423.

[21] E. Thompson, 'The "Washminster" Mutation', in *Responsible Government in Australia* (P. Weller and D. Jaensch eds., Melbourne, 1980), 32.

[22] See, e.g., *Myers* v. *United States* (1926) 272 U.S. 52; *Buckley* v. *Valeo* (1976) 424 U.S.1; *Bowsher* v. *Synar* (1986) 478 U.S. 714.

[23] See, e.g., *United States* v. *United States District Court* (1972) 407 U.S. 297.

[24] See, especially, the *Boilermakers* case: *R.* v. *Kirby, ex parte Boilermakers' Society of Australia* (1956) 94 C.L.R. 254.

[25] O. Dixon, 'The Separation of Powers in the Australian Constitution', *American Foreign Law Association, Proceedings*, No. 24, December 1942, 5. *Cf.* Dixon's evidence to the 1927 Royal Commission on the Constitution, quoted in G. Winterton, *Parliament, the Executive and the Governor-General* (Melbourne, 1983), 11.

[26] Dixon, *supra* note 25 at 5.

[27] Ibid.

[28] *Victoria* v. *Commonwealth* (the *AAP* case) (1975) 134 C.L.R. 338, 406. His Honour noted that, subject to the Constitution, '[t]he same is true of any executive power expressly conferred by the Constitution': ibid.

[29] See, e.g., G. Winterton, *supra* note 16, sections 51(xl) and 61(3).

30 See C. Bean, 'Politics and the Public: Mass Attitudes Towards the Australian Political System', in *Australian Attitudes: Social and Political Analyses from the National Social Science Survey* (J. Kelley and C. Bean eds., Sydney, 1988), 45, 49: 73% of respondents were 'satisfied...with the way democracy works in Australia'; 23% were not satisfied.

31 See 'Majority Favor a Republic', *Time* (Australia), 26 April 1993, p. 8; 'Republic Support Falters', *Time* (Australia), 3 January 1994, p.7: the figures were 73% to 22% in April 1993, and 72% to 21% in December 1993. For earlier surveys, see G. Winterton, 'Presidential Power in Republican Australia' (1993) 28 *Australian Journal of Political Science* 40, 41–2.

32 See, e.g., J.V. Poulard, 'The French Double Executive and the Experience of Cohabitation' (1990) 105 *Pol. Sc. Q.* 243.

33 The Irish Constitution expressly limits the President's power to address Parliament or the nation without the government's consent: see article 13.7. See J. Duffy, 'Ireland', in Republic Advisory Committee, *supra* note 18 at 109, 132–3 (paras. 2.60–2.62).

34 See Winterton, *supra* note 31 at 49–50.

35 Gibbs, 'Changes Would Bring Country No Material Benefit', *supra* note 15 at 34.

36 As Sir Harry Gibbs has stressed: ibid; Gibbs, 'Remove the Queen and the Whole Structure Could Fall', *supra* note 15; Gibbs, 'Republic: Difficult and Dangerous', *Canberra Times*, 28 June 1993, p.11.

37 See *supra* note 16.

38 See Republic Advisory Committee, *An Australian Republic: The Options — The Report* (Canberra, 1993), ch.6. Conversion into law need not result in justiciability; the Constitution could expressly provide that some rules be non-justiciable.

39 *Bulletin*, 19 October 1993, p.13 (popular election 80%); *Australian*, 19 July 1993, p.2 (popular election 79%); *Bulletin*, 11 May 1993, p.14 (popular election 83%); *Time* (Australia), 26 April 1993, p.8 (popular election 71%); *Time* (Australia), 3 January 1994, p.7 (popular election 76%).

40 On the other hand, some see virtue in a popularly-elected head of state 'with sufficient independence ... to provide a balance to an otherwise autocratic Prime Minister': See H. Evans, 'The Agenda of the True Republicans', in G. de Q. Walker, S. Ratnapala and W. Kasper, *Restoring the True Republic* (Sydney, 1993), 3, 6.

41 See further G. Winterton, 'Reserve Powers in an Australian Republic' (1993) 12 *University of Tasmania Law Review* 249.

42 See Australians for Constitutional Monarchy, Opinion, 8 September 1993 (unpublished). Sir Harry Gibbs appears to agree: Gibbs, *The States and a Republic* (unpublished opinion, undated, endorsed by the Legal Committee of 'Australians for Constitutional Monarchy', released 3 November 1993), 2. This opinion is noted in S. Kirk, 'Republic Move "Puts Federation at Risk"', *Sydney Morning Herald*, 4 November 1993, 5.

43 Accord Republic Advisory Committee, *supra* note 38 at 130.

44 J. Quick and R.R. Garran, *The Annotated Constitution of the Australian Commonwealth* (Sydney, 1901), 991. Accord E. Campbell, 'Changing the Constitution — Past and Future' (1989) 17 *M.U.L.R.* 1, 1 note 2.

45 The Governor-General ought to comply with such advice, but public opinion would presumably be very critical of such action. *Cf.* G.J. Lindell, 'The Arrangements for Self-government for the Australian Capital Territory: A

Partial Road to Republicanism in the Seat of Government?' (1992) 3 *Public Law Review* 5, 14–5 note 45.

[46] See further Republic Advisory Committee, *supra* note 38 at 128–9.

[47] See ibid., 126 note 14.

[48] Z. Cowen, 'Australia — Looking Ahead to the Twenty-first Century' (1993) 141 *Royal Society of Arts Journal* 296, 301. On the other hand, another commentator has asserted that 'there is no reason in constitutional logic why such a hybrid state could not exist, or for that matter thrive': G. Craven, 'The Constitutional Minefield of Australian Republicanism', *Policy*, Spring 1992, 33, 35. Accord S. M. Zifcak, 'A Modest Proposal for a Democratic Republic' (1993) 67 *Law Institute J.* 1159, 1161.

[49] Malacca, Penang, Sabah and Sarawak. See W. Hudson, 'An Australian Federal Republic?' (1992) 64 *A.Q.* 229, 238.

[50] See the Statute of Westminster 1931 (U.K.) sections 2, 4; the Australia Act 1986 (U.K.) sections 1, 3.

[51] See the Privy Council (Appeals from the High Court) Act 1975 (Cth); the Australia Act 1986 (U.K.) section 11; *Viro* v. *R.* (1978) 141 C.L.R. 88, 120–1, 130–2, 136–7, 151, 166, 175-6; *National Employers' Mutual General Association Ltd.* v. *Waind* [1978] 1 N.S.W.L.R. 466 (C.A.).

[52] See *infra*, note 58.

[53] See D. Solomon and P. Kelly, 'Depicting a Nation to its People', *Weekend Australian*, 7–8 January 1989, p.12.

[54] L. Waddy, 'Time To Put the Genie Back in the Bottle', *Canberra Times*, 6 October 1993, p.15. The complexity of the task was also stressed by former Prime Minister Malcolm Fraser a few days later: M. Fraser, 'Complex Task Goes to Heart of Government', *Weekend Australian*, 9–10 October 1993, p.33.

[55] Abbott, *supra* note 10.

[56] Gibbs, *supra* note 42, 3. Emphasis added.

[57] *Supra*, text accompanying note 52.

[58] The argument being that a separate Australian Crown existed from the enactment of the Statute of Westminster 1931 (U.K.), or at least the Royal Style and Titles Act 1953 (Cth), but that the Queen of the United Kingdom remained the head of state of the Australian States until the enactment of the Australia Act 1986 (U.K.), especially sections 7(5) and 10. The present writer disagrees with the last proposition. See generally, Winterton, *supra* note 3.

[59] The Royal Style and Title ceased to refer to 'the United Kingdom of Great Britain and Ireland' in 1927: see Proclamation of 13 May 1927, pursuant to the Royal and Parliamentary Titles Act 1927 (U.K.), reprinted in A.B. Keith, *Speeches and Documents on the British Dominions, 1918–1931* (London, 1932), 171–72.

[60] See *supra*, text accompanying note 44.

[61] Australia Acts 1986 (U.K. and Cth) section 1.

[62] Ibid. section 3.

[63] See G. Winterton, 'An Australian Republic' (1988) 16 *M.U.L.R.* 467, 479.

[64] Australia Acts section 9(2).

[65] See also Advice of Acting Solicitor-General Dennis Rose, in Republic Advisory Committee, *supra* note 18, Appendix 8, para. 42(p.306).

[66] Acting Solicitor-General Dennis Rose has commented that:

> The Constitution of any State might be capable of alteration by legislation of that State alone so as to remove the role of the monarchy. However, it might be inferred

from section 7 of the Australia Act that, in each State, there must continue to be a State Governor (as defined in section 16) appointed by the Queen, and that certain functions must continue to be exercisable by the Queen when personally present in a State … . (Ibid. at para. 44 (p.307).)

On the other hand, Professor R.D. Lumb has argued that State abolition of the monarchy is effectively prohibited by section 7 which 'both implicitly and explicitly recognises the existence of the Monarchy', in R.D. Lumb, 'The Australian States and Australia's Head of State System' (unpublished paper presented at Australians for Constitutional Monarchy Seminar, Sydney, 4 June 1993), 5.

[67] See the Australia Act section 15.

[68] This was also the view of the Constitutional Commission: 1 Constitutional Commission, *Final Report* (Canberra, 1988), paras.3.112 *ff.* (pp.121–3).

[69] See *infra* 183 note 14; Winterton, *supra* note 63 at 476; Craven, *supra* note 48 at 34.

[70] Rose, *supra* note 65 at paras. 16–18 (pp.299–300).

[71] Winterton, *supra* note 63 at 476–8; Craven, *supra* note 48 at 35.

[72] Rose, *supra* note 65 at paras. 20–25, 29 (pp.300–302, 303). But some commentators interpret section 15(3) more narrowly, and maintain that section 15(1) provides the only method of amending the Australia Act and the covering clauses, so that the consent of all States would be required: see Lumb, *supra* note 66 at 4. A similar view was expressed more tentatively in the New South Wales Government's Submission to the Republic Advisory Committee (no. 262), 14 July 1993, pp.5–6.

Sir Harry Gibbs tentatively concedes that section 15(3) may provide an alternative method of amending the Australia Act, but argues that the electors in *all* States would have to approve the Constitutional amendment pursuant to section 128: Gibbs, *supra* note 42 at 2–4.

[73] Accord Winterton, *supra* note 63 at 475–6, 479–81.

[74] See Rose, *supra* note 65.

[75] Craven, *supra* note 48 at 33.

[76] Ibid., 35. Accord G. Craven, 'Would the Abolition of the States Be an Alteration of the Constitution Under Section 128?' (1989) 18 *F.L.Rev.* 85, 102 ff. See also C. Howard, *The Constitution, Power and Politics* (Melbourne, 1980), 107.

[77] Craven, *supra* note 48 at 35: 'a fairly powerful case could be made for the constitutional indispensability of the monarchy'.

[78] Ibid., 36.

[79] Ibid.

[80] Quick and Garran, *supra* note 44 at 989.

[81] Ibid., 295.

[82] Indian Constitution article 368.

[83] *Australian Capital Television Pty. Ltd.* v. *Commonwealth* (1992) 177 C.L.R. 106, 138.

[84] See the views of Sir Zelman Cowen and Professor R.D. Lumb, cited *infra* 182 note 2; Lumb, *supra* note 66 at 8. See also Quick and Garran, *supra* note 44 at 295–6; Sir Daryl Dawson, quoted *infra* 5.

[85] A similar view is expressed by Rose, *supra* note 65 at para.47 (p.308).

[86] For the provision that ought to be made if State retention of the monarchy is to be permitted, see ibid., paras.38-43 (pp.305-7).

Chapter 1
A 'Republic'

As we approach the bicentenary of British colonization and the centenary of federation, Australians are increasingly likely to debate fundamental constitutional issues, one of which is whether we should remain a constitutional monarchy under the British Crown[1] or, in other words, whether we should become a republic.

The republic–monarchy debate is, of course, an old one, even in Australia, Australians having campaigned for a republic since at least the middle of the last century,[2] with republican agitation reaching its zenith around the time of Queen Victoria's Golden Jubilee in 1887, but declining rather dramatically within the next twenty years and remaining low for most of this century. Indeed, even at the height of republican agitation around 1887, the general public seems to have taken little interest in the question.[3] However, public interest in the establishment of a republic appears to have revived in recent years: opinion polls suggest that public support for a republic has doubled in the thirty years since 1953, when it was a mere 15 per cent.[4] Yet the findings of opinion polls on this question should be treated with greater-than-usual caution because the questions asked — such as 'Do you think Australia needs a Queen?', 'Do you think Australia needs a Governor-General?' and 'Would you prefer Australia to become an independent republic with its own elected President?'[5] — are vague and quite likely to mean different things to different people, especially since their knowledge of present constitutional arrangements will vary widely. Whether one favours retention of the Queen or the Governor-General will obviously depend upon the alternative proposed; the most diehard republican would (if a democrat) doubtless prefer the Queen to a Führer, duce, caudillo or Soviet-style 'general secretary'. Similarly, many people would find it difficult to decide in the abstract whether or not they favoured a republic because their decision would depend upon the type of republic proposed. Even among democratic republics there is, of course, considerable variety; in some, such as the United States, the head of state is also the head of the government, while in others, such as India, Ireland, Israel, Italy and West Germany, the head of state is largely a ceremonial figure. And there are numerous variations in between, such as those in Switzerland, France and Sri Lanka. Moreover, just as preferences for and against a republic may depend upon the type of republic proposed, so the type of republic favoured will often be influenced by the reasons for favouring a republic in the first place.

In other words, resolution of the republic–monarchy debate depends upon practical considerations in addition to the more philosophical reasons for favouring a republic or a monarchy. These practical questions are the subject of this book. Its concern, accordingly, is less with the question whether or not Australia should become a republic than with the options available should Australians consider departing from their present allegiance to the monarchy.

THE MEANING OF 'REPUBLIC'

A republic, unlike a monarchy or aristocracy, is a polity in which governmental power devolves by popular election, either directly or indirectly, and not by heredity; in the words of *The Oxford English Dictionary*, it is 'A state in which supreme power rests in the people and their elected representatives or officers, as opposed to one governed by a king or similar ruler; a commonwealth'. Although republicanism has wider implications of commitment to the rule of law and the separation of powers, popular sovereignty is the essential feature of modern republicanism,[6] and has been since around the 1780s, especially in America, where the 'negative senses of "republican", that is, nonmonarchical and nonaristocratic', commanded general assent by 1787.[7] However, as John Adams's numerous attempts at definition demonstrated,[8] the word 'republic' was long used in a confused way, to convey a variety of different, though frequently related, concepts. Its older meaning was simply a state or polity,[9] or a state (even a monarchical one) with a 'mixed government' or 'balanced constitution'.[10] After 1649 'republic' was frequently employed to describe a state without a king,[11] or a state in which power was derived, at least to some extent, from the people,[12] in which sense (clearly derived from the two usages previously mentioned) it was often treated as synonymous with 'democracy' or 'commonwealth'.[13] As Francis Wormuth has noted,

The terms commonwealth and republic had [in 1649] both the general meaning we attach to 'state' and the specialized meaning of non-monarchical government. The supporters of the Rump were called 'commonwealth's-men'; the title 'republicans' was first applied to them in 1659.[14]

However, the original usages of 'republic ' lingered even as new meanings developed, creating considerable lexicological confusion.

The older 'classical' concept of a 'republic' was a state in which the government was a 'mixture' or 'balance' of monarchy, aristocracy and democracy, representing the three orders in society, viz. king, nobles and people. Because the concept of 'mixed government' or 'mixed monarchy' became the dominant theory of English government in the seventeenth century,[15] especially after it was adopted by Charles I himself in answer to the Nineteen Propositions in 1642,[16] even after the demise of the Commonwealth in 1660 England could appropriately have been considered a 'republic'. As J. G. A. Pocock remarked of Charles's argument, 'The government of England, in short, without ceasing to manifest the element of monarchy, is being presented as a classical republic'.[17]

The classical concept of a 'republic' survived in England until well into the nineteenth century, when it was not uncommon for Great Britain to be described as a 'republic', especially after the House of Commons, which supposedly represented 'the people', became the politically dominant House.[18] More specifically, it was described occasionally as a 'parliamentary republic',[19] a 'disguised republic',[20] and even as a 'monarchical'[21] or 'aristocratic'[22] republic. Indeed, elements of the classical notion of a republic survive today, as in Bernard Crick's definition of 'republican government':

the form of government which attempts to solve the basic problem of the adjustment of order to diversity by conciliating different interests either by letting them share in the government or at least in the competitive and public choosing of the government or the assembly from which it is chosen.[23]

It is in this sense also that some Australian commentators have called the Senate a 'republican' institution.[24]

The modern concept of a 'republic' is a more democratic one which does not entail the 'mixture' or 'balance' of various interests or types of polity, and rejects the notion that public office can devolve by heredity.[25] It was expounded already in the 1780s by the American 'Founding Fathers'. James Madison, for instance, defined a 'republic' as 'a government which derives all its powers directly or indirectly from the great body of the people; and is administered by persons holding their offices during pleasure, for a limited period, or during good behaviour.'[26] Similarly, for Roger Sherman, what 'especially denominate[d]' a government a 'republic' was 'its dependence on the *public* or *people at large*, without any hereditary powers.'[27] A distinction was sometimes drawn between a 'democracy' or 'pure republic'[28] on the one hand and a 'republic', like the United States, on the other: in a 'democracy' the people ruled themselves directly, whereas in a 'republic' they elected representatives to rule them. As James Madison wrote in 1787, 'in a democracy, the people meet and exercise the government in person; in a republic they assemble and administer it by their representatives and agents.'[29]

Although probably the leading contemporary American student of republican government, John Adams never achieved consistency in his definition of a 'republic', although he tended generally to adopt the classical theory.[30] The tension between that theory and modern notions of a republic is illustrated well by an exchange between him and his cousin Samuel Adams in 1790. In a letter of 18 October, John

Adams enunciated the classical theory; he noted that by a 'republic' he meant 'a government in which the people have collectively, or by representation, an essential *share* in the sovereignty.'[31] His cousin's rejection of the classical theory could not have been more explicit:

A republic, you tell me, is a government in which 'the people have an essential *share* in the sovereignty.' Is not the *whole* sovereignty, my friend, essentially in the people? . . . That the sovereignty resides in the people, is a political doctrine which I have never heard an American politician seriously deny.[32]

The debate on ratification of the United States Constitution demonstrated, indeed, how political concepts can change rapidly.[33] A few years after most of them had abandoned the classical theory of a republic which still prevailed in England, Americans were debating whether the notion of 'checks and balances', an integral element of the classical theory, was compatible with republicanism.[34]

Australian republicans seek a 'republic' in the modern sense, that employed by the American Founding Fathers. But what, in practical terms, would an Australian republic entail? Donald Horne has suggested that '[p]eople are so ill-informed on this question that merely providing the most elementary information can change their minds.'[35] Misconceptions certainly abound, and not only among non-lawyers!

The Australian constitutional system embodies a number of fundamental principles, including representative government, federalism, the independence of the judiciary, judicial review of the validity of legislation, and responsible government under the Crown. The change from a constitutional monarchy to a republic would affect only the last-mentioned principle. It would, in itself, have no effect whatever on the other four principles, or on the very bed-rock of the system, the rule of law. Only responsible government under the Crown would be changed by conversion to a republic. Moreover, even that principle could remain substantively unaffected; the government could continue to be carried on by ministers enjoying the confidence of the lower house of parliament, as it is in republics such as Ireland, India and West Germany.

However, the late D. P. O'Connell held a rather different view of the impact of the advent of a republic on the Australian constitutional system. He maintained, albeit without giving any reasons, that it was '[difficult to envisage] any change in the monarchical system of government . . . without an overall dismantling of the system of Australian government, including the Federal system. The Monarchy is the keystone of the system. Remove it and the system must collapse . . .'.[36] In his opinion, conversion to a republic would, moreover, threaten not only the federal system, but even parliamentary democracy,[37] civil liberties, and the rule of law as well.[38]

With all respect, these fears are completely unfounded. There is no basis whatever for supposing that the change to a republic would be effected by unconstitutional means; as is noted below, there are no insuperable legal obstacles, either at Commonwealth or State level, to Australia becoming a republic.[39] Hence, the advent of a republic would not require the alteration of any part of the Australian constitutional system except the identity of the formal head of state. Federalism is, in fact, quite likely to be strengthened by such a change, since it would remove the Commonwealth government's potential for seeking to advise the Queen on State matters by relying upon confusion as to whether the Queen acts in State matters as Queen of Australia or Queen of the United Kingdom.[40] In Professor O'Connell's picturesque language, the States would no longer be 'vulnerable . . . to infiltration by the Commonwealth through the executive structure';[41] nor could the Commonwealth government 'capture the [State] monarchy'.[42] As Justice Dawson of the High Court of Australia noted recently,

To my mind, the final, formal end to the role of the monarchy in Australia, if it occurs, need not mean a fundamental change in our constitutional structure . . . . If it were thought desirable to substitute the Governor-General, elected or appointed, as the head of State it would, I think, be possible to achieve that in a manner which would involve little disruption to the present constitutional set-up and may even serve to eliminate some of the difficulties which still remain in discerning the role of the Crown in our federation . . . . [T]he bare change from a monarchy to a republic could be quite simple.[43]

An autochthonous, or 'We the People,' constitution is not a necessary, or even likely, prelude to a republic; the *grundnorm* of the Australian constitutional system is very likely to remain the supremacy of the United Kingdom parliament. In other words, the Commonwealth and State constitutions are likely to continue to derive their formal legitimacy from British legislation.[44] Moreover, the conversion from a monarchy to a republic is unlikely to have any adverse effect on Australian relations with the United Kingdom. Indeed, relations could well improve once the possibility of British involvement in Commonwealth-State squabbles over communications between Australia and the Queen is removed. (One has only to recall the events leading to the passage of the Canada Act 1982 (U.K.) to appreciate how British involvement in intra-federal disputation in a Commonwealth country can prejudice Britain's relations with that country.[45]) More than half the members of the Commonwealth of Nations are republics, and a republican Australia would, no doubt, remain a member of the Commonwealth on the same basis as its other members who do not recognize the Queen as their head of state.[46] Australia would continue to recognize the Queen 'as the symbol of the free

association of its independent member nations and as such the Head
of the Commonwealth', the formula adopted by the Declaration of
London in April 1949.[47]

AN ELECTED GOVERNOR-GENERAL?

As prescribed by section 2 of the Commonwealth Constitution, the
Governor-General is appointed by the Queen, who follows, in this
matter, the 'advice' of ministers: before 1930, the (British) Secretary
of State for the Colonies; thereafter, the Australian prime minister. The
simplest method of implementing an Australian republic would be to
substitute an elected Governor-General or 'president' for the present
appointive Governor-General, and to delete from the Constitution all
reference to the Queen. Since election of the Governor-General has
occasionally been advocated, and some variations of this proposal
would constitute a republic, while others would not, it is appropriate
to note the position of an elected Governor-General.

Essentially, there are four main types of elective Governor-General.

Formal Head of State under the Queen

The smallest variation of the current position would be for the prime
minister's nominee for Governor-General to be selected by parliament
(as in Papua New Guinea[48]) or the people, rather than (as now) by
the prime minister himself. A constitutional amendment would not be
required to effect this change; indeed, even legislation would be
unnecessary, except to regulate a popular election. The change could
be accomplished, *de facto*, by the major political parties undertaking
to recommend to the Queen as Governor-General only persons elected
to that position. Parliament could, probably, validly enact legislation
requiring the prime minister to nominate to the Queen only a person
elected as Governor-General,[49] but the validity of legislation requiring
the Queen to appoint the person nominated by the prime minister
would be more dubious. Of course, there would really be no practical
need for such legislation, since the Queen ultimately always follows
the prime minister's advice, just as her grandfather did in reluctantly
appointing Sir Isaac Isaacs Governor-General in 1930.[50]

An elective Governor-General of this type would not substantially
alter the structure of the Commonwealth government. The Governor-
General's powers would remain formal only (subject to rare exercises
of the so-called 'reserve powers'), and the government, which would
continue to be run by the prime minister and cabinet, would remain
responsible to the House of Representatives. However, the national
'mandate' enjoyed by a Governor-General elected by the people
doubtless would, in practical terms, increase the Governor-General's
power *vis-à-vis* the prime minister who could not claim to be directly

elected by the people.[51] This likely effect was, indeed, noted by Sir John Downer in arguing (successfully) against Sir George Grey's proposal for an elective Governor-General at the National Australasian Convention in 1891,[52] a proposal rejected again five years later at the People's Federal Convention at Bathurst.[53]

A Governor-General elected by the Australian people or their representatives would have been anomalous in the days when the Governor-General acted not only as local head of state but also as British ambassador, representing British interests in Australia. However, once Governors-General abandoned the latter role (in the early 1920s[54]), an elective Governor-General of the type postulated became feasible. Of course, such an elective Governor-General would not convert Australia into a republic because the Queen would remain the formal head of state. But because, in reality, the formal head of state would be a person chosen by the people or their representatives, Australia would become, as Sir Edmund Barton observed in 1897, 'a republic in everything but name'.[55]

Executive Head of State under the Queen

One suggestion, which appeared in the wake of the Governor-General's dismissal of the Whitlam government in November 1975 and consequent concern at the apparent ascendancy of a literal interpretation of the Governor-General's powers,[56] was that the Governor-General should become the effective head of government. The leading proponent of this idea was David Solomon, a distinguished Canberra journalist.

The Australian Governor-General has the potential power to become the active, working head of the executive government of the Commonwealth. The processes of government and the parliament would be considerably improved if the idea of a figurehead Governor-General was abandoned. And changing the Governor-General from the nominal head of government into a presidential-style political leader would be relatively easy. The constitution already gives the Governor-General more than enough powers to run the country in his own right. No further constitutional changes would be necessary but a few basic legislative changes would give the system a firm footing.

A governing Governor-General would need to have national support and a fixed term of office. He would need to be elected in a nationwide poll. ...

After the election, the winner would be chosen by the Queen as her Governor-General and appointed for a fixed term of office. The fixed term would be necessary to give the Governor-General the ability to stand up to the parliament, should it prove unwilling to co-operate with him.[57]

If the present system of parliamentary government were retained under an executive governorship-general of this type, the resulting constitutional arrangement would resemble that of France,[58] or, more accurately, Sri Lanka. However, David Solomon appears to have modelled his proposed executive on that of the United States, and would abolish the prime ministership which, after all, is not mentioned in the Constitution.

A Governor-General would have no need for a Prime Minister in his government. Abolition of the post of Prime Minister would help prevent any confusion in the public mind about where government was centred. A Governor-General would in fact be his own Prime Minister . . .[59]

Since the prospects of an elective governorship-general along these lines are minimal,[60] a few observations on this proposal will be sufficient.

The assertion that an American-style presidential executive could be substituted for the present executive, which is collectively and individually responsible to the House of Representatives, 'without a single word of the constitution being changed'[61] is simply incorrect.[62] As Quick and Garran noted in 1901, 'for better or for worse, the system of Responsible Government as known to the British Constitution has been practically embedded in the Federal Constitution, in such a manner that it cannot be disturbed without an amendment of the instrument.'[63] Moreover, constitutional amendment would probably be necessary (i.e., legislation would not suffice) to ensure that the Queen appointed as Governor-General only persons elected to that office by the people or their representatives, and that the Governor-General's term of office was fixed, for otherwise his commission could be withdrawn by the Queen whenever the House of Representatives expressed lack of confidence in him. Furthermore, duplication of the United States executive would require that the House of Representatives have a fixed minimum term, to ensure that the Governor-General could not dissolve it at any time, as he can at present. But this could not be accomplished without amending section 28 of the Constitution.[64]

Retention of the Queen as formal head of state would, of course, mean that Australia remained, at least formally, a monarchy.

Formal Head of State without the Queen

Australia's responsible monarchical government could be converted into responsible republican government by simply replacing the Queen and the present appointive Governor-General with an elected Governor-General (or 'president', if that title were preferred), and leaving the remaining machinery of government as it is. Australia would then be a 'parliamentary republic', like India, Ireland, Italy, Israel and West Germany, among others. Conversion to a republic of this type would, of course, require amendment of the forty-two sections of the Constitution which refer to the Queen or the Governor-General (if he is to have another title), but the necessary changes would be relatively straightforward. All that would need to be done is to

1. replace sections 2, 3, 4 and 126 with a provision specifying the qualifications, mode of election, term of office, method of removal, and salary of the president and, if thought appropriate, a vice-president;

2. repeal outmoded provisions providing for reservation of Bills by the Governor-General for the Queen's assent and allowing the Queen to disallow Commonwealth legislation;[65]

3. substitute references to 'the president' (if that were the preferred title) for references elsewhere in the Constitution to 'the Queen' or 'the Governor-General'.

Consideration would, of course, need to be given to the question whether the State governments should also become republican and, if so, what type of government should be adopted. This question is examined in chapter 6.

Executive Head of State without the Queen

It follows from the comments regarding an executive head of state under the Queen that replacement of the present system of responsible monarchical government with an elected Governor-General who exercised real executive powers and was the effective head of government as well as head of state would require considerable amendment of the Constitution. The necessary changes would, of course, depend upon the details of the proposed governmental structure. In addition to the requisite amendments in regard to a formal head of state without the Queen, a constitutional amendment would be necessary if the government were no longer to be responsible to the House of Representatives.[66]

DO WE NEED A HEAD OF STATE AT ALL?

Discussion of an Australian republic tends to presume that the Queen and the Governor-General would be replaced by an elected head of state (most likely titled 'president'), who may or may not also be the effective head of government, depending upon whether or not the present system of responsible government is retained. But a separate head of state is not an inexorable requirement of responsible republican government. It is quite possible to envisage a republic without any head of state at all; the monarchy and governorship-general could be abolished and the functions formerly performed by the Governor-General (including exercise of the 'reserve powers') vested in other bodies or officials, or even dispensed with altogether,[67] as was proposed (unsuccessfully[68]) by the Papua New Guinea Constitutional Planning Committee in 1974.[69] Thus, the prime minister could be elected and dismissed by the House of Representatives, as he effectively is in Ireland, West Germany, Sweden and Papua New Guinea.[70]

The formal appointment and dismissal of the prime minister need not be performed by a head of state; that function could be performed by the speaker of the House of Representatives, as in Sweden.[71] Similarly, the dissolution of parliament and calling of a general election could be left to the government subject, perhaps, to restrictions imposed by the Constitution itself, as in Sweden.[72] Functions currently exercisable by the Governor-General in council could, of course, easily be performed by the Federal Executive Council itself.

Nevertheless, some commentators have argued, or at least assumed,[73] that the Westminster system of responsible government requires a separate head of state to act as an 'umpire'[74] and supervise changes of government in accordance with the wishes of the electorate.[75] But this function need not be entrusted to a head of state; it too could be performed by the House of Representatives, as it effectively is in West Germany, Ireland, Papua New Guinea and Sweden and, indeed, ultimately is in Australia also. As Gough Whitlam has remarked,

All that is needed is transitional machinery to hand over government from one party to another when the electorate so determines. A panel of certain office-holders or the High Court . . . would probably suffice. The idea that the orderly handing over of government can be guaranteed only by a Head of State is a fallacy.[76]

However, virtually all nations appoint a head of state and, even though the head of government be effectively chosen by parliament, or its lower house, the formal power of appointing him or her is usually vested in the head of state. An Australian republic can be expected to do likewise.

Some proponents of a separate head of state under a Westminster system advocate not merely a formal or ceremonial head of state, but one with substantial discretionary powers. Surprisingly perhaps, a strong adherent of this view, even after Sir John Kerr's actions in November 1975, was Don Dunstan, the former Premier of South Australia.

In the Westminster System it is quite essential as a protection to the populace that there be a Head of State independent of Legislature, Judiciary and Executive. Without such an office one of the essential checks in the Constitution would be missing.

The chief function of the Head of State is to ensure that the Executive acts only in accordance with the power and within the limits defined by the Constitution and by Statute.

. . . If there is no independent check on the lawfulness of executive action it is extremely easy for ministers to exceed the authority which they have been given.

. . . Quite clearly, then, in a Westminster System an independent Head of State is necessary to ensure a proper check on executive power.[77]

Whether or not a head of state should have the power to supervise the legality of governmental action is, of course, a matter of opinion. Powers which ought not to be exercisable by an appointive Governor-General[78] might be considered appropriate for conferral upon an elected president. Yet it is dangerous to vest such enormous power in an irresponsible head of state[79] — even an elected one — especially when it is unnecessary, because unlawful governmental action can be left to the courts and, perhaps, an independent tribunal enforcing a leadership code, as in Papua New Guinea.[80] As the Papua New Guinea Constitutional Planning Committee noted in 1974,

It has been suggested to us that a mature and experienced person as a separate Head of State could act as an arbiter in constitutional disputes . . . . We prefer to have constitutional matters dealt with as part of the political process — for example, in discussions or negotiations among Ministers and Parliamentary leaders, or in Parliamentary debate — or, in the last resort, by a constitutional court, rather than by a kind of father figure, whose own legitimacy may not be widely accepted.[81]

However, even if a separate head of state is not mandated on constitutional grounds, practical and political considerations suggest that such a functionary can fulfil a valuable role. Although the Papua New Guinea Constitutional Planning Committee was unpersuaded by these factors,[82] a head of state can serve a useful function in acting as a personal symbol of national identity, especially on ceremonial occasions, thereby providing an alternative focus of national attention and respect, which serves to diminish somewhat the aura of importance (and, hence, the power) surrounding the head of government.[83]

In any event, for whatever reasons, virtually all countries have appointed such a functionary, and a republican Australia can be expected to follow suit.[84]

THE PROSPECTS FOR A REPUBLIC

Any assessment of the prospects of an Australian republic must be grounded on one fundamental fact: the change to a republic would require a constitutional amendment, and that, at least in practical terms, can be accomplished only by a successful referendum pursuant to section 128 of the Constitution. That provision requires a proposed constitutional amendment to be approved by an overall national majority and a majority of voters in four States, a double majority that is difficult to obtain, and virtually impossible if the proposed amendment is opposed by either of the main political parties or more than two State governments.[85]

As was noted earlier, the results of opinion polls on the monarchy v. republic issue must be treated with great caution because respondents are likely to have widely differing conceptions of what a 'republic' entails, of the effect of abolishing the office of Queen or Governor-General, and of the effect abolition of the monarchy would have on Australian-British relations. Moreover, several polls offered respondents a false dichotomy — retention of the monarchy v. a republic outside the (British) Commonwealth — whereas an Australian republic is likely to remain in the Commonwealth. Nevertheless, although the results of the twenty polls set out in table 1.1 vary quite widely — as indeed did the exact questions asked by the pollsters — some general conclusions can be drawn from them.

First, with the exception of the *Age* polls of December 1976 (which registered a pro-republic vote of almost 40 per cent) and April 1980 (36 per cent), which are considered below, the surveys between December 1975 and February 1986 suggest that republican sentiment rarely exceeded 30 per cent.[87] The level of support for a republic varied from 25 per cent in October 1976 to 31 per cent in December 1978 and November 1979. On these figures — and even on the remarkably high 39 per cent recorded in December 1976 — a referendum would obviously have no chance of success. (The simultaneous elections proposal was defeated in 1977 despite a national affirmative vote of more than 62 per cent.)

Secondly, despite the absence of any appreciable growth in republican sentiment during the last decade (the figures for December 1975 and January 1983 were identical — 28 per cent), republican sentiment appears to have doubled since the early 1950s, largely due, one suspects, to the greatly increased proportion of non-British elements in the population. Predictably, the *Age–Sydney Morning Herald* poll of 11 December 1976 found that pro-republican sentiment varied according to birthplace: British-born 29 per cent, Australian-born 38 per cent, European-born 67 per cent.[88]

Thirdly, the detailed results of the December 1976 *Age–Sydney Morning Herald* poll indicate that, as would be expected, pro-republic sentiment varies also with age, sex, education and political affiliation. Republican sentiment was stronger in men than in women (44%:34%),[89] and in those educated at university as compared with those with only a primary school education (43%:37%).[90] Republican sentiment was most pronounced in respondents aged 18–34 years, and progressively declined with each age-group surveyed thereafter; it was strongest in respondents aged 21–24 years (54 per cent), and weakest in those aged 60 years and over (21 per cent).[91] Moreover, as people familiar with Irish history would have expected, pro-republic sentiment was higher in Catholics than in Anglicans (47%:30%),[92] and was higher in Labor Party supporters (57 per cent) than in adherents of the Liberal Party (24 per cent) or National Party (16 per cent).[93]

What, then, are the prospects for an Australian republic? The advent of a republic is, undoubtedly, impossible at present — indeed none

Table 1.1   Opinion Polls on Monarchy v. Republic[86]

Date	Pro-Monarchy (%)	Pro-Republic (%)	Undecided (%)
June 1953 (Morgan Gallup Poll)[a]	77	15	8
April 1966 (Morgan Gallup Poll)[b]	65	22	13
July 1966 (Morgan Gallup Poll)[b]	63	28	9
February 1968 (Morgan Gallup Poll)[b]	53	40	7
October 1969 (Morgan Gallup Poll)[a]	64	24	12
June 1970 (Morgan Gallup Poll)[c]	68	26	6
February 1973 (Morgan Gallup Poll)[a]	50	42	8
November 1973 (Morgan Gallup Poll)[c]	53	32	15
December 1975 (*Bulletin*)[a]	61	28	11
October 1976 (*Bulletin*)[a]	60	25	15
December 1976 (*Age*)[b]	58	39	3
April 1977 (*Bulletin*)[a]	62	26	12
December 1978 (*Sun Herald*)[a]	61	31	8
November 1979 (Australian Public Opinion Polls — the Gallup Method)[a]	61	31	8
April 1980 (*Age*)[b]	61	36	3
August 1981 (*Bulletin*)[a]	59	28	13
September 1982 (Australian Public Opinion Polls —the Gallup Method)[a]	60	30	10
January 1983 (*Bulletin*)[a]	60	28	12
January 1984 (*Bulletin*)[a]	62	30	8
February 1986 (*Age*)[b]	63	30	8

Question asked:
a Retain the monarchy or become a republic?
b Retain present links with the United Kingdom or become an entirely separate republic?
c At the end of Queen Elizabeth's reign, should we recognize Charles as King or become a republic with an elected president?

of the major political parties actively proposes it — and very unlikely in the foreseeable future.[94] Yet the opinion poll published in the *Age* and the *Sydney Morning Herald* on 11 December 1976 gave cause for optimism as to the long-term prospects of an Australian republic: even without a campaign to educate the public and convert people to republicanism, overall almost 40 per cent of those surveyed favoured a republic; among men the level of support reached 44 per cent. Moreover, a majority of respondents aged 18–24 years favoured a republic — among those aged 25–34 years the level of support was still 50 per cent — while fully two-thirds of non-British European migrants favoured a republic. The level of republican sentiment revealed by that poll is, admittedly, considerably higher than the level of around 28–31 per cent usually recorded, but it is important to note that the size of the pro-republic vote corresponded with a fall in the 'undecided' vote (3 per cent compared with a usual figure of around 10 per cent), and not a corresponding fall in the pro-monarchy vote (58 per cent compared with a usual level of around 60 per cent). The same is true of the poll published in the *Age* in April 1980: the relatively high republican vote (36 per cent) was at the expense of the 'undecided' figure (3 per cent), not the pro-monarchy vote (61 per cent). (Indeed, an outstanding feature of the opinion polls over the last decade is the remarkable consistency of the pro-monarchy vote: 61 per cent in December 1975; 63 per cent in February 1986.) Hence, the results of the two *Age* polls may be less aberrant than at first appears, and may, in fact, reflect accurately the considered judgment of the respondents.

If the youth of 1976 persist in their beliefs, if the decline in the British elements of our population and culture[95] continues, and if the principal political parties or important community groups begin to espouse a republic and educate people as to its form and consequences, an Australian republic is a realistic prospect for the next generation, around the year 2000. As Senator Gareth Evans has remarked,

[A]lthough the figures have not changed over the last decade, they have changed over the last generation . . . . Over the last generation we have had [an] 80–20 ratio coming down to a 60–40 ratio. I suspect that it will take as long as another generation for that ratio to go further and become clearly pro-republican, but the trend is there.[96]

Geoffrey Sawer similarly believes that 'it is likely enough that Australia will with more or less deliberate speed become a republic.'[97]

While little practical significance can, as yet, be attached to the virtually 'accidental' inclusion of republicanism in the Australian Labor Party Platform in 1981,[98] that event was symbolic of the consistent direction of Australian history since federation (if not earlier), which indicates that an Australian republic is 'the only logical goal'.[99] An Australian republic is, ultimately, inevitable.

ADDENDUM

A poll conducted after this chapter was written supports its conclusion
that the long-term prospects for an Australian republic are good.

The poll was conducted by telephone only in New South Wales on
10 January 1985. The results, published in the *Sunday Telegraph*, 13
January 1985, p. 4 were as follows:

**Q: Do you believe Australia should become a republic or remain part of
the British Commonwealth?**

	All people 18 years and over	People aged 18 to 34 years Percentages	People aged 35 years and over
Australia should become a republic	37	44	31
Australia should remain part of Commonwealth	55	43	63
Don't know	8	13	6

A poll conducted in February 1986 among 2000 registered voters in all
federal electorates was published in the *Age*, 3 March 1986, p. 3. It is
reprinted in table 1.2 (pp. 16–17) with the kind permission of Irving
Saulwick and Associates. (Like the *Sunday Telegraph* poll above, it
offered respondents an artificial choice, because an Australian republic
will almost certainly remain in the (British) Commonwealth.)

Table 1.2   Attitudes towards Australia Becoming a Republic

(rated by respondent's sex and age)

Australia should:	Total (2000) %	Male (988) %	Female (1012) %	18–24 (344) %	25–34 (440) %	35–44 (393) %	45–59 (411) %	60 and over (412) %
Remain a member of the Commonwealth with a Governor-General	63	59	67	53	58	60	64	77
Become an independent republic with a president	30	34	26	37	35	33	29	16
Don't know	8	8	8	10	7	7	7	7

(rated by education, voting intention, religion and country of origin)

Australia should:	Primary educated (200) %	Tertiary educated (441) %	Will vote A.L.P. (900) %	Will vote Liberal (695) %	Will vote N.C.P. (127) %	Will vote Aust. Dem. (124) %	Protestant (1072) %	Roman Catholic (482) %	Born in Aust. N.Z. (1604) %	Born in U.K. (219) %	Born in Europe (117) %
Remain a member of the Commonwealth with a Governor-General	70	56	51	78	77	57	73	55	64	75	30
Become an independent republic with a president	21	38	41	17	16	40	21	36	29	24	53
Don't know	9	6	8	5	7	3	6	9	8	2	15

Note: Percentages rounded to nearest whole figure

Chapter 2
Reasons for Becoming a Republic

The form of republican government adopted by Australia will, of course, largely depend upon the reasons for making the transition from constitutional monarchy to republic in the first place. It is, obviously, impossible to predict with certainty which considerations will weigh most heavily with Australian voters of the next generation, but since republicanism has a long history — even in Australia — the likely motivations for an Australian republic can easily be identified. (As indicated earlier, it is not this book's purpose to evaluate whether or not the considerations likely to influence Australians ultimately to vote for a republic *ought* cumulatively to be persuasive enough to outweigh the countervailing arguments for retention of the status quo.)

NATIONAL IDENTITY

The principal motivation for contemporary Australian republicanism appears to be the belief that Australia should, like almost all other nations, have its own individual head of state, and should not have to share its head of state with any other country.[1]

The formal title of our present head of state is 'Queen of Australia'.[2] The King or Queen of Australia is, as the Constitution specifies, the person who is for the time being King or Queen of the United Kingdom,[3] but the *personal* unity of the British and Australian crowns (like those of England and Scotland from 1603 to 1707 and Great Britain (and later the United Kingdom) and Hanover from 1714 to 1837) has little, if any, practical significance in the Commonwealth sphere of Australian political life. The Queen of Australia acts only on the 'advice' of the Commonwealth government in all Commonwealth matters — essentially the appointment and removal of the Governor-General. Hence, to all intents and purposes, Australia practically has an indigenous monarchy — 'a monarchy exclusive to Australia in relation to Australian affairs, domestic and international.'[4] An indigenous *monarchy*, although not, of course, an indigenous monarch.*

---

* This is, at least, true in the Commonwealth sphere; the position in State matters is more complicated. At the time of writing, State governors are still appointed — and, presumably, removed — on 'advice' formally tendered to the Queen by a British

However, heads of state fulfil an important role in the national psyche, quite apart from their more mundane practical function as formal head of the machinery of state. Because a head of state is a symbol of national identity, it is not surprising that many Australians should feel that their country's retention of the head of state of its former colonial overlord as its own head of state detracts from their sense of independent nationhood. It makes them feel 'derivative, . . . provincial and second–rate',[7] as if they 'do not at heart regard [themselves] as an independent nation at all'.[8] Monarchists like Sir Garfield Barwick may well scoff that to focus attention on the 'identity of the person of the monarch', who happens to live on the other side of the globe, is a failing of 'minds unaccustomed to the subtleties of distinction and difference'[9] — minds so perverse as to regard the royal family as British, rather than Australian! — but it ill-behoves monarchists, of all people, to discount the significance of irrational psychological and sentimental factors in framing popular attitudes towards the head of state. The desire for a separate head of state symbolizing Australian independence, rather than one deriving from an era of colonial dependence, has long motivated Australian republicans,[10] and continues to foster republican sentiment in other monarchies of the Commonwealth of Nations.[11]

It has, moreover, been argued that retention of the British monarch as Australian head of state has had adverse practical consequences. It has allegedly hindered the development of an independent Australian culture which, in turn, has detrimentally affected Australian foreign policy by retarding recognition of Australia's role as an Asian Pacific nation. This argument has been expressed most forcefully by Donald Horne.

> The maintenance of the present system sustains a construction of reality, left over from the British Empire days, that is demonstrably false and dangerous to what many/most Australians might see as their interests: it does not define Australia as an independent nation adjoining Southeast Asia and the Southwest Pacific, but as a kind of sub-nation that is in some sense alien to its own environment.[12]

It has been alleged that retention of the Queen as Australian head of state can have further adverse consequences for Australian foreign relations. Complications could result, it has been suggested, from the difficulty some foreign observers might experience in distinguishing between those occasions when the Queen acts as Queen of the United Kingdom and those when she acts as Queen of one of the other

---

minister, the Foreign and Commonwealth Secretary, albeit acting, almost invariably, merely as a conduit for the State government,[5] thereby making it arguable (wrongly, in this writer's opinion[6]) that the head of state of the Australian States is the Queen of the United Kingdom, not the Queen of Australia — surely a ludicrous proposition.

Commonwealth monarchies, such as Australia. Discussion of this issue was spurred by remarks (seen by some as anti-Israeli) made by the Queen on a state visit to Jordan in late March 1984,[13] which led the editor of the *Australian* to issue the following caution:

Queen Elizabeth's journey to the Middle East is a reminder of a constitutional anomaly relating to Australia's association with the monarchy . . . .

Most of [the Queen's] time is spent in Britain and, while she is there, it has to be assumed that when she says something of a political nature she is speaking for the British Government. Similarly, when she is in one of the countries of which she is head of state, she has to be taken as speaking on the advice of that country's ministers . . . .

There is no such formal understanding of her role when she is in a foreign country. And yet there is no compelling reason why, when she is in Jordan, she should be regarded as the Queen of the United Kingdom and not, to take but one example, as Queen of Australia.

It is not absurdly pedantic to suggest that this could lead to difficulties. It is unlikely that most of the world's inhabitants fully appreciate the intricacies of our constitutional monarchy and some of them may assume that, when the Queen of Australia, in the course of her travels, says something to which they take exception, she is speaking on our behalf.[14]

Michael Pryles of Monash University went further, warning that '[i]f the British Government continues to use the Queen in this way the conclusion must be that it is intolerable to have the same person as Head of State of two independent countries.'[15] When asked a question about the matter in parliament, the Attorney-General belittled these concerns as trivial 'exotica',[16] but his detailed response some weeks later confirmed the possibility that international observers might well be confused:

The Queen is Head of State of 17 Commonwealth countries including the United Kingdom and Australia.

When the Queen visits one of these countries she does so as Head of State of the country concerned.

[When the Queen visits countries outside the Commonwealth the] position is governed largely by practice and convention and *depends upon the basis on which the invitation to visit a particular country is made and accepted*. In *most cases* the Queen will have been invited to visit the country concerned in her capacity as Head of State of the United Kingdom. The visit will therefore be undertaken in that capacity and she will speak in that capacity, acting on the advice of the United Kingdom Government. This would be understood and appreciated by the host Government.[17]

But the possibility of confusion should not be exaggerated, since officials of the host government at least will always know in which capacity the Queen is visiting their country — whether as Queen of the United Kingdom or as Queen of one of her other Commonwealth realms (or as Head of the Commonwealth).[18] However, as a debate earlier in 1984 demonstrated, opinion appears to be divided on the somewhat analogous question whether the Queen can visit a Commonwealth republic,[19] especially to attend a Commonwealth function such as a Heads of Government meeting, merely as 'Head of the Commonwealth' (in which capacity she will not be acting on the 'advice' of any responsible official),[20] or whether she can visit such a country only as Queen of the United Kingdom (acting, thus, only on the 'advice' of a British minister).[21] In this writer's opinion, the former view is preferable, and is supported by practice. During the royal tour of the United States in 1957, for example, the Queen arrived in Washington D.C. and visited the United Nations as 'Head of the Commonwealth', not as Queen of the United Kingdom.[22]

It would be inappropriate to leave this topic without acknowledging the existence of dissenting voices which argue that, far from being an archaic remnant of colonialism, the concept of a shared head of state (in the personal, rather than constitutional, sense) is a 'modern', 'internationalist' one. The clearest proponent of this view is Justice Michael Kirby:

[S]ome modernists question the beefing up of fervor for provincial patriotism. Some see such narrowly defined nationalism as the special curse of the 20th century.

Sharing a head of state with diverse countries around the world is a very modern contribution to internationalism. Fierce nationalism and promotion of 'national identity' may harken to the past and even be dangerous in the nuclear age.[23]

While the sharing by several countries of the head of state may indeed contribute to international collaboration and understanding — at least between them — the current relationship between the Australian and British monarchs cannot accurately be characterized as a 'sharing'; the equality connoted by that word is simply not present. Our head of state is, as covering clause 2 of the Constitution specifies, the British monarch. She resides in the United Kingdom, so that our *de facto* heads of state are the Governor-General and the State governors. There is, of course, no need for a Governor-General in the United Kingdom, so the practical position of the two monarchies is hardly comparable. While a truly 'shared' head of state would probably be impractical, were Australia to adopt a republican form of government with a formal (rather than executive) head of state, it might some day be considered appropriate to elect to the presidency a distinguished citizen of another country — especially a Commonwealth country, such as Canada or India. There is, indeed, no legal obstacle to following such a course at present regarding appointments to the office of Governor-General,[24] as was suggested at one time by Sir Robert Menzies.[25]

However, the yearning many Australian republicans apparently feel for a personal symbol of their national identity is unlikely to be satisfied by anything less than a separate Australian head of state. Of course, a republican form of government does not necessarily follow — the indigenous head of state could be a monarch, but the notion of a home-grown Australian king or queen is an entirely fanciful (if not ludicrous) one, with absolutely no prospect of implementation.

Finally, it should be noted that any form of republican government is compatible with this motivation for abolishing the monarchy.

OPPOSITION TO THE HEREDITY PRINCIPLE

Historically, an important motivation for republican sentiment has been opposition to the principle of devolution of public office by heredity, rather than by election or appointment on merit, and contemporary Australian republicanism can be expected to derive sustenance from this tradition.[26] Undoubtedly the most forceful critic of this aspect of monarchy was the Anglo-American political theorist and agitator, Thomas Paine (1737–1809). In his pungent, provocative tracts, especially *Common Sense* (January 1776) and *Rights of Man* (1791–92), Paine vehemently attacked hereditary government on both pragmatic and theoretical grounds. His practical objection was simply that wisdom cannot be inherited.

Admitting that Government is a contrivance of human *wisdom*, it must necessarily follow, that hereditary succession . . . can make no part of it, because it is impossible to make wisdom hereditary; and on the other hand, *that* cannot be a wise contrivance, which in its operation may commit the government of a nation to the wisdom of an idiot.[27]

I smile to myself when I contemplate the ridiculous insignificance into which literature and all the sciences would sink were they made hereditary; and I carry the same idea into governments. *An hereditary governor is as inconsistent as an hereditary author.*[28]

But Paine's detestation of monarchy went beyond pragmatic considerations. He condemned hereditary succession as 'an insult and an imposition on posterity'[29], because it denied each generation its inherent right to choose its own rulers. He characterized such 'preclusion of consent' as 'despotism'[30], and argued:

Man has no authority over posterity in matters of personal right; and therefore, no man, or body of men, had, or can have, a right to set up hereditary government. . . .

All hereditary government is in its nature tyranny. An heritable crown, or an heritable throne . . . have no other significant explanation than that mankind are heritable property. *To inherit a government, is to inherit the people, as if they were flocks and herds.*[31]

While it is, of course, true that any constitution restricts, to a greater or lesser extent (depending upon its provisions and mode of amendment), the next generation's freedom to conduct its affairs exactly as it chooses, hereditary monarchy pre-determines not merely the form of government, but the identity of the head of state as well.

Paine's call, in *Common Sense*, for independence from Great Britain had enormous impact in America, and was an important catalyst in the decision, taken within six months of its publication, to declare independence.[32] By the summer of 1776, support for a republic was widespread,[33] and even those who, like John Adams, disagreed with some of Paine's views on the organization of a government, agreed with his view of monarchy:

I know of nothing more desirable in society than the abolition of all hereditary distinctions. . . . There is nothing more irrational, absurd, or ridiculous in the sight of philosophy than the idea of hereditary kings and nobles.[34]

Moreover, opposition to the principle of heredity in public affairs was reflected and entrenched, in a more concrete form in the prohibitions against the grant of titles of nobility which appeared in State Declarations of Rights as early as 1776,[35] in the Articles of Confederation in 1777,[36] and in the United States Constitution in 1787[37] — a provision which Alexander Hamilton regarded as 'the corner stone of republican government [because] so long as [titles of nobility] are excluded, there can never be serious danger that the government will be any other than that of the people.'[38]

Paine's influence spread beyond America, Britain and France to the Antipodes, where his views on monarchy had several adherents in the 1880s[39], leading one historian of the period to note that 'hatred of hereditary monarchy and aristocracy on principle and the British monarchy and aristocracy in particular [was] the *first source* of the support for republicanism in critical circles'.[40]

However, although probably not insignificant in motivating Australian republicanism (there do not appear to be any statistics on this question), opposition to heredity in public office is unlikely to be the principal consideration for many republicans. Rather, it can be expected to have importance as an ancillary factor strengthening republican views based upon other considerations, such as the desire for a separate identifiably Australian head of state, or adoption of a presidential form of government, along American or French (or other) lines. The history of republics suggests that they are usually established either because a particular monarch or royal house is considered obnoxious (as in France (three times), Italy, Germany, Austria, Russia, China and Greece), or because a colony seeks independence (e.g. the United States, Finland, Indonesia, Burma and Zaire) or an ex-colony desires an indigenous head of state (e.g. the republics of the Commonwealth, and republics formerly in the Commonwealth, such as Ireland, Pakistan and South Africa). Australian republicanism can be expected to follow this pattern, and be motivated primarily by the aspiration for an indigenous head of state.

Of course, once again, any form of republican government would be compatible with this motivation for abolishing the monarchy.

POPULAR SOVEREIGNTY

As was noted earlier, in Western democracies republican government is government based upon 'popular sovereignty'.[41] This was recognized in the United States by the late 1770s[42]; as James Madison remarked in *The Federalist*, republican government is 'a government which derives all its powers directly or indirectly from the great body of the people'.[43] A century later, the American view of republican government was summarized admirably as 'one based on the right of the people to govern themselves, but requiring that right to be exercised through public organs of a representative character; and these organs constitute the government.'[44] Although, of course, many — if not most — of the world's republics are neither free nor democratic (in the Western liberal sense), and are certainly not models of representative government, Western democratic republics do take their foundation upon popular sovereignty seriously, and many of them assert it explicitly in their constitutions.[45]

To what extent is current Australian monarchical government based upon popular sovereignty? It should, first, be noted that some monarchies (e.g. Japan and Sweden[46]) do not regard monarchy as antithetical to a government based upon popular sovereignty, perhaps because their monarchs exercise purely ceremonial functions. The powers of the Australian Governor-General are certainly more substantial than that. Secondly, if the 'sovereign' (a notoriously vague concept with a variety of different meanings) is the body with the ultimate power to determine the form of the government, then Australian government already embodies popular sovereignty because the power to amend the Commonwealth Constitution is vested in the electors by section 128. In this respect, Australia differs from the United Kingdom, where 'sovereignty' is vested in 'the Queen in Parliament', which includes not only the popularly elected House of Commons but the appointive and hereditary House of Lords as well. Hence, strictly speaking, those who seek an Australian government based upon 'popular sovereignty' have achieved their goal already.

However, because symbolism is an important consideration in assessing the role of a head of state, a hereditary head of state is likely, notwithstanding section 128 of the Constitution, to be obnoxious to those who believe that popular sovereignty requires that governmental power should be exercised exclusively 'through public organs of a representative character'.[47] Moreover, the Australian popular tradition (somewhat mythical, perhaps), expounded so forcefully by Manning Clark in his *A History of Australia*, runs counter to the social inequality inherent (notwithstanding the best endeavours of some monarchists to deny it[48]) in the concept of monarchy.[49] Clearly, the devolution of the state's highest office within one family represents a denial at the very centre of the social and political system of the axiom that all people are born equal in status and dignity. Hence, belief in social equality inevitably leads to republicanism, a point understood by Alexis de Tocqueville more than a century ago when he wrote

In the United States the sovereignty of the people is not an isolated doctrine, bearing no relation to the prevailing habits and ideas of the people; it may, on the contrary, be regarded as the last link of a chain of opinions which binds the whole Anglo-American world. That Providence has given to every human being the degree of reason necessary to direct himself in the affairs that interest him exclusively is the grand maxim upon which civil and political society rests in the United States. . . .

Thus in the United States the fundamental principle of the republic is the same which governs the greater part of human actions; republican notions insinuate themselves into all the ideas, opinions and habits of the Americans and are formally recognized by the laws . . .[50]

An elective presidency is a more rational form of government than a monarchy for a polity, like Australia, based upon popular sovereignty. Indeed, in a general sense, republicanism might be regarded as a product of the application of reason to analysis of the forms of government, whereas monarchy derives its strength from tradition and sentiment. As Frederick Grimke argued, with the rhetorical flourish typical of his era,

In a republic men all descend into the plain; they are no longer overpowered by the indistinct notion of immensity. The understanding gains the ascendancy and they are enabled to form more just notions on all subjects. . . . [T]hey are better able to survey calmly and one by one the men and things which make up the great community in which they live.[51]

Growth in republicanism is unlikely to be an isolated phenomenon, and will probably be accompanied by other reform proposals which share its rationality and diminished deference to tradition and to institutions inherited from Britain. Such reforms might include an autochthonous constitution (one deriving its formal authority from the consent of the Australian people, rather than the British parliament), a Bill of rights, changes in the Commonwealth–State division of powers and, for some, a greater separation between legislative and executive powers. Donald Horne has argued that

For the movement for a republic to be worthwhile it must be associated with new attempts at defining Australian idealism. The ideal of the republic can become a general democratic ideal. It can become an assertion that in a democracy, as . . . the Swedish Constitution puts it, 'all public power emanates from the people'. It can become the battering ram in the demand for new political rights in Australia, embodied in a new Constitution.[52]

WIDER CONSTITUTIONAL REFORM

Some republicans might take Donald Horne's argument further and maintain that the change to a republic would not be worth the trouble unless it was accompanied by wider constitutional or governmental reform. This is especially true of those whose republicanism is based upon a preference for an American-style executive presidency.[53] They are unlikely to exhibit much enthusiasm for a republican campaign in which the only real objective is the substitution of an elected president for the present appointive Governor-General.

But displacing the Crown from the Australian constitutional set-up would, in itself, remove some of the artificial confusion of Australian constitutional law. For example, courts have occasionally sought to employ British imperial concepts, such as the 'common sovereignty' of the Crown over the whole Empire, and the role of a 'viceroy', to resolve issues concerning the power of the Commonwealth and the States to apply their legislation to one another.[54] This is a fundamental concern in all federations and must be resolved, as in republican federations like the United States and India, by deciding whether one polity in the federation can bind another, without bedevilling the issues with imperial arcana which only confuse the whole question.

In general, as was noted earlier, the role of the Crown merely confuses Commonwealth-State relations. Far from enhancing State independence, as is sometimes claimed,[55] the amorphous relationship between the Crown of Great Britain and the Crowns of the Commonwealth and the States, intermingled as it can become with Australian-British international relations, only serves to threaten State independence, not to protect it.[56] As Justice Dawson of the High Court of Australia — hardly a fervent centralist — has acknowledged, removal of the Crown 'may even serve to eliminate some of the difficulties which still remain in discerning the role of the Crown in our federation.'[57]

However, one difficulty it will not necessarily remove is the possibility of a recurrence of the events of October and November 1975, culminating in the Governor-General's dismissal of the Prime Minister on 11 November. Some of Sir John Kerr's most trenchant critics have become republicans, identifying the dismissal of the Prime Minister, followed by the Queen's refusal to intervene[58] as the catalyst.[59] But the connection between those events and the establishment of a republic is not obvious. Indeed, motivations among republicans strongly influenced by the 1975 events appear to vary.

Some believe that the Governor-General acted unconstitutionally, or at least improperly, thereby 'bringing public contempt upon his Office'.[60] Gough Whitlam, the dismissed Prime Minister, put this view to the Queen when soon after his dismissal he wrote to her that the Governor-General had 'put in jeopardy the future of the Crown in Australia and gravely undermined the respect and regard attaching to the office of the representative of the Crown and therefore, to the Crown itself.'[61] However, this is not a very persuasive reason for abolishing the monarchy. As the subsequent history of the office of Governor-General has shown, most of the contempt or rage engendered by Sir John Kerr's action was directed at him personally. Once he had resigned and was succeeded by Governors-General untainted by the 1975 events and dedicated to a public 'healing', much of the anger was spent, and the respect accorded to the office largely returned to pre-1975 levels.

Of course, objection to the Governor-General's actions was frequently combined with opposition to the very existence of the 'reserve power' which the Governor-General purported to exercise.[62] Whether or not the Governor-General acted lawfully or properly, it was claimed, he simply should not have the power to dismiss a prime minister enjoying the confidence of the House of Representatives, so these powers should be abolished by establishing a republic.[63] But this is a *non sequitur*, of course, except insofar as abolishing the Governor-General ensures that he cannot exercise an obnoxious power — or indeed any power! Merely replacing an appointed Governor-General with an elected president does not guarantee that the office-holder will not exercise certain powers.[64] It may, in fact, exacerbate the problem of 'reserve powers' because an elected head of state, perhaps even with his own popular 'mandate', no longer subject to the legal and conventional constraints of the British monarchy, is far more likely to indulge in independent exercises of power than is the present appointed representative of the Crown.[65] In short, the question of the head of state's powers must be addressed directly.[66]

Other republicans derive different lessons from the events of November 1975. For some, the constitutional language which appeared to support Sir John Kerr — if not Charles I — highlighted the fact that our Constitution is, undeniably, 'a colonial document that [says] nothing inspiring about Australia and nothing noble about ordinary human beings.'[67] Of course, one can amend the Constitution without necessarily making it republican, and one could even remove virtually all of the Crown's powers without abolishing it, as Sweden demonstrated recently.

Strangely, some republicans seem to have been surprised by the Queen's refusal to accept the Speaker's invitation to intervene and re-commission the dismissed Prime Minister.[68] They argue that, since the

Queen has no power to intervene in Commonwealth affairs (except to appoint or 'recall' (i.e. dismiss) the Governor-General), and all executive power is formally vested in the Governor-General, Australia is not a monarchy, but a 'governor-generalate'.[69] Moreover, they are justifiably concerned that the Queen's non-involvement in Australian affairs means that she can avoid responsibility for vice-regal actions, with the result that Governors-General need not share her concern to protect the monarchy, which is an important practical constraint upon the Queen's exercise of power.[70] Hence, a constitutional 'governor-generalate' inevitably has greater practical independence than a constitutional monarchy. Their conclusion is that, since our real head of state is not the Queen, but an appointed Australian official, we might as well formally dispense with the Queen and elect that Australian official. While much of this reasoning is sound, most monarchists would surely deny that their preference for retention of the monarchy is based upon any notion that the Queen can, or even should, personally intervene in Australian affairs. Indeed, they would recognize that it is precisely such an intervention which could be fatal to the monarchy in Australia, if not elsewhere as well.[71]

Chapter 3
The Crown in Australian Government

Any assessment of the governmental and constitutional changes which would be wrought by the establishment of a republic, and of the appropriate form or forms of Australian republican government, must be based upon an understanding of the existing governmental structure. This chapter outlines the current operation of Australian government at both Commonwealth and State levels.

Since the institution of a republic will transform the executive branch of government (the Queen, the Governor-General or governor, and the government headed by the prime minister or State premier), but need not significantly alter the current relationship between government and legislature, it is appropriate to consider these topics separately.

RELATIONS WITHIN THE EXECUTIVE BRANCH

The Queen

The formal head of all Australian governments is the Queen of Australia — notwithstanding the anomaly that (at the time of writing) the channel for communication between the State governments and the Queen remains the Foreign and Commonwealth Secretary, a minister in the British government.[1] The Queen of Australia's principal function is to appoint (and, presumably, dismiss) her local representatives, the Governor-General of the Commonwealth and the State governors. These powers are exercisable only on the 'advice' of the respective government, although State 'advice' is, of course, still transmitted to the Queen by the British Foreign and Commonwealth Secretary.[2]

The Queen also retains some additional powers of no practical importance, such as the power to disallow Commonwealth or State legislation within one (Commonwealth) or two (the States) years of its enactment,[3] and to assent to Bills reserved for her assent by the Governor-General or a governor. Disallowance is a dead letter and has not been exercised in this century.[4] At the Commonwealth level, the Australian Constitutional Convention has thrice recommended its abolition,[5] which would have been effected had the Constitution Alteration (Removal of Outmoded and Expended Provisions) Bill 1983 (passed by the Senate on 13 October 1983) become law.[6]

Reservation of Bills is a more complicated matter. State governors are required to reserve Bills on specified subjects by a combination of imperial and State legislation and royal Instructions,[7] and retain a general power to reserve any Bill for the Queen's assent.[8] The Governor-General has a similar power to reserve any Bill,[9] and must reserve Bills limiting appeals to the Privy Council.[10] But reservation of Bills is of no practical importance because both the governor's or Governor-General's decision to reserve a Bill and the Queen's decision whether or not to assent to it are nowadays exercised on the 'advice' of the government of the place of enactment (transmitted via the British Foreign and Commonwealth Secretary in the case of State Bills).[11] The Constitution Alteration (Removal of Outmoded and Expended Provisions) Bill 1983,[12] implementing a recommendation of the Adelaide Constitutional Convention of that year,[13] would also have formally interred reservation of Commonwealth Bills.

In three States the power to dismiss judges is formally vested in the Queen[14] but, otherwise, all Australian executive powers are exercisable by the Governor-General or the State governors, ministers and public servants. The Queen does not have power to exercise any Commonwealth executive powers vested in the Governor-General, or to give him instructions in regard to their exercise.[15] (The Queen has recognized her impotence in this respect; explicitly on 17 November 1975 in her private secretary's letter to Speaker Scholes,[16] and implicitly on 21 August 1984 when she revoked the Governor-General's Instructions of 29 October 1900 and substituted new Letters Patent relating to his office.[17]) The Queen probably has the power to exercise State executive powers not vested in the governor by statute (i.e. those derived from the royal prerogative), and to give the governor instructions in regard to their exercise.[18] But these powers of the Queen are, of course, exercisable (*de facto*) only on State government 'advice'. All powers vested in the Queen of Australia are, in short, exercisable only on the advice of local ministers, transmitted either directly (in the case of the Commonwealth),[19] or via the British Foreign and Commonwealth Secretary (in the case of the States).[20]

Governor-General and Governors

As already noted, all Australian executive powers (Commonwealth, State and territorial), apart from those few vested in the Queen of Australia, are exercisable by the Governor-General, State governors or territorial administrators (or those officers in council), and by ministers and public servants acting (generally) under their supervision. Section 61 of the Commonwealth Constitution, which provides that '[t]he executive power of the Commonwealth is vested in the Queen and is exercisable by the Governor-General as the Queen's representative', explicitly recognizes the Governor-General's formal position at the (de facto) apex of the Commonwealth executive. Although State constitutions have no provision equivalent to section 61,[21] State governors occupy a similar position because they are the formal repositories of all State executive powers except those vested by statute in some other official or body.[22] Executive powers conferred by the State (and federal) constitutions or the prerogative (or common law) powers of the Crown are vested in the governor — the former because a statutory provision expressly provides so, the latter because the governor is the local representative of the Queen, in whom the prerogative powers would otherwise inhere. The Governor-General and State governors are, in short, the de facto Australian heads of state.

General Executive Powers

Apart from the few 'reserve powers' of the Crown, in the exercise of which the Governor-General and the governors enjoy some personal discretion, all exercises of executive power in Australia are ultimately controlled by the Commonwealth and State cabinets, which are responsible therefor to the lower houses of their legislatures. Except when exercising a 'reserve power', the Governor-General or governor must act on the 'advice' of his ministers.[23] As Bagehot remarked of the monarch,[24] he is entitled to be kept informed of the activities of his ministers, and to express his opinion to them thereon, seeking to change their minds if necessary but, if they persist in their 'advice', he must ultimately give way and follow it. As Sir Paul Hasluck noted in his William Queale Memorial Lecture in 1972, the Governor-General (and, presumably, State governors) can exercise a significant influence on the operation of government by ensuring that proposed administrative action is lawful, complies with the proper forms and conventions of government and, perhaps, that it accords with government policy.[25] But, as already noted, ultimately the exercise of all executive powers (whether vested in the Governor-General or the Governor-General in council) except the 'reserve powers' is controlled by cabinet, and the Governor-General or governor has no power to refuse to follow its 'advice'. In the case of administrative powers conferred upon the Governor-General or governor by statute, Commonwealth legislation and the legislation of four States expressly provides that such powers shall be exercised with the 'advice' (or, in South Australia and Western Australia, the 'advice and consent') of the Executive Council.[26]

The 'Reserve Powers'

The position of the 'reserve powers' of the Crown — those in regard to which the Governor-General and the State governors enjoy some personal discretion and need not invariably follow ministerial 'advice'[27]

— is complicated and controversial. As a consequence, no doubt, of the anger and controversy generated by the Governor-General's dismissal of Prime Minister Gough Whitlam in November 1975, the Australian Constitutional Convention endeavoured to codify the conventions governing the reserve powers of the Governor-General,[28] and commissioned several papers on the question.[29] These papers are only a tiny portion of the enormous, and ever-expanding, volume of literature on the reserve powers of the Monarch and her representatives in Canada, Australia, New Zealand and elsewhere.[30] This is not an appropriate forum for a detailed exegesis of the reserve powers, but a brief account is necessary for an understanding of the present political and constitutional position of the Governor-General and State governors — the essential background for an assessment of the appropriate powers and functions of the head (or heads) of state in a future Australian republic.

There are, at the most, four reserve powers: the powers to appoint and (more dubiously) dismiss the prime minister or premier, and to refuse and (more dubiously) force a dissolution of the lower house of parliament or (in the Commonwealth and South Australia) a simultaneous dissolution of both houses. The Queen's powers to appoint and dismiss the (British) prime minister and to dissolve the House of Commons are common law (or prerogative) powers. Hence it is natural that their exercise should be governed by custom or convention. This is not so obvious in Australia, where the equivalent powers of the Governor-General and State governors are conferred by statute.[31] Here it is possible for constitutional neophytes (as they demonstrate whenever the reserve powers are discussed) to read the constitutional language as if it were inscribed on a *tabula rasa*, devoid of historical and conventional background. But, clearly, the conventions governing the exercise of reserve powers in Australia are essentially (if not precisely) the same as those governing the Queen's exercise of the equivalent powers in the United Kingdom. Indeed, it is arguable that the entrenchment of some Australian constitutions (especially the Commonwealth's), and their detailed provisions regarding the summoning, composition and duration of parliament, warrant an even more restrictive ambit for the reserve powers here than in the United Kingdom where the House of Commons, controlled by the government, is *de facto* supreme.[32]

The equivalence in the constitutional positions of the Queen and the Governor-General was explicitly recognized by the Imperial Conference of 1926:

it is an essential consequence of the equality of status existing among the members of the British Commonwealth of Nations that the Governor-General of a Dominion is the representative of the Crown, holding in all essential respects the same position in relation to the administration of public affairs in the Dominion as is held by His Majesty the King in Great Britain . . .[33]

In practice, the Queen is, of course, likely to exercise greater restraint than the Governor-General when contemplating the exercise of a reserve power, because an improper, or even controversial, exercise of the power could threaten not merely her tenure of office, but the future of the monarchy itself.[34] But if the positions of the Queen of the United Kingdom and the Governor-General of Australia are essentially equivalent, is this true also of State governors, who were not included in the 1926 declaration?

This oft-debated question[35] can be answered briefly: in theory, yes, but in practice, they are probably not entirely equivalent. Theoretically, the relationship between a State governor and his ministers ought to be equivalent to that of their Commonwealth counterparts because there is, in short, neither any imperial nor any federal reason for them to differ. Neither the Governor-General nor a State governor derives independent discretion from any role as a representative of the British government — the only reason in the past for according the governor of a colony enjoying responsible government powers wider than those of the Queen *vis-à-vis* her British ministers. The Imperial Conference of 1926 expressly acknowledged that the Governor-General was 'not the representative or agent of His Majesty's Government in Great Britain or of any Department of that Government.'[36] Once again, nothing was said about the position of State governors but, notwithstanding the anomalous channel of communication between the Queen and the State governments (the British Secretary of State for Foreign and Commonwealth Affairs), the declaration obviously applied *de facto* to State governors as well. It would be ludicrous and outrageous for the head of state of a constituent part of an independent nation to represent a foreign power.[37] Hence, notwithstanding the contrary implications of some archaic and obsolete provisions in the royal Instructions of State governors,[38] it is beyond question that they do not represent anyone or anything other than the Queen of Australia.

Moreover, the Commonwealth and the States enjoy equal status *vis-à-vis* one another in the federation. There is, therefore, neither any imperial nor any federal reason why a governor's relations with his ministers should not be exactly equivalent to that of his Commonwealth and British counterparts. Dr H. V. Evatt's conclusion, endorsed by Dr Eugene Forsey,[39] is undoubtedly correct.

There is really no valid argument for denying to the Australian States . . . a constitutional status in respect of internal affairs completely co-equal with the status of the central Governmental authorities. . . . It follows, of course, that no valid distinction can, or should, be drawn between the position of the

Governor-General in relation to Ministers . . . and the position of the Governors . . . in relation to Ministers . . .[40]

In practice, however, one suspects that State governors would take a more liberal view of their reserve powers than either the Queen or the Governor-General would of theirs. This probably results partly from the historical record of the exercises of such powers, which shows that governors have been more willing to refuse a dissolution of the lower house — the reserve power that has arisen most frequently in Australia — than have either the Governor-General (no refusal of a dissolution since 1909) or the Queen (no refusal since the establishment of responsible government). There have been several refusals of dissolution in the States this century, the most recent occurring in Victoria in 1952. A second factor suggesting that State governors might take a wider view of their discretion is what has been aptly described as 'the absurdly anomalous theory that the Australian States, although parts of an autonomous nation, are British colonies'.[41] The practical effect of this absurdity is noted by Professor Parker.

[T]he politically viable discretions of the Governor-General, on one view, are more circumscribed than those of a state governor, apparently because the former is appointed and therefore removable on the direct advice of Australian ministers, making it appear unthinkable for him to use his discretion against their wishes, while the Governor remains formally the nominee and agent of British ministers who have nevertheless washed their hands of his doings, so that he is left in a kind of limbo of unfettered discretion in the area not covered by specific conventions.[42]

Before examining the conventions governing the exercise of the reserve powers, it must be stressed that they constitute only a very limited exception to the fundamental rule of British constitutional monarchy — that the Queen and her representatives always follow the 'advice' of ministers responsible to parliament. Their independent discretion, which distinguishes the reserve powers from other executive powers, occupies only a very small portion of the field of exercise of the power, and can be exercised only in extraordinary, if not 'emergency', circumstances. As Dr Eugene Forsey, one of the leading authorities on the subject, has noted, '"reserve power" means what it says: a power held in reserve, to be used only on extraordinary occasions to prevent a flagrant breach of constitutional right.'[43]

Appointment of the Prime Minister

Ministers are appointed and dismissed by the Governor-General and governors on the advice of the prime minister or premier, who must at all times enjoy the confidence (i.e. command the support of a majority) of the lower house of parliament (in Queensland, the unicameral parliament) and may continue in office only as long as that confidence is retained.[44]

The principal situations in which it will be necessary to appoint a new prime minister or premier are as the result of a general election, upon the resignation or death of the incumbent, upon the deposition of the prime minister or premier by his colleagues, upon the disintegration of the government, and (in some circumstances) upon a successful vote of no-confidence in the government.

General Election   After a general election, the leader of the party (or coalition of parties) that has won a majority of the seats in the lower house must be commissioned to form a government. If that is not the incumbent prime minister or premier, the latter must resign and advise the Governor-General or governor to appoint his successful opponent. Where a party or coalition has won a majority of seats in the lower house there will be no occasion for the exercise of a reserve power (except in the fanciful circumstance that the incumbent prime minister or premier refuses to resign, in which case the Governor-General or governor could dismiss him and commission his opponent[45]). Where a party or coalition has a clear majority of seats the only contentious issue that could arise is the question whether the incumbent prime minister or premier is entitled to insist upon meeting the incoming lower house (to determine whether or not he can command a majority there) before resigning. Theoretically, he probably could,[46] but in reality a prime minister or premier would only contemplate that course if no party or coalition had secured a majority of seats and he believed that he had some chance of surviving a vote of no-confidence. As Dr Vernon Bogdanor has noted,

The truth is that whether a Prime Minister decides to meet parliament or not in a situation in which no single party enjoys an overall majority depends not upon any abstract constitutional rules, but upon whether the Prime Minister wishes, for tactical reasons, to test the *grounds* on which the Opposition seeks to displace him.[47]

The prime minister may, of course, have other motives as well. For instance, like Baldwin in December 1923–January 1924, his decision not to resign immediately may be a tactic (successful in Baldwin's case) to deflect a leadership challenge from within his own party.[48]

A fortiori, when a general election leaves no party or pre-existing coalition with a majority of seats in the lower house, the incumbent prime minister or premier is entitled to a reasonable period in which to ascertain whether he can form a government likely to secure the confidence of the house — unless, perhaps, the prospect of his accomplishing that is very remote.[49] As Edward Heath's delay in resigning in March 1974 suggests, a reasonable time is allowed even to an incumbent prime minister whose party did not win the greatest number of seats. In March 1974, Mr Heath, the incumbent Conservative Prime Minister, whose party won 297 seats to Labour's 301 (in a House of Commons of 635 seats) did not resign for four days, during which he tried (unsuccessfully) to form a coalition with the Liberal Party (14 seats).[50]

In Australia there is little prospect nowadays of the Australian Labor Party forming a coalition or even a *modus vivendi* (like the 'Lib-Lab Pact' of March 1977–July 1978 in Britain[51]) with either the Liberal Party or the National Party (except, perhaps, with the Liberal Party in Queensland). If a general election left neither the Labor Party nor the Liberal Party–National Party coalition with a majority, the incumbent prime minister or premier would be allowed a reasonable time in which to negotiate with the minor parties or independent members holding the balance of power in the house. If he failed to attract sufficient support to make it likely that he would win a vote of confidence when the house met, he ought to resign and advise the Governor-General or governor to commission the leader of the opposition.

A Governor-General or governor would have occasion to exercise independent discretion in choosing a prime minister or premier only in the event that the state of the parties in the lower house was so fluid that there was no obvious person (such as the leader of the opposition) to commission once the incumbent prime minister had failed to form a government likely to command the confidence of the lower house. Such a situation is very improbable in contemporary Australia with its system of two well-disciplined party groups (the Labor Party and the Liberal Party–National Party coalition). Minor parties have hardly ever secured representation in lower houses, and independent members have been rare in the House of Representatives, although not in the States.[52] In short, a contemporary Australian Governor-General or governor would need to exercise independent judgment in choosing a prime minister or premier only if no party or coalition secured a majority of seats at a general election and the incumbent prime minister or premier had lost his seat, died or become disabled. In that event, the Governor-General or governor should first approach the leader of the party that won most seats and ask him or her to attempt to form a government. If that course was patently doomed to fail, or if it had failed, the Governor-General or governor would have to consult the various party leaders and independent members of the lower house, and then commission the person who seemed most likely to be able to secure the confidence of that house.

However, when no party or pre-existing coalition secures a majority of seats in the lower house, it would be preferable for the Governor-General or governor to forgo the exercise of any independent discretion and leave the choice of prime minister or premier to the lower house,[53] as in Ireland, West Germany, Japan and Papua New Guinea, among others.[54] Since the Governor-General and the State governors must avoid even the appearance of partiality, they should decline to exercise any independent discretion unless it is absolutely unavoidable. The wisest principle in contemplating the exercise of any reserve power surely is that 'matters which are capable of political resolution ought to be left in the hands of politicians.'[55]

Resignation   There will be no occasion for the exercise of independent vice-regal discretion when a prime minister or premier resigns his office upon retirement or on account of ill health (unless he is suddenly and seriously incapacitated, in which event the position is essentially the same as that arising on the death of a prime minister or premier).[56] In Australia, as in the United Kingdom (since 1965), Canada and New Zealand, all political parties elect their leaders. Hence, the governing party or coalition will elect a new leader following the prime minister or premier's announcement of his intention to resign but before his actual resignation. The prime minister or premier should advise the Governor-General or governor to commission his party's new leader — so that he gives advice while still in office[57] — and then resign. The Governor-General or governor will then appoint the new leader as prime minister. Thus, neither the Queen nor her representative exercised any independent discretion when James Callaghan succeeded Harold Wilson in Britain (1976), when John Turner succeeded Pierre Trudeau in Canada (1984), and when Harold Holt succeeded Sir Robert Menzies (1966) and William McMahon succeeded John Gorton (1971) in Australia. There have been similar recent transitions of power in State premierships, with Lewis succeeding Askin (1975) and Willis succeeding Lewis (1976) in New South Wales, Hamer succeeding Bolte (1972) and Thompson succeeding Hamer (1981) in Victoria, Corcoran succeeding Dunstan (1979) in South Australia, and O'Connor succeeding Court (1982) in Western Australia. (Of course, not all these resignations were voluntary.)

Death   When a prime minister or premier dies in office, the Governor-General or governor obviously must appoint his successor without obtaining the advice of an incumbent chief minister. But this does not mean that he does not have the benefit of ministerial advice, nor that he is entitled to exercise independent judgment in choosing the new chief minister. As Professor Sol Encel has remarked, 'In principle, the party system effectively eliminates uncertainty as to the choice of the leader of a new government.'[58] This is certainly true of Australian Labor Party governments (and will continue to be, unless the ALP is forced to govern in coalition with another party or parties). The elected deputy leader of the ALP is the deputy prime minister or premier, and will be appointed interim prime minister or premier upon the leader's death.[59] Caucus will then elect a new leader; if that is not the interim prime minister or premier, the latter will advise the Governor-General or governor to commission the new leader, and then resign. This is exactly what transpired upon the death of Prime Minister John Curtin on 5 July 1945. F. M. Forde, the deputy Prime Minister, was appointed interim Prime Minister next day. Caucus elected J. B. Chifley party leader on 12 July, and next day Forde resigned and Chifley was appointed Prime Minister.

However, the position is more complicated when the leader of a coalition government dies in office (unless, of course, the coalition parties have a pre-arranged plan for such an eventuality). This was demonstrated on the deaths of J. A. Lyons, leader of a United Australia Party–Country Party government, in April 1939, and Harold Holt, leader of a Liberal Party–Country Party government, in December 1967. The difficulty in following the same procedure as under a Labor government is that the deputy prime minister in a Liberal–National Party coalition government (and its predecessors) is the leader of the National Party (formerly the Country Party), the junior partner. Yet on both occasions, the deputy Prime Minister was appointed interim Prime Minister, pending the election of a new leader of the senior coalition partner. However, on each occasion the circumstances were so unusual as to render it doubtful that they established a 'convention' or, perhaps, even a reliable precedent for future vice-regal action.

The unusual situation upon Lyons's death on 7 April 1939 (without being able to give the Governor-General any advice as to his successor) was that the deputy leadership of the United Australia Party was temporarily vacant, R. G. Menzies having resigned three weeks earlier. This fortuitous circumstance appears to have been the principal justification for the Governor-General's appointment of Sir Earle Page, the Country Party leader, as interim Prime Minister on the day Lyons died. In a statement to the House of Representatives a fortnight later (much quoted after Holt's death), Page commented:

The position [upon Lyons's death] was that the United Australia party, which was in partnership with the Country party in the government of the country, and which being the larger party, had always provided the leader of the Government, was temporarily without a deputy leader; therefore, no officer of that party could rightly be said to be in the direct line of succession. *In those circumstances*, and without any advice from me,[60] the Governor-General decided to commission me to form a government to carry on the affairs of this country. . . . The Governor-General issued his commission to me without any qualification whatever. . . . Although I had been given an unqualified commission my wish was that the *status quo ante* should be re-established at the earliest possible moment. I told my colleagues, without any pressure at all, . . . that when the United Australia party elected its leader I would tender my resignation to the Governor-General and give to him whatever advice he sought. That is the position I am still in.[61]

Menzies was elected U.A.P. leader on 18 April, whereupon Page resigned, and the Menzies government was sworn in on 26 April. That government included no Country Party members.

When Prime Minister Harold Holt disappeared on 17 December 1967 the Liberal Party, the senior partner in the Liberal Party–Country Party coalition government, had a deputy leader, Treasurer William McMahon. But the Governor-General, Lord Casey, did not appoint him interim Prime Minister. Instead, as in 1939, the Governor-General commissioned the deputy Prime Minister and Country Party leader, this time John McEwen, giving him a formally unqualified commission.[62] Upon John Gorton's election as leader of the Liberal Party, McEwen resigned and Gorton was sworn in as Prime Minister.

On this occasion the unusual circumstance which prevented the deputy Liberal leader's appointment was that McEwen had informed the Governor-General that the Country Party would not support a government led by McMahon.[63] A government led by McMahon could not have survived a motion of no-confidence if the Country Party had voted with the Labor Party in the House of Representatives. But that contingency was very unlikely; at the most Country Party members probably would have abstained from voting, giving the Liberals a clear majority. In any event, the House was in recess at the time, and was not due to meet until March, long after the Liberal Party would have elected its new leader. Hence, it is doubtful whether the Governor-General was justified in concluding that McMahon should not be appointed interim Prime Minister on the ground that he could not command the confidence of a majority in the House of Representatives.[64]

In December 1967, unlike April 1939, the Governor-General held discussions with several leading ministers, including McEwen, McMahon and other contenders for the Liberal leadership (Paul Hasluck, Allen Fairhall and John Gorton), as well as chief government whip Dudley Erwin, and the Secretary of the Prime Minister's Department, Sir John Bunting. He learned that most, if not all, of these ministers were willing to serve in an interim McEwen administration (in fact all of them did), but that neither McEwen nor Hasluck was willing to serve under McMahon.[65] Alan Reid's fascinating detailed account of these events suggests that in at least some of these discussions, especially those with McEwen, the Governor-General went beyond merely seeking advice, and instead sought to exert his considerable influence, as a former colleague, to ensure that the coalition government survived.[66] (Although he retired from parliament in February 1960, Lord Casey continued to take a close interest in coalition politics before, during and after his term of office as Governor-General.[67]) Alan Reid has described Lord Casey's general approach to his vice-regal office as follows:

While to suggest that the Governor-General advised rather than was advised may appear to attribute to Casey a role that went beyond the functions of his office, there is evidence that Casey, despite his 77 years, was very much an activist. He does not appear to have taken a narrow view of his constitutional functions but to have accepted that his task was to assist the government in power, whatever its political complexion, and that he had a responsibility to maintain stability of government.[68]

Don Aitkin, who conceded that Reid's account was 'substantially true',[69] nevertheless concluded that 'the Governor-General acted in a perfectly proper manner throughout.'[70]

Whether or not McEwen's appointment as interim Prime Minister was justified, what ought a future Governor-General or governor to do upon the death in office of the prime minister or premier of a Liberal–National Party coalition government, assuming that (a) the deceased prime minister or premier had not recently given him advice on the matter, (b) the Liberal Party has a deputy leader in whom the National Party will not express no-confidence in the House of Representatives, and (c) there is no current agreement or under-standing between the coalition parties as to what should occur in such an eventuality?

It is submitted that the deputy leader of the Liberal Party should be appointed interim prime minister or premier because he is the heir apparent, the person who is 'in the direct line of succession', as Sir Earle Page put it in 1939,[71] even though the Liberal Party has, admit-tedly, often bypassed the deputy leader in selecting its new leader. Two propositions combine to justify the appointment of the deputy Liberal leader: first, the interim prime minister ought to be a member of the larger party in the coalition which commands a majority in the House of Representatives; secondly, there is no justification for commissioning the leader of the smallest party in the House, especially if his commission is unqualified, so that the interim government is not merely a 'caretaker' administration (one which effects no appointments or dismissals and initiates no new policies).

A possible objection to the appointment of a Liberal member is that the Governor-General or governor may thereby influence, or appear to be endeavouring to influence, the choice of the new Liberal leader; in other words, that the deputy leader may be unduly advantaged in the election of a new leader. But appointing the National Party leader could also influence the selection of the new prime minister: in 1939, Page, while interim Prime Minister, sought (with R. G. Casey) to persuade S. M. Bruce, the Australian High Commissioner in London and a former Prime Minister, to return to Australia (from the United States) to form a government,[72] and in 1967–68 there were moves, whether or not supported by interim Prime Minister McEwen, to make his premiership permanent by amalgamating the coalition parties and electing him leader.[73]

As Lord Casey's statement in December 1967 suggests, the principal reason for appointing the National Party leader interim prime minister is that he is the deputy prime minister of the coalition government and acts as prime minister in the absence of the prime minister.[74] But there is a significant difference between acting as prime minister when the prime minister is alive and contactable (and can reverse decisions to which he objects) on the one hand, and enjoying an unqualified commission to run one's own administration on the other.

In sum, as things stand, a Governor-General or State governor may have to exercise independent judgment in choosing an interim prime minister to succeed a deceased coalition prime minister or premier. As adverse comment (from some quarters) on Lord Casey's actions following the death of Harold Holt demonstrated, an exercise of independent judgment inevitably leads to criticism of the Governor-General or governor, and suspicion of bias and partisanship on his part.[75] The coalition parties would be well advised, it is submitted, to reach an agreement or understanding as to what should happen on the unexpected death in office of a prime minister or premier.

Deposition   A change in the premiership may result from a prime minister's deposition by his colleagues, as occurred in Britain in May 1940 when Winston Churchill replaced Neville Chamberlain, and in Australia in March 1971, when William McMahon replaced John Gorton. Yet here again, no occasion need arise for the exercise of independent vice-regal discretion.

If a party or coalition enjoying the confidence of the lower house voted to replace the prime minister or premier, the incumbent ought to advise the Governor-General or governor to appoint the new leader, and then resign. Reserve power enthusiasts sometimes hypothesize, however, a defiant prime minister who ignores his party's decision to depose him, and seeks either to carry on as if nothing had happened, or to dissolve parliament. Surely, they argue, in these circumstances the Governor-General would be justified in refusing a dissolution, and dismissing him and commissioning the new leader. But the notion that a prime minister, who had just been deposed by his party and had not yet regrouped his forces and formed another, would seek to wage an election campaign on that basis is so fanciful as not to warrant serious consideration. If the House of Representatives were in session, a Governor-General faced with such a request would be well advised to defer consideration of it until the House had had the opportunity to consider whether or not the prime minister still enjoyed its confidence. If the House were not in session, the Governor-General might suggest that the House of Representatives be recalled, warning the prime minister that the ultimate consequence of a refusal could be dismissal. If a defiant prime minister rejected that suggestion, the Governor-General could possibly still check him by addressing the nation on radio and/or television, outlining what had transpired, and calling upon public opinion to bring the prime minister to his senses. However, if all else failed and it was clear beyond reasonable doubt that the prime minister did not enjoy the support of a majority in the House, but that the leader elected by the governing party or coalition did, the Governor-General probably could dismiss the prime minister and commission the new leader in his place.

However, it is fanciful to suppose that a prime minister would defy the unambiguous decision of his party unless he was able, like W. M. Hughes (November 1916–February 1917), to form a new party likely to control a majority in the House of Representatives. Realistically, as the Chamberlain–Churchill and Gorton–McMahon transitions demonstrate, a prime minister deposed by his own party will go quietly.

Governmental Disintegration   The circumstances attending the disintegration of a governing party or coalition are so multifarious that it is difficult to discuss the role of the Governor-General or a State governor in a general way. However, if a governing party or coalition disintegrated into various factions or groups there would be no immediate need for the exercise of independent vice-regal discretion because the incumbent prime minister or premier would be entitled to remain in office until he lost the confidence of the lower house. This is supported by the experiences of two Labor leaders, Prime Minister W. M. Hughes of the Commonwealth and Premier W. A. Holman of New South Wales, who, after losing their party's support at the end of 1916 (Holman in October, Hughes in November), retained office with the support of the erstwhile opposition with whom they then formed new Nationalist Party governments enjoying the support of a majority in the lower house (Hughes in February 1917, Holman in November 1916).[76]

Vote of No-confidence   Finally, the premiership may have to change as the consequence of a vote of no-confidence in the prime minister or premier which is, of course, a vote of no-confidence in the government he leads. If the lower house of parliament (in Queensland the unicameral parliament) passes a simple vote of no-confidence in the prime minister or premier he must either resign or advise a dissolution of the lower house (or, at his option, in the Commonwealth and South Australia, a dissolution of both houses if the constitutional prerequisites for it have been satisfied).[77] (If some unpaired members of the governing party or parties were absent from the House when the vote was taken, and their presence might have saved the government, the incumbent prime minister or premier ought to be allowed a reasonable time to secure a reversal of the vote.) If the Governor-General or State governor accedes to the request for a dissolution, the government will continue in office as a 'caretaker' administration until the election result is known.[78]

There are, therefore, only three situations in which the premiership will change virtually immediately as the result of a lower house vote of no-confidence.

1. If the house resolves that it has no confidence in the prime minister or premier but names a person in whom it would have confidence (a 'constructive' vote of no-confidence),[79] the prime minister or premier must resign, and his nominated successor is entitled to be commissioned. In the (highly unlikely) event that the incumbent refused to resign, the Governor-General or governor could dismiss him.

2. Although the house may not have expressed its confidence in another person, it may be apparent that another person, such as the leader of the opposition, the leader of a minor party, or even another member of the governing party, would enjoy that confidence, or at least has a good prospect of securing it. In that case, the incumbent prime minister or premier may advise the Governor-General or governor to commission that person, and then resign. (Commonwealth examples are the transition from Deakin to Watson in April 1904, from Deakin to Fisher in November 1908, and from Fadden to Curtin in October 1941.) The prime minister's only alternative would be to seek a dissolution of parliament. At the Commonwealth level, dissolutions have twice been granted in such circumstances (to Bruce in September 1929 and Scullin in November 1931), and thrice refused (Watson in August 1904, Reid in July 1905 and Fisher in May 1909).

3. If the house's vote of no-confidence immediately followed a general election, so that it was the government's first test of its ability to command the support of a majority in the house, the prime minister or premier would not be entitled to another dissolution, unless it were clear that no alternative government could be formed from the current house. In the extremely unlikely event that the incumbent chief minister refused to resign, the Governor-General or governor probably could dismiss him and commission a new chief minister.[80] (However, if the latter failed to secure the confidence of the house, and there was no further alternative prime minister or premier, the Governor-General or governor ought to re-appoint the original incumbent and grant him a dissolution of parliament.[81])

The situation in the last category is, therefore, the only realistic one in which a Governor-General or governor may have to exercise independent judgment consequent upon a house vote of no-confidence in the government.

Dismissal of the Prime Minister

The conventions governing the exercise of the power to dismiss the chief minister, the most dramatic and, hence, controversial of all the reserve powers, are somewhat speculative because there have been so few exercises of this power — none in the United Kingdom since the establishment of responsible government,[82] and none in New Zealand or, at the federal level, in Canada. But the power has, of course, been exercised twice in Australia, on both occasions against governments commanding a majority in the lower house: in New South Wales in May 1932, when Governor Sir Philip Game dismissed Premier J. T. Lang, and in the Commonwealth in November 1975, when Governor-General Sir John Kerr dismissed Prime Minister Gough Whitlam.

The power to dismiss the prime minister (i.e the government) is regarded as virtually obsolete by British commentators; the Judicial Committee of the Privy Council regarded it as beyond 'the scope of practical politics',[83] and a leading authority has described its corollary, when exercised against a government enjoying the confidence of the lower house — the forced dissolution of parliament — as 'obsolete' and even 'unconstitutional'.[84] As Professor S. A. de Smith has noted, this reserve power, 'the most drastic form of royal initiative, must be a recourse of last resort, an ultimate weapon which is liable to destroy its user.'[85] It certainly destroyed Sir John Kerr.

However, its exercise twice in Australia within the last half-century or so suggests that the power is not obsolete here, even though the conventions governing the exercise of the reserve powers are essentially the same here as in the United Kingdom.

In the aftermath of the Governor-General's dismissal of Prime Minister Whitlam, the South Australian parliament resolved (on the following day) that the governor of South Australia 'should act on the advice of his Ministers, and should not dismiss a Ministry' except in two situations: (i) 'in the case of that Ministry's acting in breach of the law' or (ii) 'its losing the confidence of the Lower House.'[86] This resolution, which has no legal force but would, undoubtedly, influence State governors, especially South Australia's, is a reasonably concise statement of the *maximum* reserve power possibly consistent with the principles of responsible government, but the power conceded to the governor is still really much too generous, as is discussed below.

If the purpose of the reserve powers — to protect the fair operation of responsible parliamentary government — is borne in mind, the Governor-General or State governor will be allowed no personal discretion beyond that *absolutely necessary* to ensure the effective operation of parliamentary democracy. If other means exist, the Governor-General or governor does not need to exercise a personal discretion and, therefore, should not have one. As Professor K. H. Bailey, a future Commonwealth Solicitor-General, suggested, the only acceptable reserve powers are those which 'are not the antithesis but the corollary of the democratic principle that political authority is derived from the people.'[87]

Undeniably, a government must not ignore an expression of 'no-confidence' by the lower house; nor is it entitled to act contrary to law, whether it be the Constitution or statute. But it is a gratuitous and unwarranted assumption that the Governor-General or governor is obliged, or even empowered, to act as enforcer of the government's constitutional duties. As one judge has noted, '[j]ust because a Chief Minister . . . does not go when he ought to go is not sufficient reason for implying in the Constitution an enforcing power vested in some individual'.[88] One important consideration frequently overlooked is that, in the remote event that a government does act unconstitutionally, the Governor-General or State governor is not faced with a choice of absolutes — either dismissing the government or doing nothing at all. Public opinion can exert immense influence on a democratic government, and there is no reason whatever why a Governor-General or governor could not appeal to it for assistance in a crisis. If the government were acting unconstitutionally, the Governor-General or governor could issue a press statement or even address the nation or State on radio and/or television, outline the circumstances of the constitutional crisis, and call upon the government to do its duty. Such an appeal would almost certainly succeed in persuading the government to resile from its unconstitutional course. Moreover, the vice-regal image of neutrality and impartiality would be compromised far less by such a public appeal to the government's sense of duty than by dismissing the government, an act which cannot avoid the odium of partisanship since it inevitably favours the opposition.

However, if all vice-regal persuasion and exhortation to the government to do its duty failed, the Governor-General or governor would be entitled to terminate the commission of a prime minister or premier without, or contrary to, his advice in three circumstances.

1.   If the lower house of parliament (in Queensland the unicameral legislature) has passed a 'constructive no-confidence' resolution (i.e. one calling for the appointment of a specific person as prime minister or premier) and the incumbent prime minister or premier refused to resign (after being allowed a reasonable time to secure a reversal of the resolution), the Governor-General or governor would be entitled to dismiss him.

2.   If the lower house passed a simple no-confidence resolution and the incumbent prime minister or premier (again, after being allowed

a reasonable time to secure a reversal of the vote) refused either to resign or advise a dissolution of parliament, he could be dismissed.[89] As noted above, the option of a dissolution may not be available if the house's no-confidence resolution immediately follows a general election; a prime minister or premier who loses a simple no-confidence vote immediately after a general election must resign if there is a realistic prospect of forming an alternative government from the existing house. If he refused to resign, he could be dismissed.[90]

3. More doubtful is the proposition that the Governor-General or a governor may be entitled to dismiss a government if (a) it is clear beyond reasonable doubt that it has persisted in breaching a fundamental constitutional provision, (b) the Governor-General or governor has called upon it to desist but the government has ignored that plea, and (c) the contravention is not justiciable (i.e. cannot be brought before the courts). Examples of such conduct might include refusing to summon parliament, refusing to call a general election when the house's term had expired[91] and, perhaps, persisting in spending funds not appropriated by parliament (i.e. both houses).*

This last category is based upon the dismissal of Premier J. T. Lang by Governor Game of New South Wales in 1932 on the ground of illegal behaviour,[92] but it is widely conceded that Lang's dismissal was probably improper because the government's alleged illegality was justiciable.[93] Moreover, Game himself had second thoughts on his 'assassin's stroke',[94] and the Dominions Office in London, in a memorandum to the Governor prepared too late and, hence, never sent, also advised against dismissal where the unlawful governmental action was justiciable.[95]

Since the reserve powers are in effect emergency powers to protect the fair operation of responsible parliamentary government, they should be exercised only as a last resort, if there is no other remedy. This is especially true of the power to dismiss a government, the most extreme and the most dangerous (especially to the Crown) of all the reserve powers. As Dr Geoffrey Marshall has remarked of the Queen's power to dismiss a government which 'by illegal or unconstitutional administrative action' had violated 'some basic convention of constitutional behaviour', the breach must be 'a profound one for which *no other remedy could be found, either political or legal.*'[96]

Finally, the present writer's omission to mention an upper house's denial of supply (appropriation for the ordinary annual services of the government) as a circumstance justifying dismissal of a government

---

* However, at least some of these matters may be justiciable, in which case the government would almost certainly comply with a High Court ruling that its action was unconstitutional. In the extremely remote contingency that it defied the High Court after the governor or Governor-General had called upon it to desist, the governor or Governor-General could dismiss the government.

should not be attributed to oversight. As is well known, Governor-General Sir John Kerr dismissed Prime Minister Gough Whitlam on 11 November 1975 on the ground that he was unable to obtain supply because the Senate continually deferred the Appropriation Bills.[97] On the previous day, Chief Justice Barwick had advised the Governor-General that he had the 'constitutional authority' to dismiss the Prime Minister,[98] but Sir John Kerr went further and asserted a 'duty' to do so. By the time he published a book on the question eight years later, the former Chief Justice's opinion had become identical to Kerr's: the vice-regal 'authority' of 1975 had become a 'constitutional *duty*' to dismiss a prime minister unable to secure supply from the Senate as soon as it appeared likely that the Senate would persist in its view.[99]

However, there never was any authority for the Kerr–Barwick thesis of the dismissal power, and there still is none.[100] The exercise of power — especially on a single occasion — is no evidence that it exists. The fact that Mr Whitlam's commission was terminated does not establish that the termination was proper or even lawful. Because the Commonwealth and State governments are not responsible to the upper houses of their parliaments (and no one, including Sir Garfield Barwick, has suggested the contrary), an upper house's rejection of supply is constitutionally irrelevant *until* the treasury's funds are exhausted — which was not the case in 1975. Once that occurs, the government will run the risk of dismissal for persistent violation of the constitution if it withdraws funds without parliamentary appropriation (which requires the approval of both houses). But it may have no alternative, except to succumb to the upper house's demands, since the government obviously requires funds to run the administration. These remarks do not, however, apply to Queensland or New South Wales, because the former abolished its upper house in 1922, and Bills appropriating moneys for the ordinary annual services of the government can become law in New South Wales without the approval of the Legislative Council.[101]

Hence, the relevance of denial of supply by an upper house is that it may, ultimately, lead to the government's dismissal under the third category noted above. Of course, a denial of supply by the lower house would be a vote of no-confidence and would, therefore, fall within the second category, were dismissal ultimately necessary.

Refusal of a Dissolution

The vice-regal power to refuse advice to dissolve parliament (i.e. the lower house) has been exercised more frequently than the other reserve powers, although refusals to dissolve have nevertheless been extremely rare. (The Governor-General has never refused a double dissolution, and none has been sought in South Australia.) A dissolution has not been refused in the United Kingdom since the establishment of responsible government, in New Zealand since 1877, in the Commonwealth since 1909, and in Canada since 1926, but dissolutions have been refused very occasionally in the Australian States, most recently in Victoria in 1952. It is noteworthy, however, that the three Commonwealth refusals of dissolution (in August 1904, July 1905 and May 1909) and the State refusals all occurred before the modern system of stable two-party groupings was established.

Although refusals of dissolution have been very infrequent, the views of monarchs and their representatives, statesmen — including Asquith, Churchill and Attlee — and other commentators (not necessarily listed in order of decreasing importance!), almost all of them *obiter*, support the continued existence of the power to refuse a dissolution in extra-ordinary circumstances.[102] Apart from the Governor-General's refusal in Canada in 1926 and South Africa in 1939 — the former highly controversial,[103] and the latter the consequence of dissension within the cabinet and the governing party (in both of which the Prime Minister, General Hertzog, was in a minority) on the eve of war[104] — King George V may initially have refused a dissolution in November 1910, but subsequently granted it when the Asquith government threatened to resign.[105] In October 1924 the same King sounded out the party leaders (through his private secretary) before granting MacDonald a dissolution, having ascertained that no alternative government could be formed from the existing house.[106] However, it should not necessarily be inferred that if it had been possible to form an alternative government the King would have refused a dissolution to the first Labour administration. The most significant aspect of both episodes surely is that, notwithstanding his reluctance to do so, in each case the King accepted the Prime Minister's advice to dissolve parliament. Similarly, although on three occasions in the 1950s (in March 1950, September 1956 and April 1959) the Queen's Tasmanian representative denied that the premier was automatically entitled thereto, the dissolution was granted on each occasion.[107]

What, then, is the ambit of vice-regal authority to refuse a dissolution? In an injudiciously phrased passage in his Queale Memorial Lecture in 1972, Governor-General Sir Paul Hasluck appeared to suggest that a prime minister will be granted an early dissolution only if parliament is 'unworkable'.

If a situation arises, however, in which it is proposed that the House be dissolved sooner than the end of its three-year term, . . . a solemn responsibility rests on [the Governor-General] to make a judgment on whether dissolution is needed to serve the purposes of good government by giving to the electorate the duty of resolving a situation which Parliament cannot resolve for itself. If a Prime Minister were to advise a mid-term dissolution simply because 'he would like to have an election', a Governor-General would quite reasonably ask for additional reasons to support a general argument that

Parliament had become unworkable or that some exceptional and unforeseen situation had arisen which could not be resolved by Parliament itself.

The key question is whether in fact Parliament has become 'unworkable'.[108]

Sir John Kerr, when Governor-General, virtually repeated Hasluck's remarks,[109] but he was obliged later to 're-interpret' them, because they endorse an unrealistically generous view of vice-regal discretion unsupported by either constitutional practice or the accepted commentaries. As Sir John Kerr later conceded, any vice-regal discretion to refuse a dissolution on the ground of parliament's 'workability' must be confined to requests by a minority government.[110] This is clearly correct: a dissolution cannot be refused to a prime minister or premier with a secure lower house majority because the governor or Governor-General's inability to commission a viable alternative government means that the chief minister can always achieve his objective by threatening to resign.[111] The Governor-General could, of course, seek to persuade the prime minister to withdraw his request[112] — as George V sought to do in November 1910 and November 1918[113] — but, if a prime minister or premier with a secure majority in the lower house persists in his advice to dissolve, the Governor-General or governor *must* comply, regardless of the portion of the parliamentary term which remains to be served. Dr Geoffrey Marshall has suggested that even a secure majority government might be denied a dissolution if it sought 'a series of dissolutions aimed at securing successive increases in its majority.'[114] However, this contingency is not only extremely improbable, as Dr Marshall admitted, in view of the expense of holding general elections (among other reasons); it is, surely, also unrealistic because a Governor-General or governor unable to find an alternative government enjoying the confidence of the lower house must ultimately concede the prime minister's request, even in this extreme case, and leave the infliction of appropriate punishment to the electors.

The government's position is obviously weaker when it does not command a secure majority in the lower house. A view widely accepted by commentators is that the Queen or her representative can refuse a dissolution to a government lacking the confidence of the lower house if it is clear that an alternative government enjoying that confidence can be formed.[115] The classic modern statement of the principal considerations is probably that of Sir Alan Lascelles, Private Secretary to King George VI, in May 1950.

[N]o wise Sovereign . . . would deny a dissolution to his Prime Minister unless he were satisfied that: (1) the existing Parliament was still vital, viable and capable of doing its job; (2) a General Election would be detrimental to the national economy; (3) he could rely on finding another Prime Minister who could carry on his Government, for a reasonable period, with a working majority in the House of Commons.[116]

However, these criteria, and many of the other factors suggested occasionally — such as the portion of the parliamentary term remaining, whether the previous dissolution was granted to the government or the opposition, the importance of the question at issue (if there is one), whether the government has been voted adequate supply, whether the prime minister is in a minority in the cabinet (as General Hertzog was in 1939), and whether the country is at war[117] — depend upon the subjective judgment of the Monarch or her representative, and some, at least, are likely to be highly controversial. Clearly, the Monarch or her representative should avoid such matters if possible. The considerations favouring a narrow scope for this reserve power have been well summarized.

[T]here are difficulties inherent in the proposed . . . rule stated by some of the authorities, namely that the Governor-General should prima facie refuse a dissolution to a Ministry defeated in the House where an alternative Ministry exists. First, such a rule requires the Governor-General to have regard to matters of a political nature in reaching his decision. . . . Secondly, if the Governor-General's decision that there is a viable alternative Ministry turns out to be incorrect, that decision itself will inevitably be the subject of political debate and the Governor-General will find himself embroiled in the political crisis.[118] Thirdly, . . . where a government has been formed as a result of the expression by the people of their political preferences, it ought to be for the people to decide whether they wish the representatives who formed that government before its defeat in the House to continue to govern. Finally, . . . matters which are capable of political resolution ought to be left in the hands of politicians.[119]

Surely the final consideration, that *'matters which are capable of political resolution ought to be left in the hands of politicians'* (emphasis added), is the key to the resolution of this question. The onus of choosing the chief minister falls primarily on the lower house, not on the Queen or her representative. Accordingly, a prime minister or premier in whom the lower house had confidence but has now lost it should be entitled to a dissolution unless, within a reasonable period, the house calls upon the Governor-General or governor to commission someone else. The house's failure to nominate a new chief minister within a reasonable time should be taken to indicate its inability to do so.[120] As Dr Vernon Bogdanor has noted

If government and Parliament cannot work together, . . . the dispute should be resolved by the real political sovereign, which in a democracy is the electorate. A change of government which occurs without an election can, as the West German example in 1982 has shown, provoke resentment that democratic norms are being ignored, and it would be dangerous for the Sovereign to allow herself to be exposed to criticism on this score.[121]

In sum, it is submitted that there are only three situations in which a chief minister should not be entitled to a dissolution:

1.   When the lower house has passed a 'constructive no-confidence' resolution; i.e. has expressed lack of confidence in the chief minister, but would confer its confidence upon another person were he commissioned.

2.   When a government which has just lost a general election seeks a second dissolution in the hope that it might fare better on the second occasion — unless no alternative government can be formed from the existing house.[122] It is difficult to imagine any modern prime minister or premier attempting this; if he did, it would be so obvious an abuse of power that a vice-regal address to the nation on radio and/or television would almost certainly persuade the chief minister to withdraw his request.

3.   Where parliament is given a fixed term by law, as in Victoria and South Australia since 1985,[123] the governor would, of course, be obliged to refuse to dissolve contrary to law. Similarly, the Commonwealth Governor-General and the governor of South Australia would be obliged to refuse to dissolve both houses if the constitutional prerequisites for a double dissolution had not been satisfied.[124]

Forcing a Dissolution

A forced dissolution of parliament (i.e. one contrary to the wishes of the government) can only occur as the consequence of the dismissal of a government under the third category noted above (or, conceivably, pursuant to the unwarranted Kerr–Barwick thesis of 1975). In other words, a forced dissolution can occur only as a result of the dismissal of a government (especially one with a majority in the lower house) for gross violation of the constitution (or, conceivably, according to Sir John Kerr and Sir Garfield Barwick, upon the denial of supply by an upper house). Thus, dissolutions followed the dismissals of the Lang government in May 1932 and the Whitlam government in November 1975 (a double dissolution in the latter case) — both of which commanded the support of a majority of the lower house. Although in each case the dissolutions were formally requested by the new chief minister (the erstwhile leader of the opposition), in reality they were forced dissolutions.

Notwithstanding Dr Forsey's view that a forced dissolution may be appropriate in a wider range of circumstances,[125] it is submitted that the better view is that the forced dissolution is 'obsolete' and 'unconstitutional',[126] except in the limited circumstances noted above.

RELATIONS BETWEEN LEGISLATURE AND EXECUTIVE

The constitutional relationship between Australian legislatures and executives can be stated succinctly as one of 'responsible government':

the government is 'responsible' to the lower house, and only that house, in those jurisdictions in which the legislature is bicameral (all except Queensland and the self-governing Territories). Although ministers, who by law (in the Commonwealth, Victoria and South Australia) or convention (in the other States) must be members of the legislature,[127] are *accountable* to both houses of parliament for the administration of their departments — and thus subject to inter-rogation at Question Time, criticism in debate, and even censure — the government is not *responsible* to the upper house because it does not need to retain the confidence of that house in order to stay in office.[128] Upper house resolutions censuring a minister or the govern-ment are constitutionally (although not necessarily politically) irrele-vant, and can be — and have been — ignored. As the Tasmanian Royal Commission on its Constitution noted, 'a vote of no confidence in the [Legislative] Council does not have any direct effect. In that sense, therefore, the Government does not depend on the "confidence" of the Upper House and is not "responsible" to it.'[129]

Of course, if an upper house (except in New South Wales where it can delay supply for only one month[130]) sought to enforce its lack of confidence in the government by persisting in refusing to grant supply, its lack of confidence would become constitutionally significant once previously appropriated funds had been expended and the government was faced with the dilemma of either running an admin-istration without funds (which would be impossible) or withdrawing funds from the treasury without parliamentary authorization (which would be unlawful and/or unconstitutional).[131]

While constitutionally the government is responsible to the lower house, politically the position is, of course, rather different. Under the current Australian system of a lower house comprising two reasonably stable party groups, a government enjoying a secure lower house majority can rely on party discipline and prime ministerial power to control government backbenchers and, thus, in effect, the lower house. Hence, while in theory that house controls the government, in reality the converse is often closer to the mark. This question will be considered further when the Australian and United States systems of government are compared in chapter five.

Finally, as noted at the beginning of this chapter, there is, of course, no reason why the current legislative-executive relationship need change substantially under an Australian republic.

ADDENDUM

On 29 July 1985 the Brisbane session of the Australian Constitutional Convention 'recognize[d] and declare[d] that the following principles and practices should be observed as Conventions in Australia:

A   The basic principle is that the Ministry has the confidence of the House of Representatives.

B   Following a general election in which the Government is defeated, the Governor-General, having taken the advice of the outgoing Prime Minister as to the person who the outgoing Prime Minister believes can form a Ministry that has the confidence of the House of Representatives, appoints as Prime Minister the person who, in his opinion, can form a Ministry that has the confidence of the House of Representatives.

C   If the Prime Minister resigns, the Governor-General, having taken the advice of the resigning Prime Minister as to the person who the Prime Minister believes can form a Ministry that has the confidence of the House of Representatives, appoints as Prime Minister the person who, in his opinion, can form a Ministry that has the confidence of the House of Representatives.

D   If the Prime Minister dies in office, the Governor-General, having taken the advice of the next most senior Minister as to the person who that Minister believes can form a Ministry that has the confidence of the House of Representatives, appoints as Prime Minister the person who in his opinion can form such a Ministry.

E   If following a defeat in the House of Representatives, the Prime Minister, acting in accordance with Practice F, advises the Governor-General to dissolve the House of Representatives or to send for the person who the Prime Minister believes can form a Ministry that has the confidence of the House of Representatives, the Governor-General acts on the advice.

F   In advising the Governor-General for the purpose of Practice E, the Prime Minister acts in accordance with the basic principle that the Ministry should have the confidence of the House of Representatives and if, in his opinion, there is another person who can form a Ministry which has the confidence of the House of Representatives, he advises the Governor-General to send for that person.

G   The Governor-General appoints and dismisses other Ministers on the advice of the Prime Minister.

H   The resignation of a Prime Minister following a general election in which the government is defeated or following a defeat in the House of Representatives terminates the commissions of all other Ministers, but the death of a Prime Minister or his resignation in other circumstances does not automatically terminate the commissions of the other Ministers.

I   The Governor-General dissolves the House of Representatives only on the advice of the Prime Minister.

J   When a Prime Minister who retains the confidence of the House of Representatives advises a dissolution of the House of Representatives, the Governor-General acts upon that advice.

K   The Governor-General, having satisfied himself on the advice of the Prime Minister that the conditions in section 57 of the Constitution have been met and that a double dissolution should be granted dissolves both Houses of the Parliament simultaneously on the advice of the Prime Minister.

L   All advice tendered by the Prime Minister to the Governor-General in connection with a dissolution of the House of Representatives or a dissolution of both Houses of Parliament and the Governor-General's response thereto, should be committed to writing and published before or during the ensuing election campaign.

M   In advising a dissolution, the Prime Minister must be in a position to assure the Governor-General that the government has been granted sufficient funds by the Parliament to enable the work of the administration to be carried on through the election period or that such funds will be granted before the dissolution.

N   Subject to the requirements of the Constitution as to the sittings of Parliament, the Governor-General acts on prime ministerial advice in exercising his powers to summon and prorogue Parliament.

O   In advising a prorogation, the Prime Minister must be in a position to assure the Governor-General that the government has been granted sufficient funds by the Parliament to enable the work of the administration to be carried on through the period of prorogation or that such funds will be granted before the prorogation.

P   The Governor-General, having satisfied himself on the advice of the Prime Minister that the conditions in section 57 of the Constitution have been met, acts on prime ministerial advice in exercising his power to convene a joint sitting of the members of the Senate and of the House of Representatives.

Q   The Governor-General acts only on the advice of the Prime Minister in submitting a proposed law for the alteration of the Constitution to the electors, whether the proposed law has been approved by both Houses or by one House only.

R   In the exercise of his constitutional powers and responsibilities, the Governor-General always has the right to be consulted, to encourage and to warn in respect of Ministerial advice given to him.'

Chapter 4
Types of Republican Government

The second most important question the Australian people will have to consider when deciding whether or not to become a republic is the type of republican government to adopt. For many voters, the form of republican government proposed will doubtless determine whether or not they vote for a republic at all. Although the world's democratic republics manifest a fairly wide variety of governmental structures, and a fertile constitutional imagination could invent many more, the Australian people are very unlikely to choose between more than three models of republican government, if that.

PARLIAMENTARY EXECUTIVE

Most of the republics of Western Europe have adopted a form of government modelled, in many cases, on that of Britain, the essential elements of which are a head of state with largely ceremonial functions combined with a separate head of government (prime minister) responsible, with his ministerial colleagues, to the lower house of parliament (in Italy, responsible to both houses). The prime minister and the other government ministers are usually members of parliament, although that is infrequently constitutionally mandated (it is in India, Ireland and, for the prime minister, in Israel). Republics with this form of government include India, Ireland, Israel, Iceland, Italy, Austria, West Germany and Greece, although there is considerable diversity among them. The Greek president, for example, is more powerful than his Indian or West German counterparts (although the present Socialist government proposes to reduce his powers by early 1986).

This form of republican government would involve very little constitutional change in Australia, and even less governmental adaptation; in essence it could be implemented by abolishing the monarchy and electing the Governor-General, probably re-designating him 'president'. Accordingly, when this form of republican government is compared with the American system in the next chapter, it will be assumed that, insofar as legislative–executive and intra-executive relations are concerned, it represents, in essence, a continuation of the present system of Australian government.

EXECUTIVE PRESIDENCY

Under a presidential form of government, the archetype of which is that of the United States, the functions of head of state and head of government are combined in one person, the president, elected directly by the people (albeit, in the United States, through the medium of the popularly elected electoral college). The president and the members of his administration, who are appointed by him, are neither members of, nor responsible to, the legislature, which enjoys a fixed term and, hence, cannot be dissolved by the president. In short, the executive branch is (in theory) a unity (unlike the Australian or French executives), with the president at the apex — indeed, constitutionally, he *is* the executive — and the relationship between the legislature and the executive can be characterized as one of separated powers and functions combined, however, with a system of 'checks and balances', as will be seen in the next chapter.

HYBRID EXECUTIVE

There is an almost infinite variety of possible combinations of elements of an executive presidency with those of a parliamentary system. It might, for instance, be proposed that the functions of head of state and head of government be combined in one popularly elected officer (as in the United States), but that, unlike the American president, he be responsible to the legislature, so that the consequence of a parliamentary vote of no-confidence is a new presidential election combined, perhaps, with a dissolution of parliament. Such a system operates in Kiribati and, to some extent, Kenya, but, with respect, would not be an improvement on the present system of Australian government which, in bare essentials, it vaguely resembles. The principal defect of the Kiribati model is that it would deprive Australian government of the benefits derived from separating the functions of head of state and head of government. These include having a respected, impartial officer to represent the nation and, thus, serve as a focus for national identity and pride — a 'fixed point of reference for [the] nation', as Governor-General Sir Ninian Stephen expressed it recently,[1] — to deflect public attention and, hence, power from the prime minister or premier, who already has more than enough of both as it is, and to implement the machinery of responsible government. Hence, combining the office of head of state with that of chief minister and leaving the Australian system otherwise intact would, it is submitted, be a retrograde step.

The form of hybrid presidential-parliamentary regime most likely to be considered by Australian reformers is the French, which divides the powers and functions of a head of government between a popularly elected President with a fixed term of office, who is not responsible to the National Assembly (the lower house of parliament) and a prime minister, appointed by the president, who is responsible to the National Assembly. The system of government of the Fifth French Republic (founded in 1958) was the model for that of the Second Republic of Sri Lanka,[2] and bears some resemblance to the earlier Finnish system, although the Finnish president is, admittedly, considerably weaker *vis-à-vis* the prime minister than his French or Sri Lankan counterparts.

Historical, political and, above all, cultural considerations combine to make the United States system of republican government the principal alternative to the parliamentary form — essentially the current form of Australian government — in a future Australian republic. Because the debate on the form of Australian republican government is very likely to focus upon a choice between the United States model on the one hand and the present Australian model (without the monarchy) on the other, a comparison between those two systems will be the subject of the next chapter.

However, it is true that, throughout her history,

Australia's mistake has been to assume that if it drops the British way of doing things, it must adopt the American way, just as it seems to feel that if it drops the Westminster form of government, it should adopt the Washington model.[3]

Hence it is appropriate to examine here the only realistic alternative (for Australia) to the American or parliamentary models — the French.

THE FRENCH PRESIDENCY

On its face, the constitution of the Fifth French Republic appears to create a 'dyarchy at the top, a twin-headed or bicephalous executive',[4] with executive powers and functions shared — albeit unequally — between president and prime minister.

The president of the Republic, who also presides over and represents the French Community (the French equivalent of the (British) Commonwealth), is elected by direct universal suffrage for a term of seven years, and is removable only for high treason upon impeachment by parliament and conviction by the High Court of Justice (comprising parliamentarians elected, in equal numbers, by the two houses of parliament). The president is the guarantor of national independence and the independence of the judiciary, and is constitutionally enjoined to ensure, 'by his arbitration' the regular functioning of public authorities and 'the continuity of the State'. He appoints the prime minister, and appoints and dismisses the other ministers (in theory) on the proposal of the prime minister, presides over the Council of Ministers, and dissolves the National Assembly (the lower house of parliament) after consulting the prime minister. The president is commander of the armed forces, and appoints the principal civil and military officers of state, including judges, ambassadors, Councillors of State (*conseillers d'Etat*), the president and one-third of the members of the Constitutional Council (which can review the constitutionality of legislation before promulgation), members of the High Council of the Judiciary (which oversees the judiciary), and receives foreign ambassadors. His powers include the negotiation and ratification of treaties and the power to pardon offenders and, although the president can request parliament to reconsider legislation (which it cannot refuse to do), he has no power to veto it. Two additional, and important, presidential powers are the power to submit certain questions, including government Bills dealing with the organization of the governing authorities, to referendum on the proposal of the government or parliament (a power exercised on five occasions, two of them unconstitutionally), and the power to 'take such measures as the circumstances require', after consultation with the prime minister, the presidents of both houses of parliament and the Constitutional Council, whenever the independence or institutions of the nation are threatened, an emergency power exercised only once — by President de Gaulle from 23 April to 30 September 1961, after an attempted *coup* by four army generals in Algeria.

On the other hand, it is not the president but the government which is constitutionally enjoined to 'determine and direct the policy of the Nation.' The activities of the government are directed by the prime minister (appointed by the president), who is responsible for national defence and for ensuring the enforcement of the laws. The prime minister's specific powers include the appointment of subordinate civil and military officers, exercise of the executive rule-making power, and, like the president of the Republic and the presidents of both houses of parliament, the power to submit laws and treaties for review by the Constitutional Council. Although the government is responsible to the National Assembly and, hence, must resign when censured by it, ministers may not be members of parliament — a provision which President Giscard d'Estaing hoped to abolish.[5] (By contrast, membership of parliament is a prerequisite for ministerial office in Sri Lanka.) French ministers are, however, entitled to address both houses.

The French Constitution clearly envisaged the government as a co-operative venture between the president and the government headed by the prime minister. As Prime Minister Chaban-Delmas noted in January 1970, the Constitution 'requires close and almost intimate relations between the President . . . and the Prime Minister and an almost total confidence in each other.'[6] This intention is manifested most clearly in article 19 which requires the prime minister, or other appropriate minister, to countersign (and, hence, both approve and bear responsibility for) all presidential acts except (to mention the principal items) appointment of the prime minister, dissolution of the National Assembly, exercise of the emergency power to rule by decree, submitting, or refusing to submit, a Bill to referendum, and appointment of members of the Constitutional Council. Small wonder, then, that early in its history, President de Gaulle characterized the Fifth Republic as 'both parliamentary and presidential',[7] a description echoed by Michel Debré, principal draftsman of the Constitution and first prime minister — 'a mixed regime'[8] — and Georges Pompidou, his successor — 'half-way between a regime squarely presidential and a regime squarely parliamentary'.[9] One parliamentarian, André Chandernagor, aptly described the government as 'hybrid'.[10]

Other commentators have been less charitable, however, and have tended to suggest that 'schizoid' might be a more appropriate adjective than 'hybrid' or 'mixed'.

[T]he result of [concessions by General de Gaulle to Parliament and vice versa] was not a happy compromise but a *constitutional mess*. The unfortunate constitutional experts of the Council of State were called upon to juxtapose and superimpose conflicting ideals, and in the resulting lengthy text *confusion competed with contradiction and ambiguity with obscurity*. In essence, the lawyers were trying to fuse two ultimately incompatible notions: on the one hand, the separation of powers with a strong Head of State (which smacked of presidentialism), and on the other, the principle of governmental responsibility to Parliament (which implied a parliamentary regime). The central question of any constitution — who rules? — is fudged. . . . Certain articles of the Constitution clearly suggest that the Prime Minister governs, whilst successive Prime Ministers and Presidents of the Republic have so far claimed that the President rules: *with the French Constitution of 1958 we enter the world not of Descartes but of Lewis Carroll* . . . . [T]he Constitution clearly establishes a dyarchy at the top, a twin-headed or bicephalous Executive. In practice, the problem has been solved by prime ministerial acceptance of presidential supremacy, but such a happy situation may not last, and the prospect of a major constitutional crisis has haunted the minds of politicians throughout the Fifth Republic.[11]

Whatever the picture suggested by the bare constitutional provisions, there is no doubt that, in practice, 'there is only one head'[12] — the President. As Presidents de Gaulle and Pompidou agreed, there is 'no dyarchy at the summit'.[13] Just as the essential character of the American presidency was established by its first occupant, General Washington (although the office has obviously evolved greatly since then), so General de Gaulle set the pattern of the presidency of the Fifth Republic, and his presidency has provided the model followed by his successors.[14] As one commentator noted, 'The constitutional text of the newly established Fifth Republic was to prove less important than de Gaulle's views of leadership.'[15]

De Gaulle, heavily influenced by his perception of the weakness of presidents of the Third and Fourth Republics, held an almost mystical view of the presidency as the embodiment of the French state (Louis XIV was not the only Frenchman to believe that '*L'Etat c'est moi*'), a view which 'bore little resemblance' to the constitutional text.[16] At a press conference on 31 January 1964, de Gaulle remarked:

It should obviously be understood that the indivisible authority of the State is entrusted completely to the president by the people who have elected him, that there is no other authority — either ministerial, civilian, military, or judicial — which is not entrusted and maintained by him.[17]

De Gaulle was able to implement his view of the supremacy of the presidency through the combination of several factors.

First, and undoubtedly the most important, was his personal prestige derived from his role as leader of the Free French during the Second World War, President of the provisional government of 1944–46, and his role as 'statesman in waiting' throughout the history of the Fourth Republic (1944–58), culminating in his return to office in June 1958 as the only person with sufficient stature to save France from civil war over Algeria. In addition to his personal prestige, he possessed a powerful and imperious personality, which was well displayed at his press conferences — the regime's 'absolute weapon', according to one commentator[18] — which resembled Louis XIV holding court.[19] One writer has described the French head of state as 'a sort of president-king'[20] and this conception of the office also owes much to de Gaulle, who adopted a 'self-consciously regal style',[21] to which future presidents have tended to succumb, no matter how egalitarian their intentions upon entering office; Giscard d'Estaing, for instance, who commenced his term by strolling up the Champs Elysées in a lounge suit and inviting rather astonished dustmen to breakfast at the Elysée ended by allowing no one to sit opposite him at dinner and insisting that his family be served before their guests.[22]

Perhaps the clearest demonstration of President de Gaulle's identification of the state with himself in his role as 'national arbitrator'[23] is his persistent violation of the Constitution — in particular, his assumption of emergency powers following the attempted *coup* in Algiers in April 1961 in circumstances which did not appear to constitute a 'grave and immediate' threat to the independence or institutions of France, as article 16 requires (although the institutions of Algeria were certainly threatened); his refusal (contrary to article 29) to convene an extraordinary session of parliament in March 1960, although requested to do so by a majority in the National Assembly; and, above all, his insistence upon holding referenda to amend the

Constitution in October 1962 and April 1969, contrary to the constitutional requirements for amending the Constitution, as interpreted
by the Council of State and the Constitutional Council, both of which
were ignored by de Gaulle.[24]

Other factors serving to establish the supremacy of the presidency
under de Gaulle were the Algerian war and public perception that he
was the only person who could bring it to an honourable end, his
secure majority in the National Assembly, a majority which favoured
a strong presidency and, above all, the (unconstitutionally wrought)
constitutional amendment of 1962 changing the method of electing the
president from election by an electoral college to election by direct
universal suffrage.[25] One commentator expressed a widely shared
view:

The political significance of the October 1962 reform cannot be over-esti-
mated, for it completely upset, in favour of the President, the uneasy and
ambiguous balance established in the 1958 Constitution. As President de
Gaulle claimed in his January 1964 press conference, 'we behave in such a way
that power . . . emanates directly from the people, which implies that the
Head of State, elected by the nation, must be the source and holder of power
. . . that is what was made clear by the last referendum'.[26]

The pattern set by de Gaulle has continued under his successors;
indeed, most observers see the power of the French presidency as
constantly expanding.[27] Among the main factors which have fostered
the growth of presidential power are the general acceptance by the
public, prime ministers and parliament of the powerful presidential
role established by de Gaulle and his successors, media reluctance to
criticize or even scrutunize too closely presidents who seek — at least
between elections — to foster an image as 'national arbiter' above the
political fray,[28] France's fortune (in contrast to the United States) in
electing presidents with a high level of intelligence, competence and
integrity,[29] and the fortuitous circumstance that, so far, no president
has faced an opposition-controlled National Assembly.

The result has been an ever-expanding sphere of presidential interest
and activity, and an increasing tendency for presidents to act independently of the government in areas beyond those in which French
presidents, like British monarchs, have traditionally shown greatest
interest[30] — foreign relations, defence, and European and French
Community affairs — the field to which President de Gaulle more or
less adhered, when acting independently of the government,[31] although
he certainly denied that any sphere of activity was beyond his
authority.[32]

The French Constitution provides that the president shall appoint
the prime minister and shall dismiss him 'when [he] presents the
resignation of the Government'.[33] Thus, the president is not expressly
authorized to dismiss a prime minister contrary to the latter's wishes,

as General de Gaulle acknowledged during the drafting of the Constitution in 1958. De Gaulle's reply to a direct question from former Prime Minister Paul Reynaud as to whether the president could dismiss the prime minister was:

No! For, if it were like that, [the Prime Minister] could not govern effectively. The Prime Minister is responsible to Parliament and not to the Chief of State in what concerns policy matters. The Chief of State has as his essential role to ensure the regular functioning of the branches of government. So, he names the Prime Minister. . . . The Prime Minister, then, forms his government and the President . . . signs the decree, but he does not take the initiative for the decision on his own. If it were not like this, the balance would be compromised. The President . . ., I insist on this, is essentially an arbiter who has the mission of ensuring, no matter what happens, the functioning of the branches of government.[34]

It would be difficult to imagine a statement more at odds with the practice of the Fifth Republic, especially after 1962. That practice indicates that, whatever the letter of the Constitution, presidents can, and do, dismiss prime ministers who have not lost the confidence of the National Assembly. President de Gaulle dismissed two of his three prime ministers — Michel Debré in April 1962 and Georges Pompidou in July 1968 — and President Pompidou dismissed his first Prime Minister, Jacques Chaban-Delmas, in July 1972.

The prime minister is constitutionally enjoined to 'direct the activities of the Government',[35] which 'shall determine and direct the policy of the Nation'.[36] However, once again, in practice the supremacy of the president has negated the language of the Constitution.[37] President de Gaulle's attitude toward his government — which provided the model for his successors — was that it was for him to determine the government's 'overall direction';[38] the government could 'not act on crucial matters except on his directives'.[39]

One commentator has aptly remarked that 'presidential supremacy is not inscribed in tablets of stone but depends upon a willing Prime Minister.'[40] Presidents have decided policy and taken administrative action,[41] and even given directions to other ministers and officials,[42] without informing the prime minister — the officer constitutionally empowered to 'direct' the government's activities — and have appointed and reshuffled ministers without consulting the prime minister[43] in direct contravention of the constitutional stipulation that ministers be appointed 'on the proposal of the Prime Minister'.[44] And, generally speaking, prime ministers have been prepared to accept or, at least, endure this unconstitutional presidential domination. No wonder François Mitterrand 'likened the Prime Minister to a political strip-teaser who, under the greedy eyes of the President, steadily shed the prerogatives clearly conferred upon him by the constitution.'[45] The only exception was Prime Minister Jacques Chirac, who resigned in August 1976 protesting at President Giscard d'Estaing's encroachment upon his prime ministerial domain.[46] But, in assessing the significance of the Chirac resignation, one should not overlook the fact that he was the leader of a different political party from the president — the much larger Gaullists (RPR) — and had presidential ambitions of his own.

In view of the pusillanimity of most Fifth Republic prime ministers, it is hardly surprising to find them agreeing with presidential assessments of the relationship between the two principal executive officers. Indeed, prime ministerial descriptions of the president–prime minister relationship are both colourful and revealing. Echoing de Gaulle,[47] Prime Minister Chaban-Delmas explained, in September 1970, that 'the President is captain of the ship, the Prime Minister his first lieutenant';[48] two years later he told the National Assembly that his role 'consisted of directing governmental action according to the larger orientation defined by the President of the Republic'.[49] Similarly, Prime Minister Chirac regarded the prime minister as the conductor of the orchestra, but the president composed the music.[50] Undoubtedly the most enjoyable comment is that of the satirical weekly magazine *Le Canard enchaîné*:

A Prime Minister must have no merits. . . . He must take responsibility for all errors, especially if they are those of the President. He must not fail, otherwise he runs the risk of being sacked or being forced to resign for incompetence. Still more, he must not succeed, for to do so would be the ultimate impertinence, and his disgrace would then be even more terrible. . . . A Prime Minister must maintain himself in an honest, active and competent mediocrity, half-way between obvious failure which would harm the President and striking success which would put the President in the shadows.[51]

Lest it be thought that this cynicism is misplaced, it should be recalled that two prime ministers were sacked apparently because they were too successful — Georges Pompidou, immediately after winning the general election of June 1968, and Jacques Chaban-Delmas after obtaining an overwhelming vote of confidence from the National Assembly in July 1972.[52] Hence, it is not surprising to find *The Times* of London endorsing *Le Canard enchaîné* — surely not an every-day occurrence!

The role of the prime minister in the Fifth Republic is an ungrateful one. If he is generally perceived as successful he tends to strike the President as having grown too big for his boots, and must therefore be got rid of. If he is generally seen as a failure his usefulness gradually diminishes and his last service must be to make way for a new face.[53]

The important question for Australians is whether a republican Australia should seriously consider adopting the French system of government. It is submitted that it should not, principally on two significant grounds.

The first is the presence of a serious structural defect — indeed time may yet show it to be a fatal flaw — in the French model of government. The defect, in essence, is that the terms of office of the president and National Assembly deputies do not coincide (unlike the position in Kiribati), with the consequence that a president could face an opposition-controlled National Assembly, leading to governmental stalemate, or worse. Stalemate is, of course, possible also in the United States when the presidency and Congress are controlled by different parties (and even when they are not) but, whereas in the United States the executive branch can continue to function, however ineffectively, when faced by a hostile Congress, in France and Sri Lanka a similarly placed government could virtually collapse because, unlike its American counterpart, the government is responsible to and, therefore, needs to retain the confidence of, the National Assembly.

The terms of office of seven years for the presidency and five for the National Assembly were adopted from the Fourth Republic where the difference in the terms of office was not critical because, by and large, the president exercised mainly ceremonial functions, and the effective head of government was the prime minister. However, the spectre of presidency and National Assembly falling into the hands of opposing parties[54] — the Constitution's 'Achilles heel', according to Prime Minister Chaban-Delmas[55] — haunts the Fifth Republic, although, so far, it has been spared, largely through the fortuitous victories of the centre-right in the parliamentary elections of March 1978, and of the left in those of June 1981.

A reduction in the presidential term to five years, that of National Assembly deputies, has received wide support (64 per cent of those polled in an opinion poll published by Le Monde on 5 September 1984),[56] including that of Presidents Pompidou and Mitterrand.[57] Early in his term, President Giscard d'Estaing argued that a seven-year term was simply too long, but he finally rejected the proposed reform in 1980, the sixth year of his term of office.[58] In any event, while reducing the presidential term to five years would reduce the risk of the presidency and the National Assembly falling to opposing parties, it would not remove the problem entirely. As in Sri Lanka,[59] where both the president and members of parliament serve six-year terms, the political colour of the two institutions could still differ because the president can dissolve the lower house at any time, thereby destroying the synchronization of their terms of office. Moreover, as American experience confirms, electors may well vote differently in presidential and parliamentary elections, even if they occur simultaneously. Only if a constitutional amendment stipulated that presidential and National Assembly elections must coincide would the problem be greatly ameliorated, but such a reform would transform the French/Sri Lankan system — one with an effective head of government whose tenure of office is unaffected by a parliamentary vote of no-confidence — into one resembling that of Kiribati, whose Beretitenti (president) must retain the confidence of the Maneaba ni Maungatabu (parliament).[60]

President Mitterrand faces the prospect of having to govern with a hostile National Assembly by mid-1986. Upon his election in May 1981, the socialist Mitterrand dissolved the opposition-controlled National Assembly, and won the consequent general election. However, that National Assembly, elected in June 1981, must face the electors by June 1986. Current opinion polls suggest that the opposition will win,[61] so that President Mitterrand, whose term expires in May 1988, may have to govern with a hostile National Assembly for a full two years. Speculation is already rife as to how he will cope with that challenge.[62]

Apart from resignation, which is unlikely to be considered seriously,[63] two possible courses of action are open: the president could either choose a prime minister (and, consequently, a government) acceptable to the opposition (the course proposed by Presidents Mitterrand and Giscard d'Estaing had they lost the National Assembly elections of June 1981 and March 1978, respectively[64]), or dissolve the National Assembly and hold fresh elections (the course of action threatened by President Pompidou in 1970 and, probably, 1973).[65] If the opposition again won control of the National Assembly, the president's only alternatives would be to resign — it has been suggested that a president who loses two consecutive general elections ought to do so[66] — or to commission a government acceptable to the opposition for at least one year, since the National Assembly cannot be dissolved more than once every twelve months.[67] No doubt relations between a president and a prime minister from opposing parties could prove to be very difficult; it is even conceivable that they might spend their time sabotaging each other's efforts as they jockey for position in the next presidential election, with chaotic effects, especially on the national economy.[68]

The periodic threat of deadlock between the executive and parliament, or between president and prime minister is a very serious defect of the French system of government and surely constitutes a sufficient reason for ruling out its adoption in Australia.

But there is a further ground for rejecting the French system: it is, simply, too undemocratic, a judgment shared by French commentators.[69] In their effort to overcome the governmental instability of the Fourth Republic (1946–58), the founders of the Fifth Republic deliberately made parliament weak — too weak, it is submitted. (They even denied it the full field of legislation, vesting some of that field exclusively in the government,[70] an aspect of the French system which Sri Lanka wisely declined to follow.)

In the Fourth Republic, firm government had been impossible: there had never been a parliamentary majority willing to give regular support to a government when unpopular decisions had to be faced. Any question to the government could end in a vote of no confidence and a new, short-lived coalition would have to be found. The Fifth Republic Constitution was a reaction to this state of affairs and *there cannot, in consequence, be a constitution in history to compare with it for laying down in such meticulous detail all the ways and procedures by which the executive can avoid parliamentary harassment.*[71]

Because the French president can dissolve the National Assembly while his own tenure is legally unaffected by the National Assembly's lack of confidence in him, he 'cannot be called to account at all except by the electors at the end of his exceptionally long seven-year term of office.'[72] As one commentator has noted,

The problem in France is that the government, provided it has the support of a parliamentary majority, is just a little too safe from parliamentary scrutiny or criticism or control. Constitution, procedure and parliamentary practice are too restrictive of the opposition. . . .

France is still a country where *executive power remains almost immune from parliamentary scrutiny. The main reason is that the President, who makes all the important policy decisions, is not responsible to Parliament.*[73]

It has rightly been remarked that 'France has the most remarkable and uncontrolled concentration of executive power to be found in any Western democracy.'[74] 'The French presidential regime is *hyper-presidential* because it compounds the strengths of the executives of the U.S.A. and Britain while being subject to the limitations and constraints of neither.'[75] Unlike a British or Australian prime minister, the French president is 'constitutionally irresponsible and neither accountable to nor removable by the legislature.'[76] The American president shares these characteristics, but, unlike his French counterpart, he cannot dissolve a troublesome legislature and is subject to a wide range of 'checks and balances', including a powerful legislature with powerful committees, the requirement of Senate confirmation for major appointments and Senate ratification of treaties, a powerful, judicially enforced Bill of Rights and, perhaps above all, a well-educated and independent-minded citizenry informed (and manipulated?) by a powerful press and other media protected by the First Amendment.[77] François Mitterrand was correct in asserting, in 1980, that the French president had 'infinitely more power than the president of the United States.'[78]

Australia does not suffer from the Fourth French Republic's disease of weak governments at the mercy of unstable parliamentary majorities; therefore, we have no need for the cure the French adopted in the form of the Fifth Republic. Australian governments should, if anything, be made more, not less, accountable to parliament. Since the subject of this chapter is the type of government Australia should adopt under a future republican regime, it is appropriate to conclude by quoting, and endorsing, the 'personal note' on which the English scholar, John Frears, concluded his masterly study of *France in the Giscard Presidency*, published in 1981.

Many British people . . . admire and rather envy the vigorous and effective way that France has set about its political and economic renewal in the last twenty-five years. The French are very fortunate to have had leaders of the intelligence, clarity and authority of de Gaulle, Pompidou and Giscard d'Estaing. In the case of the latter, I admire greatly his capacity to rise above day-to-day concerns and to try to prepare his country for the future. However, I think that few English people would care to live under a regime in which such unrestricted power was conferred even on such a sage. The problems of Great Britain, and of America too, are the problems of democracy — that is to say, they stem from a political system in which the authorities cannot compel people to accept even what is considered good for them. It is very irritating to live with Anglo-Saxon pluralist democracy at the present time, where pressure groups have acquired the power to frustrate all policies including those which seem manifestly to be in the public interest. If you ask me if I admire the lucidity and authority revealed by the French political system under Giscard d'Estaing and his predecessors, I have to say yes. If you ask me, however, do I want the same style of authority here, I have to reply: not on your life.[79]

Chapter 5
Parliamentary Executive or Executive Presidency?

As suggested in the previous chapter, the debate on the appropriate form (or forms) of republican government in a country with Australia's cultural, historical, political, economic and military ties with the United States is very likely to resolve itself into a choice between adopting an executive presidency modelled on that of the United States or essentially retaining the present system of Australian government.

There are, of course, forms of executive presidency other than that of the United States (which was easily the first), and 'executive presidency' and 'parliamentary executive' are not necessarily incompatible or alternative forms of government, since an executive president could be a member of, and responsible to, the legislature, as he is in Kiribati. These considerations would need to be addressed if the focus of this chapter were upon a comparison between these two forms of government in abstract. However, such an abstract analysis would have little practical benefit in the Australian context given that the debate on the appropriate form of republican government will probably centre upon a choice between the present form of Australian government (without the monarchy) on the one hand, and a system resembling that of the United States on the other.

Hence, this chapter will compare the Australian and American systems of government. The comparison will, of course, concentrate upon the essential features of each system, since it is unlikely that either system would be adopted without at least limited amendment. Moreover, both systems of government will inevitably undergo considerable further evolution and change before Australian republican government becomes a reality.

UNITED STATES GOVERNMENT

The American system of government is founded upon four great political principles: representative government, the rule of law enforced by judicial review, federalism, and the separation of powers. The United States Constitution appears to envisage a tripartite division of governmental powers and functions into legislative, executive and judicial, and vests each power or function in a separate branch of government. Thus, legislative power is vested in Congress, executive power in the president, and judicial power in federal courts headed by the Supreme Court. Each branch was to be independent and free from control by the others; accordingly, each was to have its own personnel and not share them with any other branch.

However, the constitutional framers recognized that merely vesting different powers or functions in separate branches of government — 'a mere parchment delineation of the boundaries'[1] as Alexander Hamilton expressed it — would not guarantee the independence of the branches from encroachment by other branches. Demonstrating great practical wisdom, they realized that a thoroughgoing separation of powers would, in fact, be counterproductive; it would not preserve the independence of the branches, but would probably compromise it, because the legislature would tend to prevail over the other two branches.[2] Hence, ironically, in order to preserve the separation of powers *in practice* it was necessary to temper that separation by allowing each branch to 'check' or 'balance' the other branches' exercise of their principal functions.[3] The role of these 'checks and balances' has never been expounded better than by James Madison in *The Federalist* in February 1788:

[U]nless [the legislative, executive and judiciary] departments be so far connected and blended, as to give to each a constitutional control over the others, the degree of separation which the maxim ['that the legislative, executive and judiciary departments ought to be separate and distinct'[4]] requires as essential to a free government, can never in practice, be duly maintained.

. . . [T]he great security against a gradual concentration of the several powers in the same department, consists in giving to those who administer each department, the necessary constitutional means, and personal motives, to resist encroachments of the others. . . . Ambition must be made to counteract ambition. The interest of the man must be connected with the constitutional rights of the place. . . . In framing a government which is to be administered by men over men, the great difficulty lies in this: You must first enable the government to controul the governed; and in the next place oblige it to controul itself.[5]

Alexander Hamilton concurred, noting that a 'partial intermixture' of functions was 'not only proper, but necessary to the mutual defence of the several members of the government, against each other.'[6]

Richard Neustadt has aptly characterized the relationship between the branches of the federal government as one of 'separated institutions *sharing* powers'.[7] Thus, the legislative power of the United States is vested in Congress, but the executive and judicial branches have power to check abuse of power (real or perceived) by Congress: the president has power to veto legislation (although this power is itself checked by being subject to a congressional power to override it by two-thirds majorities in both houses), the vice-president presides over the Senate (where he can exercise only a casting vote), and the judiciary has power to review the constitutional validity of legislation. Moreover, bicameralism provides a further, internal, check on each house of Congress.

Similarly, federal executive power is vested in the president, who is elected by the people (through the medium of an electoral college) for a fixed term of four years and, thus, is not removable by Congress on political grounds. But he effectively shares certain powers with the Senate, which must ratify his appointment of judges, ambassadors and public officers, as well as (by a two-thirds majority) treaties executed by the United States, and he is subject to removal from office upon conviction by the Senate (after impeachment by the House of Representatives) for treason, bribery, or other high crimes or misdemeanours. The president's handiwork is, of course, like Congress's, subject to judicial review.

The judiciary, which the framers perceived as 'the least dangerous' branch of government[8] because it 'has no influence over either the sword or the purse' and possesses 'neither Force nor Will, but merely judgment',[9] is also subject to certain checks, but these must be more limited than those of the political branches in order to preserve judicial independence from political influence. Thus, federal judges who hold office 'during good behaviour' are removable (only?)[10] upon conviction by the Senate (after impeachment by the House) for the same offences for which the president and other civil officers are removable and, as mentioned, their appointment by the president is subject to confirmation by the Senate.

The constitutional separation of legislative and executive powers and, hence, of Congress and the president, had two important corollaries, both of which distinguish the American system of government from the Australian. First, both Congress and the president enjoy fixed terms of office; the president cannot dissolve either house of Congress, and Congress cannot dismiss the president (except through impeachment). The mutually independent tenure of these branches (indeed, of all three branches of government) is the foundation upon which the legislative–executive relationship is built and has, of course, had profound political consequences, some of which are noted below.

Second, the president enjoys a sphere of action in which he is immune from congressional control, although not, of course, from political influence. Congress cannot deprive him of his constitutionally conferred powers and offices, such as his power to appoint federal judges, ambassadors and other officers[11] and to dismiss officers of the executive branch,[12] or his office of commander-in-chief of the armed forces.

However, in what may be regarded as the substantive counterpart of the structural 'checks and balances' noted earlier, in most areas of national concern, executive action is impossible without the concurrence of Congress. As a recent commentator observed, 'on a host of matters there can be no effective governmental policy until the branches reach, if not an agreement, at least an accommodation.'[13] The most obvious example is the legislative power of the purse; all executive action requires funds, which only Congress can appropriate. Indeed, history — including very recent events — demonstrates that Congress's power over appropriations constitutes by far the most effective check on executive power, both in domestic and in foreign affairs.

But Congress's power of the purse is not the only power it possesses to stymie presidential action. To take an obvious example, presidential power over the disposition of the armed forces, conferred by the constitutionally conferred office of commander-in-chief, would be rendered vacuous without armed forces, which only Congress can provide and regulate because it controls the purse and is empowered 'to raise and support armies', 'to provide and maintain a navy' and 'to make rules for the government and regulation of the land and naval forces'. Similarly, the president's power, as commander-in-chief, to direct the armed forces during war depends upon a declaration of war, which only Congress can authorize. (Although it must be conceded that formal declarations of war appear to be an irrelevant minor technicality nowadays.)

Indeed, even after Watergate, Congress's power to check the president is occasionally regarded as excessive and as leading to governmental stalemate. But the constitutional framers recognized that liberty could be threatened by a powerful single executive with guaranteed tenure and a sphere of action legally beyond legislative control, and intended that 'effectiveness [should take] second place to the preservation of liberty'.[14] Apart from the Bill of Rights — adopted four years later — their principal device for protecting liberty from governmental power was to divide that power — between the national government and the States and, among the branches of the national government, through the separation of powers, bolstered and enforced by a system of checks and balances.

Separation of powers and checks and balances prevented the Framers from being impaled on the horns of the dilemma of the necessity for a strong executive on the one hand and the apparent incompatibility of a strong executive with republican principles on the other.[15]

Comparison of the Australian and American systems of government will be facilitated by examining separately relations within the executive branch and the relationship between the legislative and executive branches of government.

Intra-executive Relations

Constitutionally, the outstanding feature of intra-executive relations in the United States government is that the executive branch consists of one person: the president. Although the constitutional framers predicted correctly that presidents would appoint 'a principal officer in each of the Executive Departments'[16] — who collectively constitute 'the cabinet' — the existence of these officers is not constitutionally mandated and the Constitution confers no powers upon them. All federal executive powers are vested in the president alone.

Of course, the president cannot run the country from the White House, even with the assistance of a large staff. As in many countries, the executive branch comprises several departments, established by legislation, headed by a cabinet officer, and staffed by a vast public service, together with many other bodies — such as the Office of Management and Budget, the National Security Council and the Central Intelligence Agency — some established by statute and others by executive decree. All these bodies have heads appointed by the president, and countless public servants. Thus, whatever the constitutional position, the executive branch in fact includes hundreds of thousands of people in addition to the president, and their institutional interests do not always coincide with his. In the opinion of Nelson Polsby, an eminent student of the presidency,

In the longer view, perhaps the most interesting development of the fifty-year period [1933–83] is the emergence of a presidential branch of government separate and apart from the executive branch. It is the presidential branch that sits *across* the table from the executive branch at budgetary hearings, and that imperfectly attempts to coordinate both the executive and legislative branches in its own behalf. Against this development — this growing estrangement if not outright hostility of the presidential branch — the executive branch has been helpless, and that is the root cause of the decline in the caliber of the career bureaucracies, which is only beginning to become visible to thoughtful students of public administration.[17]

The significance of the constitutional unity of the executive branch is that much of its legitimacy is derived from the president; he appoints the senior officials, and much of their activity is an exercise of power conferred upon him by statute or the Constitution, especially his power to ensure that the laws are faithfully executed, and his (implied) power to conduct foreign relations. (Of course much, if not most, federal administrative action is an exercise of power conferred by Congress.)

The constitutional unity of the United States executive contrasts starkly with the position of its Australian counterpart. The focus of any theoretical unity of the Australian executive is the Crown, not the prime minister, who, in theory, is merely the Crown's principal adviser, and is not even mentioned in the Commonwealth Constitution.

The presidency of the United States combines the functions of both head of state and head of government. Apart from supervising the executive branch and directing its overall policies, the president sends and receives ambassadors, receives and visits foreign leaders, throws first baseballs and kicks first footballs of the season, opens Olympic Games, awards honours, and generally performs the functions of a head of state. Former President Ford estimated that these 'perfunctory, ceremonial things' occupied 'about 15 per cent to 20 per cent of a President's time — more in election years'.[18] He regarded them as 'the worst waste' of his time, yet these ceremonial activities, in which the president is widely perceived (and certainly seeks to be) not as a politician, but as the personal embodiment or representative of the nation — as a focus of national identity — are a significant adjunct to his other functions because they undoubtedly enhance his authority and prestige, which inevitably augments his political power.

In view of the experience of the United States presidency, is too much power entrusted to one person? And is it wise for one person to combine the functions of head of state and head of government?

Notwithstanding Watergate, most students of the American presidency appear to be reasonably satisfied with it. Far from suggesting that the president enjoys excessive power, such criticism as there is usually focuses on the president's perceived weakness relative to Congress. Thus, with the rhetorical overstatement so characteristic of American discussion of the presidency, Clinton Rossiter described it as 'one of the few truly successful institutions created by men in their endless quest for the blessings of free government',[19] and Thomas Engeman called it 'the finest institution of democratic statesmanship currently known to us, and perhaps of all time'.[20] Theodore Sorensen remarked, more soberly, that 'the actual legitimate power now granted by the Constitution to the Presidency is not unreasonable or dangerous',[21] and may even be *too little* . . . to tackle fast-changing economic problems effectively'.[22] In 1974, at the height of Watergate, with President Nixon still clinging to power, and after years of abuse of presidential power — Watergate, Vietnam, Cambodia — which he had chronicled so masterfully the previous year,[23] Arthur Schlesinger could still describe the presidency as 'a superb instrument of American democracy'[24], even though he advocated a reduction in presidential deification, suggesting that 'What we may need is a little studied disrespect for the Presidency.'[25]

But there are — or, at least, were — dissenting voices. Several scholars have joined Arthur Schlesinger in calling for a demystification of the presidency, although not necessarily an actual reduction in its powers.[26] (But it is probably an uphill battle: one of the most distinguished scholars of the office felt obliged to commence his study of it (in 1956) with an admission of his 'feeling of veneration, if not exactly reverence, for the authority and dignity of the Presidency.'[27]) One of its most trenchant critics was Philip Kurland, who regarded Watergate as an 'evil' of the presidency, not merely its occupant. He described the office as 'bloated with unrestrained power, available for use for good or evil, with little or no accountability for the use to which it is put.'[28]

Inevitably, some critics have proposed that the president's ceremonial functions be separated from his office and conferred upon a separate head of state.

> If we had our way we would have some figurehead President, with a big salary and no power, who would live in the White House and lay cornerstones to the awe and veneration of the populace, and lead worship, and we would let some shrewd political leader from Congress head the government, answer opposition questions, consult his cabinet, and fight no-confidence votes. We would secularize the chief executive.[29]

Although proposals along these lines, which would entail conversion to some sort of parliamentary executive, might reduce presidential power *within* the executive branch, they would probably also have the consequence of *strengthening* the president's powers relative to Congress, not reducing them.[30] Indeed, conversion to some system of responsible government — with or without a parliamentary executive — has been proposed over the years by astute critics of the American system of government who see its great defect as the president's inability to implement his legislative programme in the face of a recalcitrant Congress.[31] However, the prospect of achieving conversion to some form of responsible government or parliamentary executive — whether motivated by the objective of increasing or reducing presidential power — must be rated as minimal.[32]

American perceptions of the adequacy or excess of presidential power are not, of course, determinative of the question whether such an office would be appropriate in Australia, with its different political traditions and environment, especially its strong party discipline and the absence of a constitutional Bill of Rights. That question is best deferred until the final section of this chapter, after an examination of the Australian system of government.

Legislative–Executive Relations

Legislative–executive relations in democratic polities depend upon so many variables — including the personalities of (at least) the principal protagonists, the strength of their electoral 'mandate', their current standing with the public, their political affiliation, the strength of the parties in each house of the legislature, the leading political issues of the day, and the contemporary political climate — as well as more stable institutional factors — such as the applicable constitutional and statutory provisions, and the political and constitutional conventions and traditions of the various governmental organs — that it is rather difficult to describe such relationships in general terms.

In a system, like Australia's, based upon responsible parliamentary government, the constitutional requirement that the political complexion of the executive be compatible with that of the lower house of the legislature imposes greater stability in legislative–executive relations than is possible under the American system of separated institutions sharing, and competing for, power. Hence, the variable factors have less impact in Australia than in the United States. In Australia they are influential at the periphery of the legislative–executive balance, determining the finer details and nuances of the relationship, whereas in the United States they determine the core of those relations as well. Hence, legislative–executive relations fluctuate much more widely in the United States than in Australia, making it hazardous to attempt a general overall assessment of those relations in the United States.

The different governmental functions performed by Congress and the president provide the foundation upon which their relationship is based. The president, the only officer (apart from the vice-president) enjoying a national 'mandate', is the principal initiator of government policy and legislation, the national representative in foreign relations, and the main source of energy and motive power in the federal government.[33] Congress, on the other hand, although certainly not without energy of its own, is primarily the deliberative branch of government. Its members represent local and State interests while, hopefully, endeavouring also to promote the wider national interest — an effort which is not always successful, according to critics, who charge congressmen with excessive parochialism.[34] But close attention to local projects and events is frequently necessary if the congressman hopes to be re-elected.[35]

The relationship between Congress and the president is essentially competitive, as the constitutional framers intended; there would have been little point in separating the branches of government and establishing mechanisms enabling them to 'check' and 'balance' one another if close co-operation were the desired norm. The framers' intention was 'not to avoid friction, but by means of the inevitable friction incident to the distribution of the governmental powers among three departments, to save the people from autocracy.'[36] Hence, 'if the Constitution can be said to grant legitimacy to anything, surely it legitimizes conflict between Congress and the President.'[37]

On paper, the contest between the president and Congress would appear to favour the latter: although both branches were invested with important powers, Congress certainly received the lion's share,[38] including, above all, the appropriation power, and each branch was given the means to protect itself against encroachment by the other. But, in fact, the executive prevailed; although presidential supremacy developed slowly and somewhat fitfully in the nineteenth century, it has become well-entrenched and virtually institutionalized in this crisis-ridden century.[39] Moreover, the executive has prevailed even apart from crises, because it is the active, initiating branch and here, as elsewhere, possession is nine-tenths of the law. As Louis Koenig has noted,

In the interbranch struggles over the concurrent powers, advantage most often lies with the branch that outraces the other in taking the initiative; whoever 'gets there first' prevails. Generally, the president has run faster than Congress and therefore usually occupies a far greater sector of the gray area.[40]

Consequently, one governmental branch is now 'permanently "more equal" than the others: as the Supreme Court and Congress are preeminent in constitutional theory, so the President is preeminent in constitutional fact.'[41]

Like most democratic legislatures, Congress has two main functions: legislation and oversight of the administration.

Legislation

The president's constitutionally assigned role in legislation — Congress's central function — is relatively modest. He is obliged to give Congress periodic information on 'the State of the Union' and to 'recommend to [its] consideration such measures as he shall judge necessary and expedient'[42] but, once he has sent his proposed legislation to Congress, Congress has complete control over the legislative process, and determines whether, and in what shape, it emerges. However, the president enjoys a limited power of veto, his principal power regarding legislation, and his main weapon with which to resist congressional encroachment on his domain. But Congress can override his veto by two-thirds majorities in both houses.[43] Apart from requiring taxation Bills to originate in the House of Representatives,[44] the Constitution does not otherwise regulate the legislative process; there is, for example, no constitutional requirement that Bills — even appropriation Bills[45] — must originate in the executive branch, and, in fact, many do not.

Presidential success in securing passage (in recognizable form) of legislative proposals largely depends upon the variables mentioned at the beginning of this section. Hence, presidential success waxes and wanes depending upon the president's personality and political strength and, above all, his capacity for dealing with Congress. An ability to deal with Congress — by persuasion, cajolery, bullying, bribery, compromise and co-operation — is probably the most important asset a president can have, yet relatively few have possessed it in abundance. In the twentieth century, only Woodrow Wilson, Franklin Roosevelt and Lyndon Johnson stand out, and even they lost their magic touch after a few years. The most recent president to enjoy excellent relations with Congress was Johnson, a former Senate majority leader, who was fortunate (in regard to handling Congress) in coming to office in circumstances which fostered national cohesion (the assassination of President Kennedy), securing a landslide election victory the following year, and facing a Congress controlled by his own party, many members being former colleagues. In Johnson's early, halcyon years (1964–66), it was still possible for a president to secure passage of legislation by enjoying good relations with a few congressional leaders, and Johnson's relations with those leaders was so close that one observer remarked that 'the system more resembled the parliamentary form of executive–legislative relations than the presidential'.[46]

However, such a close relationship was exceptional, even when Congress and the presidency were in the hands of the same political party (contrast, for example, the experience of President Carter). Of course, relations were usually much worse when they were not (as under Truman, Eisenhower, Nixon, Ford and Reagan). The legislative–executive relationship has frequently been characterized as one of 'stalemate' with presidents having great difficulty in securing passage (in relatively intact form) of even their most important legislative and budget proposals.[47] In 1970, George Reedy, a former special assistant to President Johnson, described the history of the previous thirty-three years as 'a rarely broken record of presidential swimming in hot congressional water'.[48] In many respects, legislative–executive relations have worsened since then; after all, 1970 was supposed to be the zenith of the imperial presidency.

Congressional power has undergone a resurgence since Watergate (1973–74). Insofar as congressional opposition to the president was a reaction to Watergate, it was a temporary phenomenon and appears to have subsided, as was to be expected.[49] However, important legal and institutional reforms since the Watergate era (not all — especially the institutional reforms — directly attributable to Watergate) have both strengthened Congress institutionally (especially its budget process) and made presidential negotiation with Congress more complicated than in earlier times when a deal struck with a few congressional leaders could secure the passage of legislation. The principal statutory reforms, which sought to roll back the imperial presidency — the Congressional Budget and Impoundment Control Act of 1974, the War Powers Resolution of 1973 and the National Emergencies Act of 1976 — strengthened Congress's budgetary process, and information and staff resources but otherwise their main overall impact on legislative–executive relations was to raise congressional morale — a not insignificant contribution to congressional resurgence.

The institutional changes in Congress since the mid-1970s have undoubtedly had the greatest impact on the presidential–congressional equation. The main institutional reform was the overthrow of the seniority system. As a result, 'The former ability of the President to sit down with ten or fifteen leaders in each House, and to agree on a program which those leaders could carry through Congress, has virtually disappeared.'[50] From the democratic point of view, that may not seem a disaster, but that was certainly not ex-President Ford's view. He regarded the presidency as 'imperiled, not imperial' and laid the blame squarely on 'some misguided "reforms"', especially 'the erosion of the leadership in the Congress.'

Party leaders have lost the power to tell their troops that something is really significant and to get them to respond accordingly. . . . Part of this erosion of the congressional leaders' power has come from the 'reform' of the procedures in the Congress. We went on a wild nightmare of reforms, and *we really messed up the way the Congress effectively works.* You could run down a list of things that have been done under the title of reform, and they all look good, but the net result is that the *Congress has really lost its capability to respond.* I think all the so-called reforms since the late 1960s ought to be reviewed to see whether or not they have been counterproductive.[51]

The demise of the congressional seniority system has exacerbated the effect of a fundamental and long-term phenomenon of the American political order: the decline of the political party.[52] The result is 'an ever more rampant individualism',[53] which has become the 'dominant element of the new political order.'[54] As James Sundquist has noted,

Political individualism — the antithesis of party regularity and party cohesion — is at once a cause and a product of the decay of the strong political party organizations that once dominated American politics, a decay that dates from the Progressive Era and has been accelerating especially since World War II.[55]

Congressional individualism has served to render legislative–executive relations more fluid than ever. Contemporary presidents are unable to negotiate permanent congressional coalitions, but must construct a separate congressional majority for each legislative proposal. Moreover, it seems that lobbying in Congress by political action committees (PACs), local interests and even fellow congressmen employing internal PACs is out of control and urgently in need of reform.[56] According to one recent study, which (impliedly) suggests that 'bribery' would be a better description of what often occurs than 'lobbying',[57] 'congressmen now owe their first loyalty to PAC interests rather than to party or public interests.'[58] Greater individualism is not necessarily detrimental to presidential bargaining with Congress, since it enables the White House to pick off congressmen one by one,[59] and to exploit PAC and local pressures on congressmen.[60] All in all, Congress appears to be too beholden to special interests to instil confidence that the national interest is its primary concern.

Were Congress itself able to supply greater legislative initiative and leadership, presidential difficulty in securing passage of legislation might not constitute a serious defect of the American political system. But the 'institutional structure of the Congress and its patterns of behaviour have evolved to enable it to follow and to respond, but not to lead. . . . [T]o *the extent that presidential leadership is rejected, there is no substitute.*'[61]

Is stalemate between the two political branches necessarily a symptom of failure of the governmental system, or can it be argued that the electors mandated it by choosing a president of one political party and a congressman of another (not that stalemate is confined to that situation)? James Sundquist believes not:

Even when the voters give the president an uncooperative Congress, *he remains the only source of effective leadership, and the people understand that as a fact of life and expect him to be the leader.* He is still the one person who presented a philosophy and a program to all the voters, asked for a mandate to lead the country in a more or less defined direction, and received it. The people sent him to Washington to take charge, and one of his jobs is to lead the legislature, to stop the incessant bickering and get things done. Even when they elect a president of one philosophy and congressmen of another, it is surely doubtful that the people are mandating deadlock and inaction. They may be expressing ambivalence and uncertainty, but they are more likely to be simply paying respect to incumbency or personal acquaintanceship in voting for Congress — particularly for members of the House. *The superior mandate is still the president's.*[62]

Oversight

The second great power shared by both houses of Congress[63] is the power to examine the operations of all branches of the government — 'oversight' as it is commonly termed. This power is incidental to Congress's legislative power because reliable information on the workings of government and the operation of existing legislation is an essential pre-requisite for intelligent and effective legislation. The House of Representatives also derives investigative power as an incident of its power to impeach all civil officers of the United States, including the president, vice-president, cabinet members and judges, for 'treason, bribery, or other high crimes and misdemeanors'.[64]

Insofar as the two aspects of the legislative process can be separated from one another, it is the congressional oversight power, rather than the legislative (presidential–congressional bargaining) process, which foreign admirers of the American system find so appealing. This is especially true of observers from countries, like Australia, with a responsible parliamentary executive which dominates the legislature, or at least its lower house. They see powerful congressional committees 'grilling' witnesses from the executive branch, perhaps on national television, and apparently probing the darkest recesses of the White House and the executive departments. In the public mind, this somewhat mythical view of Congress as super-sleuth probably reached its apogee in the Senate Watergate Committee (formally the Senate Select Committee on Presidential Campaign Activities) hearings of May–September 1973. But other recent congressional investigations — such as those into the assassination of foreign leaders, the Central Intelligence Agency and, of course, the House Judiciary Committee hearings on the impeachment of President Nixon — stand out as causing the executive far more embarrassment than parliament or its committees are usually able to inflict in 'Westminster' systems.*

In theory, the great difference between legislative oversight of the administration in the United States and Australia lies in the wider range of sanctions available to Australian legislatures. In reality, however, the opposite is the case.

In Australia, the House of Representatives' ultimate sanction is a vote of no-confidence and the Senate's is a refusal to grant supply. The consequence thereof is that sooner (the House's no-confidence resolution) or later (exhaustion of appropriated funds) the government will fall. The president of the United States, in contrast, enjoys a fixed term of office (subject only to impeachment); hence, whether or not Congress has confidence in his administration is *constitutionally* irrelevant.[66] Indeed, during Watergate the inability of Congress to remove from office a president abusing his power (short of committing an impeachable offence) or whose political views had fallen grossly out of alignment with those of Congress and the people was perceived by some as a serious weakness of the American political system. Several congressmen and academic commentators proposed constitutional amendments to enable Congress (usually by more than a simple majority) to remove a president from office without having to employ the highly impractical impeachment process.[67] (Predictably, once Nixon had gone most of these proposals evaporated.) A much-debated question was whether a British or Canadian (or Australian) prime minister who behaved as Richard Nixon had would have survived in office as long as he did. He probably would not have, but whether so many of his erstwhile associates would have been brought to justice — or at least trial — is much more questionable.

Now that the legislative veto has been effectively removed,[68] the principal sanctions available to Congress are to refuse to pass legislation or appropriate funds (for example, to bomb Cambodia, continue a high level of military aid to South Vietnam after the Paris Peace Accord of 1973, assist rebels in Angola, or finance the 'contras' in Nicaragua)[69] and, perhaps most important of all, to embarrass the administration publicly by exposing its failings though the media.

---

* Of course, one ought not to forget some rather less savoury congressional investigations, such as the 'witchhunts' a generation ago by Senator Joseph McCarthy and the House Un-American Activities Committee.[65] Perhaps these only serve to remind us that all power can be abused.

Apart from extreme cases, these are also the only sanctions realistically available to Australian parliaments and, here also, adverse publicity is by far the most effective weapon. As has been noted of Britain, 'It is not the loss of a vote of confidence which the British executive must dread but the loss of face.'[70]

Hence, in reality the sanctions underpinning legislative oversight are similar in both countries, but Congress, in practice, commands a greater range of weapons. A consequence of the control of Australian lower houses by governments is that their only weapon is the ability of the opposition in the house to embarrass the government publicly. When they are not controlled by the government parties, Australian upper houses can deploy a wider range of sanctions against the government and its political allies in government elsewhere in Australia.

How effective, then, is legislative oversight in the United States? Informed observers, including congressmen, are rather critical. One Senator remarked in 1965 that 'regular committee oversight . . . is not carried out to any degree whatever.'[71] Eight years later, representatives told a House enquiry that Congress had been 'derelict', because oversight was inadequate and 'pathetic'.[72] Although the *quantity* of oversight 'increased markedly' in the 1970s, its *quality* did not;[73] in 1979, representatives were still condemning it as a 'total failure'.[74] Members of both branches of government have alleged that congressmen frequently interfered in administrative details on behalf of constituents or special and local interests, instead of engaging in detached oversight in the national interest:[75] 'what we've got now, instead of oversight, largely is intervention.'[76] A 1981 assessment by James Sundquist, a highly respected student of American government was that

To the extent that oversight has been intensified, so have certain questions of impropriety associated with the process. At its best, congressional oversight exposes and prevents misconduct, helps to maintain a salutary degree of constituency influence on administration, and in doing so protects the country from imperial presidencies and bureaucratic arrogance.[77] But, at its worst, oversight becomes irresponsible meddling in administrative matters, producing undesirable strain and tension between the branches, imposing burdens of time and paperwork and harassment on the executive, blurring lines of responsibility, and inducing administrators to stretch or even violate the law to give preferential treatment to particular constituents at the expense of others, sometimes with added cost to the treasury.[78]

A recent study of Congress confirms that, all too frequently, legislative oversight merely serves to attract publicity to sub-committee chairmen at the expense of a serious waste of government resources.

Subcommittee hearings held primarily to showcase the chairman waste not only the sub-committee members' time: someone must testify at those hearings. Secretary of State George Shultz was called to Congress for formal testimony twenty-five times in 1983, or every other week; all told, high State Department officials made nearly 400 appearances. Senator Robert Kasten, of Wisconsin, says that officials appearing before redundant committees not only discuss the same topics but use the same words. 'Often I'll say to myself, Where have I heard that before? and realize that it's the exact same speech that was read by the same man, the week before, at another hearing. If you miss part of his speech, just go to the next hearing, because he'll be giving it again.'

Constantly going up the Hill to testify — and constantly having to defend budget requests, which in the multi-tier system are subject to some kind of challenge somewhere almost daily — affects the efficiency of executive agencies.[79]

The chairman of one regulatory commission was obliged to spend four days a week for six consecutive weeks testifying before eight congressional committees.[80] This sort of behaviour led one critic to complain in June 1979:

With the democracy within the committee system, one of the ways to get elected committee chairman is by . . . having a lot of subcommittees. . . . Everybody gets to chair one, and each one has its own staff and its own offices. Once you've got a subcommittee with a staff, they've got to do something, so of course they hold hearings and . . . summon administration witnesses. There was a period for about six months at the beginning of this administration, when everybody was always up on the Hill testifying, and you wondered who the hell was running the departments.[81]

In sum, legislative oversight in the United States should not be viewed through rose-tinted spectacles. But, for all its failings, oversight by congressional committees is still far more effective than any Australian counterpart.

AUSTRALIAN GOVERNMENT

Intra-executive Relations

As in other 'Westminster' systems, the 'supreme governing body'[82] in Australian governments is cabinet, whose members must (by law or convention, depending upon the jurisdiction) be members of the legislature. Cabinet ministers, together with any ministers outside the cabinet, are collectively responsible to parliament: if the lower house loses 'confidence' in them, the government must resign or call a general election.

The prime minister or premier heads the government. In non-Labor administrations he appoints and dismisses ministers; caucus elects them in Labor governments, but the chief minister allocates portfolios and decides (with his deputy and the two Senate leaders) which ministers sit in cabinet if it does not comprise the full ministry. The prime minister or premier also settles the agenda of cabinet meetings, presides over them, and decides which non-cabinet ministers should be invited to attend. Theoretically, he is simply the Crown's first or chief minister — *primus inter pares*, or first among *equals*, as it is often expressed.

How accurately does this aphorism reflect the true position? As is so often the case, comparison with another system of government helps to illuminate our own. An Australian or British prime minister's relationship with his ministerial colleagues differs markedly from that which exists between an American cabinet secretary and the president. This difference, moreover, is a fundamental one of *function*, and is far from being merely a matter of degree. British and Australian cabinets *decide*; American cabinets do not. They merely *advise* the president; he decides. Executive power is vested in the president, not his cabinet. Therefore, he alone, not the cabinet, makes the decisions, after receiving advice from the cabinet and elsewhere. Whether true or not, the apocryphal anecdote concerning President Lincoln's response upon finding his Cabinet unanimously opposed to him — 'seven noes, one aye; the ayes have it'[83] — captures nicely cabinet officers' subordinate status and purely advisory relationship with the President.

In Australia, in contrast, ministers are the prime minister's colleagues, not his subordinates.[84] Like him, they have been elected to parliament and in Labor governments elected (by caucus) to the ministry as well, and have often previously held several portfolios and served in parliament for many years. Unlike their American namesakes ('counterparts' would be an overstatement), they are certainly not merely creatures of the prime minister. When they lose ministerial office they do not (as in the United States) simply disappear into private life (like Walter Hickel or Alexander Haig), but remain members of parliament and, therefore, of the governing party's caucus. If their departure from office was involuntary they are, thus, provided with a public platform from which to criticize the prime minister (for example, Malcolm Fraser's attacks on John Gorton in 1971 and Andrew Peacock's on Fraser a decade later), and the means to plot a party-room deposition of the prime minister, a fate which befell Robert Menzies in 1941 and John Gorton thirty years later.

Central to any assessment of prime ministerial power within the executive branch is his relationship with his cabinet. If he is astute and well-informed he can dominate its deliberations[85] and, occasionally, he can bypass it with the support of the relevant ministers, and present cabinet with a *fait accompli*, especially in the fields of foreign affairs and internal security;[86] examples from the Hawke government include the framing of policy on Timor, the establishment of the Hope Royal Commission, and the abortive decision to co-operate with the United States in testing the MX missile.[87] But prime ministers, even those as powerful as Margaret Thatcher, do not always carry the cabinet with them,[88] and must, like their colleagues, accept defeat under the doctrine of cabinet solidarity — at least until they have managed to eliminate their opponents from cabinet (Mrs Thatcher's tactic), an option not available to Australian Labor chief ministers.

For at least a generation, some observers of British government, led by the late Richard Crossman, have suggested that the power of the British prime minister within the executive branch has come to approximate that of an American president.[89] (That opinion has, of course, been strongly contested.[90]) It is, therefore, somewhat ironic to find Sir Winston Churchill, under whom, according to Crossman, cabinet government 'finally disappeared'[91] drawing a parallel between a British prime minister's relations with his cabinet colleagues and an American president's relations with Congress. 'You, Mr President', he told Franklin Roosevelt,

are concerned to what extent you can act without the approval of Congress. You don't worry about your Cabinet. On the other hand, I never worry about Parliament, but I continuously have to consult and have the support of my Cabinet.[92]

This comparison was reiterated, albeit without reference to Churchill's remarks, by Richard Neustadt, one of the foremost scholars of the presidency.

The functional equivalence between a British Cabinet and our set of influentials — whether Secretaries, Senators, White House staffers, Congressmen, or others — is rendered plain by noting that, for most intents and purposes, *their Cabinet members do the work of our congressional committees, our floor leaderships, and our front offices downtown, all combined.* . . . One of the checks-and-balances in Britain's system lies between the PM and his colleagues as a group. . . . *So a British Premier facing Cabinet is in somewhat the position of our President confronting the Executive Departments and Congress combined.*[93]

It is interesting to note that, although he was writing during the Vietnam War and Lyndon Johnson's 'imperial presidency', Neustadt's conclusion was that American government was 'more prime-ministerial than we are inclined to think'.[94] Although the British prime minister was 'not yet a President', the president of the United States was 'a sort of super-Prime Minister'.[95] Hence, it is not clear whether Neustadt's comparison between the 'checking' roles of the British cabinet and the American Congress reflects his perception of the former's strength or the latter's weakness. In any event, he appears somewhat to overstate the British cabinet's ability to check and control the prime minister.

Prime ministerial authority within the executive branch depends primarily upon his strength in cabinet and within his party, and control over the public service. His power derives from many sources: the prime minister's role as party leader, his authority over his ministerial colleagues and his ability to control the direction and duration of their careers, his power largely to control the proceedings of cabinet, its committees and (to a lesser extent) parliament, to decide when to dissolve parliament, the patronage at his disposal, his control over senior appointments to the public service, and his ability to command media attention. How effectively he deploys these great powers will, of course, depend on many factors which determine the environment within which prime ministerial power is exercised. These factors, which obviously vary widely among incumbents, include the ability, health and temperament of the leading members of the government and parliament (including the opposition), party strength in both houses, and the political and economic climate of the country and the world. But, even when these variables produce an environment least conducive to prime ministerial power, his power over cabinet, the public service, his party and parliament will far exceed that of any other minister; he is *first*, and not among equals.[96] This is as true of the Australian prime minister as it is of his British and Canadian counterparts, who are generally in a stronger position *vis-à-vis* their colleagues.[97] As Patrick Weller concluded, after a wide-ranging survey of prime ministers in Britain, Canada, Australia and New Zealand, 'Within the political machine, prime ministers remain the most powerful individuals, perhaps to an even greater degree than in the past,' — but 'they are often more limited than they appear'.[98]

One frequently admired aspect of the United States executive is the president's unlimited freedom of choice in selecting his cabinet. In particular, his field of choice is not confined to members of Congress, and any congressman chosen must resign his congressional seat.[99] Pursuant to the separation of powers doctrine, membership of the executive is incompatible with membership of the legislature.

Australian ministers are in a very different position. By law (in the Commonwealth, Victoria, South Australia and Tasmania) or convention (in New South Wales, Queensland and Western Australia), ministers must be members of either house of parliament.[100] Section 64 of the Commonwealth Constitution, which was modelled on the South Australian provision,[101] provides that 'no Minister of State shall hold office for a longer period than three months unless he is or becomes a senator or a Member of the House of Representatives.'[102]

Several commentators, including Prime Minister Bob Hawke (before he became a member of parliament) have argued that in selecting his ministry a prime minister should be free to look beyond the ranks of the members of parliament of the government party (or parties).[103] Mr Hawke recommended that 'as an initial step' one-quarter of the ministers should be non-members of parliament.[104] The non-parliamentary ministers would (like French ministers) be entitled to speak, but not to vote, in parliament, and would be answerable to parliament for the administration of their departments, but Mr Hawke may have contemplated a looser doctrine of cabinet solidarity for them, because he envisaged them '[not necessarily] fully embracing the total philosophy of the Government in which they were prepared to serve'.[105]

Complete or partial abandonment of the requirement that ministers must sit in parliament is not, of course, dependent on Australia becoming a republic. That requirement is absent in Japan and several West European monarchies; on the other hand, it is constitutionally mandated in republics such as Ireland, India and Sri Lanka. However, since presidential (or prime ministerial) power to choose non-parliamentary ministers may be a factor leading some republicans to favour the American (or French) system of government, a brief comment thereon may be apposite.

It is, of course, impossible to predict the practical effect on Australian government of allowing chief ministers to select at least some of their ministry from outside parliament. There are, moreover, persuasive arguments both for and against the proposal.

Several considerations commend the proposal. First, even if the general level of competence of members of parliament is viewed favourably,[106] a prime minister (or caucus) must nevertheless experience difficulty in selecting a highly competent ministry of twenty-seven from the relatively small number of government party (or parties) members in the Commonwealth parliament (117 in April 1985), not all of whom would be both qualified and willing to serve in the ministry. Moreover, as the experience of Senator (now former Justice) James McClelland (Minister of Labour in the Whitlam government and a man of recognized ability) demonstrates, finding a competent minister is easier than finding one qualified (in ability, interest and temperament) for the allotted portfolio.

So long as it is necessary to be a politician in order to become a minister, cabinets of all political colourations will tend to be mediocre at best, incompetent at worst. . . . The considerable ability of the mandarins of the Public Service provides a further reason why we should seek to have ministers of the highest calibre and experience. Twenty years as an industrial lawyer did little to prepare me to cope adequately with my first portfolio (Manufacturing Industry), and at no stage did I feel on terms of equal expertise with the permanent head or the top echelon of my department. . . . [I]f I had kept the job for the life of the Parliament, I do not believe I would have known enough about it to be the minister in fact as well as name.[107]

If the prime minister were free to choose ministers from outside parliament, he could select ministers technically competent in the fields covered by their portfolios.

Secondly, the level of competence of parliament is reduced because so many of the governing party's most talented members join the ministry, and thus have little or no time to participate in *real* parliamentary activity, such as service on parliamentary committees. As of April 1985, one-quarter of the Australian Labor Party representatives are ministers, as are one-sixth of its Senators.[108] (In the United Kingdom, with its much larger House of Commons, on average, 28 per cent of government members serve in the ministry, although under the Wilson government of 1964–70 and the Callaghan government of 1976–79, the figures were as high as 37 per cent and 36 per cent respectively.[109]) Moreover, proponents of non-parliamentary ministers argue, members of parliament might be less consumed by ambition to become ministers. They 'might develop some sharper sense of special function',[110] and devote themselves more assiduously to their parliamentary functions — examining proposed legislation and overseeing the executive — without seeking to curry favour with the prime minister. This was the view of Senator Don Chipp, leader of the Australian Democrats.

I see the real benefit of recruiting Ministers from outside Parliament in the area of responsible government, for if the Executive are not Members of Parliament, then Parliament has no vested interest in allowing the Executive a free and sometimes irresponsible reign. In fact, it is *in Parliament's interest* to defend itself against abuse of Executive power.[111]

However, one may remain sceptical regarding the supposed effect which the appointment of some non-parliamentary ministers would have on members' ministerial ambitions. The effect would surely be slight unless members of parliament were disqualified from ministerial service. But, even then, concern to curry favour with the government might still influence members if, as in France, ministers were frequently chosen from the ranks of parliamentarians who are then obliged to vacate their parliamentary seats.

Finally, reducing the proportion of ministers chosen from parliament might confer greater freedom of action on the governing party caucus. In the 1985 Hawke government, the ministry constituted 23 per cent of the members of caucus; under the last Fraser government, the figure was 36 per cent.[112] Since cabinet solidarity binds all ministers — even those not in cabinet[113] — in caucus, as elsewhere,[114] it is relatively easy for the prime minister and a few ministerial colleagues to dominate caucus. A decision of the prime minister and one or two colleagues in a cabinet committee, for example, could effectively determine cabinet policy which, in turn, would bind the entire ministry in caucus. The prime minister would need to persuade only a few members more than a quarter of caucus (less than a third of the backbenchers) in order to secure a majority in caucus. Thus, what appears to be the decision of a majority of caucus may, in fact, be the view of a minority as small as 30 per cent, including the prime minister and a few of his colleagues. The introduction of non-parliamentary ministers who would not, of course, be members of caucus would clearly reduce cabinet and, hence, prime ministerial, influence in caucus.

On the other hand, several countervailing considerations should be noted. First and foremost, the introduction of non-parliamentary ministers would effect a considerable increase in prime ministerial power. In Liberal-National Party coalition governments (and, perhaps, in Australian Labor Party governments also), these ministers would be selected by the prime minister and would be entirely beholden to him and him alone. They would be the prime minister's creatures and would owe allegiance only to him.[115] Unlike present ministers, they would lack the independent status conferred by popular election and membership of parliament.

Secondly, although cabinet might be strengthened in terms of technical expertise, the introduction of non-parliamentary ministers would probably weaken it politically, because it would no longer constitute a microcosm of the governing party, with most major interest groups represented. As Sir Douglas Wass remarked in his 1983 BBC Reith Lectures,

Cabinet represents a cross-section of the majority party, and its decisions in my view are more likely to command parliamentary support than decisions of the Prime Minister alone. For these reasons, I would not favour any further strengthening of the Prime Minister's position in relation to his colleagues.[116]

Parliament as well as the cabinet could be weakened by the introduction of non-parliamentary ministers, because these ministers would probably make only sporadic appearances in parliament, would have little interest in, or sympathy for, the institution and, perhaps most important, would not be directly subject to parliamentary authority and discipline. As one English commentator observed, in rejecting this proposal,

The Commons believes that it controls ministers because, apart from peers, they are members of it, subject ultimately to all the authority vested in the House. It has never in its history shown the slightest inclination to believe that it can properly control those who do not, as elected members, enjoy equal rights within it.[117]

Finally, appointment of non-parliamentary ministers would probably increase the risk that ministerial portfolios may be 'captured' by 'special interests', which appears to happen quite frequently in the United States. Senator Chipp has unconsciously highlighted this danger:

If Ministers were chosen from outside Parliament, I believe many of the deficiencies of our Westminster System would be relieved. The Ministers in the American system are experts in their own fields. For example, the President of the Board of General Motors may become Minister for Manufacturing

Industry, or the Treasurer may be attracted from the board of a leading bank or financial institution.[118]

The chairman of BHP, borrowed *temporarily* from his company, will indeed enjoy greater technical competence in the field of manufacturing industry than any politician, no matter how experienced. But which will be better able to balance or reconcile the interests of industry with those of labour and the general public? Running the Department of Manufacturing Industry requires very different skills from running a manufacturing industry. Knowledge of the industry is certainly an asset for the former, but experience in the reconciliation of various aspects of the public interest — *politics* in other words — is more important. After all, provision of technical information is the function of the department's public servants. The minister's role is to provide the *political* expertise.

Overall, the countervailing arguments are more persuasive. The probable effect of introducing non-parliamentary ministers would be to bolster the prime minister's position within the government. Not surprisingly, his power within the executive branch would come to resemble closely that of the president of the United States. In the writer's opinion, that power is excessive; consequently, the introduction of non-parliamentary Ministers would be a retrograde step.

Finally, it should be noted that, notwithstanding its pivotal role in the day-to-day operations of government, a study of the role of the public service — 'the bureaucracy', as it is so often tendentiously called — is omitted here because this chapter is not concerned with relationships within the executive branch *per se*, but rather with a comparison between such relations in the United States and Australia. From that perspective, the role of the public service need not be examined for two reasons. First, despite important differences between them, especially regarding political neutrality in their upper echelons, the public services occupy broadly similar positions in both countries. Secondly, and more important, conversion to republican government is unlikely to affect the role of the Australian public service significantly, because its role and the political neutrality of its upper echelons are matters not directly related to the question whether Australia becomes a republic or remains a monarchy.

Legislative–Executive Relations

Constitutionally, the relationship between Australian governments and legislatures is one of individual and collective ministerial responsibility to the lower house of parliament (in Queensland the unicameral parliament). The government must, at all times, enjoy the confidence of the lower house; that is, it must retain the support of a majority of its members. Hence, the political colour of the government will be identical, or at least compatible, with that of a majority in the lower house.

Unlike their American counterparts — Congress and the president — parliament and the executive are not co-equal branches of government in Australian constitutional theory. Parliament is supreme in our system, and ministerial responsibility to parliament was the mechanism developed to implement that supremacy. Hence, in theory, the lower house of parliament controls the government, ultimately through the device of the government's collective responsibility to that house. If that house loses confidence in the government, it must dissolve parliament and call a general election, or resign to enable the Governor-General or governor to appoint a new government able to command the confidence of the lower house.

However, in 'Westminster' systems, such as Britain, Canada, Australia and New Zealand, political reality bears little resemblance to constitutional theory. Because, initially, governments subsisted at the mercy of changing majorities in the lower house, political parties developed (among other reasons) to ensure governmental stability. Once stable, well-disciplined parties developed, a government whose party had secured a clear majority of the seats in the lower house was virtually guaranteed tenure for a full parliamentary term because party discipline strongly discouraged the defection of erstwhile supporters, especially on crucial matters of 'confidence'. Consequently, in all four countries, instead of the lower house of parliament controlling the government as constitutional theory suggests, by and large, the opposite is true: the government controls the lower house because the party leaders who head the government control the party to which the majority of lower house members belong. (Of course, the prime minister's role as party leader is only one source of power, among many others, especially his power of patronage.)

Party discipline is especially strong in Australia — certainly stronger than in Britain,[119] and, perhaps, 'much more intense and rigid than . . . in almost any other democratic country'.[120] As Sir Garfield Barwick (a minister for more than five years before becoming Chief Justice) noted, its effect is 'to rob [members of Parliament] of a sense of responsibility to the electorate'.[121] Harry Evans, a senior officer of the Australian Senate, has similarly remarked that 'members of Parliament regard themselves not primarily as legislators or as controllers of the executive but as representatives of parties which are either in or out of power'.[122] The consequence, he argues, is that 'the distinction between executive and legislative powers has entirely disappeared; both functions are exercised by one body, the majority party'.[123] Parliament, he believes, has been 'virtually killed' by '[t]he growth of party machines and the intensity of modern party discipline';[124] it has become merely 'a debating panel appended to the ministry'.[125]

Although perhaps exaggerated, and expressed with unusual acerbity, this perception of legislative–executive relations is quite widely shared. Colin Howard, for example, regards parliament as a 'cipher',[126] 'totally dominated by the executive',[127] and other commentators have argued that parliament's 'nominal control over the executive is non-existent'[128] and that, consequently, ministerial responsibility to parliament is 'moribund'.[129] Even those, like Gordon Reid, who deny that ministerial responsibility is defunct,[130] have acknowledged that the executive dominates the House of Representatives, if not parliament as a whole.

The contemporary state of the Australian Parliament . . . is an elected House of Representatives with its parliamentary effectiveness undermined by the domination of the Executive Government — its Speaker is drawn from and owes allegiance to the Government party; the 'Leader of the House' is an Executive Minister of State advised by departmental officials; the Government determines when the House will be summoned and adjourned; the Government dominates the business of the House; it claims the chairmanship of every parliamentary committee; the Government claims a monopoly over financial initiative in the House; Ministers have important advantages and priorities entrenched in parliamentary rules; the Executive Ministers claim extensive territorial rights in the parliamentary building (ironically they seldom claim rights in the administrative buildings); and both major parties when in government show a preference for party committees over parliamentary committees. The elected Senate, on the other hand, has managed initiatives independently of the Executive Government but it is a threatened institution for doing so.[131]

Party discipline certainly ensures that, barring extraordinary circumstances, the House of Representatives *as a corporate entity* (i.e. a majority of its members) will not enforce ministerial responsibility by passing votes of no-confidence in a government whose party holds a majority of House seats. To that extent, party discipline has indeed emasculated ministerial responsibility. If ministerial responsibility were measured solely by successful votes of censure deposing chief ministers, one could reasonably conclude that Australian governments are *responsible* only to caucus, and not to the House of Representatives. As Lord Shawcross noted of British government, 'Responsibility to Parliament means in practice at the most responsibility to the party commanding the majority there.'[132] Richard Crossman has, similarly, remarked that

the British Cabinet's concern today is not for its majority over the Opposition, because that is almost automatic, but for its majority inside its own Party. The key to power is inside the Party. It is not in Parliament as such, it is in the Party. And the opposition the Government fears is not that of the Opposition on the front bench opposite. Anybody knows the official Opposition is going to remain in opposition and is going to be defeated in every division until the next election, from the first day to the last. Everybody knows that.
The only doubt the Prime Minister has is about his own supporters. They are the people who can challenge him and, in the last resort, overthrow him.

In choosing his Ministers, therefore, one of his first preoccupations is to form a Cabinet which reduces rebellion to zero in his Party.[133]

Hence, a chief minister whose party holds a majority of lower house seats can be removed from office only if he loses the confidence of his party colleagues, as happened to Prime Minister John Gorton in March 1971 and New South Wales Premier Tom Lewis in January 1976.

However, although governments may not be effectively *responsible* to the lower house, they are *accountable* to both houses of parliament: they must explain and defend their actions and policies, and debate proposed legislation and public issues with the opposition with whom they are constantly compared. An Australian opposition has at least two significant advantages denied its American counterpart. First, question time enables the opposition to focus public attention on the government's mistakes and peccadillos; as the loans affair of 1975 — admittedly an extreme case — demonstrated, a determined opposition with public support can continually harrass and embarrass a government over a prolonged period of weeks, even months, causing it to lose its nerve and plunge into a fatal abyss of self-destruction. Secondly, the United States has no official leader of the opposition (or, of course, shadow cabinet); opposition party leadership is diffused among several leading personalities and presidential aspirants in both houses of Congress and even among State governors. In Australia and other 'Westminster' systems, the official leader of the opposition is the officially recognized alternative prime minister with whom the prime minister is constantly compared, and their performances evaluated, both by parliament and the general public.

Hence, the picture brightens considerably if attention is diverted from ministerial *responsibility* to ministerial accountability or answerability to parliament. As David Butler has noted,

The idea seems quite widespread that dismissal, or self-enforced resignation, is the only real sanction over ministerial conduct. But ministers are, in fact, insecure people desperately seeking to stand well before the rest of the world, and especially before the elites of Canberra or Westminster. *Admitting to error, being made a fool of, is for them a very real sanction.*[134]

An American student of British politics has made the same point:

The power of the House of Commons to control and oversee does not, in fact, depend upon its ability to register a formal vote of no confidence in the prime minister and thereby compel his resignation. It consists rather in the ability to compel him and his Cabinet colleagues to continuously justify their conduct before a large, politically sophisticated and critical audience, with potentially the entire world watching and listening. *It is not the loss of a vote of confidence which the British executive must dread but the loss of face.*[135]

His contrast between British and American 'oversight' of the administration is particularly instructive:

But in the conduct of debate on national policy, the British House effects an exposure of the executive through direct confrontation which is wholly lacking in the American system and whose importance ultimately may be far greater for the democratic conduct of public affairs than the power of individual, sometimes obscure legislative committees to exercise a parochially-oriented, haphazard, and frequently capricious initiative with respect to sundry items of legislation.[136]

The opposition's ability to question and embarrass the government may oblige it to alter its policies, endeavour to improve its public image, or even call an early general election (as in New South Wales in March 1984), and can force the prime minister to dismiss a culpable or burdensome minister. But the actions of a house minority are a poor substitute for action by the House of Representatives as a whole. The opposition in the House cannot, of course, defeat a Bill; hence, no government legislation has been defeated in the House of Representatives for forty years.[137] Moreover, the public's memory is short and easily distracted, as Mrs Thatcher demonstrated in the United Kingdom in 1982–83. Embarrassing a government — probably only temporarily in any event — is a very poor substitute for throwing it out of office by passing a vote of no-confidence in it.

Any assessment of the role of Australian parliaments in controlling, or even embarrassing, their governments must take account of their relatively infrequent sessions. In the 1970s (the most recent figures available) the average annual sittings of other 'Westminster' parliaments in non-election years greatly exceeded those of the Commonwealth parliament; New Zealand by 38 per cent, and Britain and Canada by more than 100 per cent. Their average number of annual sitting days in non-election years were:[138]

United Kingdom 1977–80	168 days
Canada 1971–75	187 days
New Zealand 1971–76	109 days
Australia 1971–76	78 days

The average number of annual sitting days of the House of Representatives over the twenty years 1962–82 was only 65,[139] and the average number of hours per year between 1971–80 was 716.[140] Moreover, the State parliaments sit even less frequently. Their average number of annual sitting days over recent years were:[141]

New South Wales 1979–83	
Legislative Assembly	51 days
Victoria 1978–83	
Legislative Assembly	56 days
Legislative Council	47 days

Queensland 1978–83 (August)	49 days (386 hours)
South Australia 1977/78–83 (2 December)	
House of Assembly	63 days
Legislative Council	58 days
Western Australia 1978–83	
Legislative Assembly	59 days
Legislative Council	52 days
Tasmania 1978–83	
House of Assembly	55 days
Legislative Council	54 days

Although the Commonwealth government, like its State counterparts, is not *responsible* to the Senate, it is *accountable* to it, as it is to the House of Representatives.[142] Hence, no examination of parliamentary control over the executive can afford to overlook the crucial role played by the Senate, especially since it effectively toppled the Whitlam government (albeit with vice-regal assistance) in November 1975.

Constitutionally, the government party (or coalition of parties) does not need to hold a majority of Senate seats and has not done so for thirty-eight of the Commonwealth's eighty-five years.[143] The introduction of proportional representation for the Senate in 1949 and the consequent near equality in representation of the two principal party groups (A.L.P. and L.–N.P.) has meant that the balance of power in the Senate is frequently held by minor parties and/or independents. Indeed, governments have controlled the Senate for only thirteen years between 1949 and 1985, and for only five years between 1962 and 1985 (1976–81). However, the position of governments in the Senate has not been as difficult as these figures might suggest because, for most of those years, the balance of power was held by the Democratic Labor Party (D.L.P.), a political ally of Liberal–Country Party governments and, since 1981, by the Australian Democrats who have undertaken not to block supply and have not obstructed governments of either political hue. Only during the Whitlam Labor government (1972–75) did the Senate seek deliberately (and successfully) to obstruct, if not destroy, the government.[144]

Although (perhaps 'because') the public profile of Senate opposition leaders is lower than that of their House colleagues, Senate scrutiny of proposed legislation, delegated legislation, executive action and the activities of statutory authorities is superior and probably more effective than that of the House of Representatives. Several factors are responsible for this, foremost among them being the frequent inability of the governing party or coalition to control the Senate in its own right. Other factors include the Senate's more effective committee system, and the weaker party loyalty displayed by senators, especially when participating in committee work.[145] Consequently, it has been suggested that responsibility for effective parliamentary control of the executive will increasingly fall upon the Senate, rather than the House of Representatives. Senator David Hamer, a strong proponent of this view, has argued that

A possible answer to [the problem of government by the public service] lies in the gradual development of the Westminster system to a point somewhat closer to the American system, with a strong questioning Senate balancing the Executive. In this process the Senate, unlike any other chamber in the Westminster system is uniquely placed to play a key role, since it cannot effectively be whipped into line by the threat of an election or of abolition. . . .

The Senate is desperately needed in roles which *it alone* can perform, as a watchdog on the proper decentralisation of Executive power and as a public chamber of review of the implementation of the policy decisions of the Executive.[146]

In some respects the Senate, the institution copied most closely from the United States, already occupies a position relative to the executive somewhat akin to that of Congress, with the government bargaining with senators to secure the passage of legislation or prevent public issues being brought before the Senate or one of its committees. Jonathan Gaul, who served on the staff of Liberal Party leaders in the early 1970s and deprecated this development, has noted that Prime Minister Menzies recognized the potential power of the post-1949 Senate sooner than most and began to negotiate 'deals' with the D.L.P.

This undercover horse-trading between the Executive and the Senate had become a fairly regular part of political life before November 11, 1975. Since, it has become almost an everyday affair.

The development of Senate power in this process began with dealings between the [L.–C.P.] Coalition and the DLP. Envious of the greatly disproportionate power of this rump, other senators of both major parties sought methods of wringing concessions from the Executive. . . .

This uncertainty of numbers and a growing appreciation of their real power by more and more senators transformed the Senate by the early 70s into something very different from the Westminster model. *Its political nature instead resembles more closely that of Washington*, with the Executive negotiating deals . . . with individual senators, or groups of senators. The 1975 crisis merely reinforces these trends.

The growing strength of the Senate has now reached the point where it is quite clearly *an embryonic development of the US-style separation of powers*. No one who follows the progress of proposals from policy into actual legislative detail in Canberra should doubt that the Senate is exercising its power in a very formidable way.[147]

The Commonwealth's form of government has indeed been aptly described as a 'Washminster mutation'.[148] To adapt an Indian Supreme

Court judge's 'riverine imagery', both the Thames and the Potomac flow into Lake Burley Griffin.[149]

Is the Senate's power beneficial to Australian government? Provided that the Senate does not — by denying the government supply — seek to appropriate to itself the House of Representatives' constitutional function of selecting the government, in general the more legislative scrutiny there is of executive action, policies and proposed legislation, the better. However, while bargaining and 'deals' are the very essence of politics, the political balance established by the electors would be unhealthily, if not dangerously, distorted were minor parties and independents holding the balance of power in the Senate to use their bargaining position to extort excessive favours from the government. Moreover, two additional caveats should be entered. First, the Senate, in which all States enjoy equal representation despite great disparity in population, and whose members serve terms double those of representatives, clearly cannot be said to represent the people of Australia as directly and proportionately as the House of Representatives does. Hence, the Senate should not replace the House as the principal forum for legislative debate and democratic accountability and control of the government. While Senate 'oversight' of the government is to be encouraged, House scrutiny of the executive is even more important and should be strengthened by whatever structural and procedural devices are available. These include a more independent speaker, as in Britain, and a more effective committee system, which former Speaker Sir Billy Snedden regarded as 'the most fruitful method by which backbench members can call ministers and their advisers to account',[150] a path pursued with some success by the British House of Commons since 1979.

Secondly, greater Senate power would be more compatible with the democratic foundations of our polity if the requirement of equal State representation were removed. Various methods of electing the Senate could be adopted and could be combined with proportional and preferential voting: Senators could represent electorates with roughly equal numbers of electors selected on a national or a State basis,[151] or the entire Senate could be elected on a national basis with the whole country as one electorate. As John Uhr, a senior officer of the Senate has argued, 'equal State representation should be seen as a concession and *not as an essential attribute of a federal upper chamber*'.[152]

COMPARISON

It is not the purpose of this chapter to compare the American and Australian systems of government in abstract, but to consider whether the former is so obviously superior to the latter that an Australian republic should adopt it, or a variant of it, with all the constitutional and governmental uncertainty and dislocation the conversion to that form of government would entail. Hence, the American system clearly must bear the burden of proof of superiority.

It is submitted that the standard against which the two systems must be measured and compared — both as to intra-executive and legislative–executive relations — is: how effectively do they combine and balance the twin objectives of power and accountability? For, as Woodrow Wilson remarked in 1885, *'Power and strict accountability for its use* are the essential constituents of good government'.[153]

The government should be able to implement at least the essential elements of the programme it was elected to achieve; it should be able to pursue the policies and secure the legislation for which it has an electoral 'mandate'.[154] At the same time, since power corrupts and is easily abused, the government must be made effectively accountable for the *manner* in which those policies are pursued, to ensure that they are implemented efficiently and are responsive to the public interest.[155] Although courts, tribunals, ombudsmen, the media and individuals (for example, employing freedom of information legislation) all help to make governments more accountable, the principal enforcer of accountability must be the legislature, which is elected for that purpose, as well as to enact legislation by mutual accommodation with the executive. Hence, the legislature's proper role is not to obstruct the government and prevent it from implementing its legislative programme — much less to drive it from office — as long as it behaves lawfully, honestly and reasonably, and is responsive to public opinion. Although, admittedly, accountability to the legislature (among others) diminishes a government's power to achieve its objectives, legislative 'oversight' should not significantly diminish the government's *proper* power, since it will primarily control the *manner* in which the government accomplishes its objectives, rather than prevent it pursuing them.

Hence, power and accountability are not incompatible. Indeed, quite the opposite: they complement one another because, in a democratic society ruled by law, accountability makes the exercise of power acceptable.[156] *It legitimates it.*[157]

In comparing the Australian and American systems of government, it is essential to note that the United States constitutional order has traditionally emphasized *liberty* — protected by a judicially enforceable Bill of Rights and by dividing power through devices such as federalism, the separation of powers, and checks and balances — more than accountability.[158] In the United States, unlike Australia which lacks a Bill of Rights, 'effectiveness has always taken second place to the preservation of liberty'.[159]

How, then, do the two systems of government compare when measured against the standard of effective combination of power and accountability?

Accountability in intra-executive relations is provided by the chief executive's need to consult and bargain with cabinet and party colleagues. Although, of course, the position varies with each incumbent, in general the United States fares rather poorly in this respect: the presidency simply 'puts too much power in one man',[160] who consequently can easily become isolated from reality,[161] as President Kennedy demonstrated over the Bay of Pigs incident, President Nixon over Watergate and the invasion of Cambodia, and President Reagan when planning his visit to West Germany in May 1985.

In contrast, in 'Westminster' systems like Australia's, the supreme executive organ is cabinet and the prime minister must, like other ministers, bargain with his colleagues if his proposals are to secure cabinet approval. (This is not to suggest, however, that his power is not greater than that of any other minister.) Moreover, especially when Labor is in office, the prime minister and his colleagues must pay close attention to the views of their party caucus, and they cannot afford to ignore the views of the wider party, especially the policies endorsed by the party conference.

The separation of the functions of head of state from leadership of the government provides a further check on prime ministerial power,[162] if only (ultimately) to ensure that proper governmental procedures are followed.[163]

In sum, it is submitted that the United States compares unfavourably with Australia insofar as intra-executive relations are concerned. The Australian prime minister's power is more than adequate to direct the framing and implementation of coherent policies and generally provide effective governmental leadership. At the same time, he is undoubtedly more accountable to his ministerial, party, and public service colleagues for the exercise of power — especially under Labor governments with their powerful and suspicious caucuses — than is even a weak United States president, like Ford or Carter, who has no constitutional equal within the executive branch.

As was noted above, 'Westminster' executives undoubtedly enjoy greater power than their American counterparts (federal and State) *vis-à-vis* their legislatures. Although the president of the United States, unlike 'Westminster' executives possesses constitutionally conferred powers beyond legislative control[164] (although still subject to Congress's appropriation power), the weak American party system does not enable the president to control Congress, even when his party 'controls' both houses. Hence, except in times of military or economic crisis, the president must negotiate with Congress widely and exhaustively on virtually every legislative proposal. Whether or not this is seen as a virtue of the American system naturally varies with one's perception of the relative merits of the policies pursued by Congress and the president (not that Congress always has a 'policy'). Thus, many who condemn the Senate for refusing to ratify the Treaty of Versailles in 1920 and criticize congressional resistance to President Roosevelt's desire to end neutrality in the early stages of the Second

World War also applaud congressional obstruction of presidential belligerence toward Vietnam, Cambodia, Angola and Nicaragua. In short, whether or not Americans favour an imperial presidency often depends on who the emperor is, and what he offers.[165] But, whether beneficial or detrimental to American and other interests, Congress's ability and willingness to obstruct the president's legislative and policy proposals undoubtedly provides a powerful check on presidential power.

Congress is far more independent of the executive than Australian legislatures,[166] in which party discipline ensures that lower houses (at least) are virtually rubber stamps in the hands of their executives. Although obviously overstated, an English scholar's colourful remark that 'the Executive today has *more* control over the Commons than Charles I had at any period of his reign'[167] captures nicely the executive's dominance of 'Westminster' lower houses. Seven years after his dismissal, Gough Whitlam noted that '[t]here are some respects in which the Australian Prime Minister or the Australian Government has, fortunately, more power than the US President',[168] and he is unlikely to have overlooked the role of the Australian Senate![169]

If Australian governments undoubtedly enjoy greater power than their American counterparts *vis-à-vis* parliament (including the Senate and Legislative Councils), which system imposes stricter accountability on the executive?

In Australia, on the positive side is the government's exposure to public interrogation and criticism by the opposition, with which it must debate proposed legislation and the great issues of the day. But this is balanced by the infrequency of parliamentary sessions (even the Commonwealth parliament sits for less than 25 per cent of the year and State legislatures meet even less frequently), and party discipline which ensures that a successful resolution censuring the government or a minister is possible only from the Senate, and even then only when the government lacks a majority in that house. (Moreover, Senate votes of no-confidence are constitutionally irrelevant.) Legislative oversight would, of course, be more effective if the government were in a minority in the House of Representatives, because it would then face a real possibility of censure by a no-confidence vote, as last occurred in Australia in October 1941, Britain in March 1979 and Canada in December 1979. Moreover, even though no majority government has lost a confidence vote since the advent of organized political parties, the lower house's power to sack a government by passing a vote of no-confidence is a vital constitutional safeguard — which the United States lacks — which, in extraordinary circumstances, could be employed against a majority government guilty of gross abuse of power.

In the United States, on the other hand, positive considerations are the scrutiny of proposed legislation and executive operations by powerful well-staffed congressional committees willing to question and criticize the administration, even when that house's majority party occupies the White House. (Although party loyalty must not, by any means, be discounted entirely.) Moreover, civil liberties are afforded much greater legal protection against both legislative and executive action than they are in Australia. Negative factors are the *ad hoc* nature of much of the oversight conducted by congressional committees, the president's power to veto legislation (subject to Congress's power to override it by two-thirds majorities in both houses), his general immunity from (involuntary[170]) congressional interrogation, and his fixed term of office which makes congressional lack of confidence *constitutionally* irrelevant. The president cannot be removed from office merely because his policies clash with those of Congress, or because his competence or integrity are suspect. He and his principal subordinates can be removed from office by Congress only through the quasi-judicial impeachment process, which is impractical because it takes too long and would entirely disrupt the normal legislative and executive processes, making government impossible in the interim, as President Nixon noted in his resignation address of 8 August 1974.

Overall, then, there are pluses and minuses on both sides, with power and accountability varying on a spectrum depending upon the factors mentioned earlier. In Australia, Labor governments, facing a strong caucus and frequently hostile media, have usually been more accountable than their opponents, especially when low in public esteem and facing an opposition-controlled Senate. All these elements coincided during the Whitlam governments of 1972–75. Liberal–National Party governments, on the other hand, have usually been less accountable, especially when they controlled the Senate, as Malcolm Fraser's did between 1976 and 1981. The spectrum in the United States depends upon many considerations, especially the president's public standing, whether his party controls both houses of Congress, and whether the country is facing some sort of crisis.

It is difficult, and ultimately unnecessary, to attempt to reach any overall conclusion as to the relative success of the two systems in combining and balancing power with accountability in legislative–executive relations. An American scholar who compared the British and American systems of government in 1974 concluded that the 'pros and cons for the respective systems' ability to keep the executive under popular control' were 'more or less balanced'.[171] That assessment could probably be fairly applied to the American and Australian systems as well. Hence, especially in view of the latter's more effective balance of power and accountability in intra-executive relations, it may be concluded that, notwithstanding its many virtues, the United States system has not discharged the heavy burden of proof of superiority.

AUSTRALIA'S DECISION: A WORD OF CAUTION

If Australia is to make an informed decision on the critical question of the appropriate form of republican government, it must engage in a wide-ranging debate on the relative merits of various systems of government, including its own. The debate about a republic is still at an early stage in Australia, so it is not surprising that forms of government have, so far, excited relatively little discussion. A few republicans, led by Colin Howard, have advocated adoption of the American system[172] or some variant of it[173] while, naturally enough, others — some of them certainly not republicans[174] — favour retention of the present system,[175] a course also advocated in the republican proposals of the General Constitutional Commission of Papua New Guinea and the Committee on the Constitution of the Canadian Bar Association.[176] A December 1978 Gallup Poll conducted throughout Australia among almost 2000 respondents aged sixteen and over revealed a strong preference (63%:30%) for retention of a separate, largely ceremonial, head of state over an American-style executive presidency.[177] However, one may wonder how many respondents would have been familiar with the American system — or the Australian, for that matter.

Even if the American system of government were considered clearly superior to ours, Australians should exercise great caution before contemplating its translation to an alien political, constitutional and cultural environment. Vital components of the American environment — a powerful constitutional Bill of Rights, a population of more than 200 million, imbued with a strong sense of the value of personal initiative, distributed over fifty States, a powerful, independent, relatively fearless press protected by the First Amendment,[178] and uniquely American governmental conventions and practices[179] — could not be replicated in Australia. Yet, without them, a translated American presidency would bear little (substantive) resemblance to the original. As one American scholar noted, 'our presidency is *sui generis* — . . . it represents a case of its own, based on long and difficult historical adjustments, *which it would be impossible to transfer to other countries*.'[180] Harold Laski argued, similarly, that both the parliamentary and presidential systems 'have [their] special merits, and neither is likely to be capable of transference to another environment, where alien traditions are deep-rooted, without becoming something very different from what it was in the country of its origin.'[181] He likened a system of government to a pair of shoes: 'it grows to the use of the feet to which it is fitted'.[182]

Among the constituents of America's political and cultural environment, none is more important than the party system. The strength of party loyalty usually depends upon the nature of the political system; the weakness of American party loyalty is a reflection of the system's separation of powers and checks and balances.[183] In general, party loyalty is only as rigorous as it needs to be.[184] Thus, in Australia it is stronger in the House of Representatives, whose confidence the government must always retain, than in the Senate, where a vote of no-confidence is not fatal.

If the American system of government were adopted here, how would the party system react? This is the great imponderable. Party discipline would probably relax somewhat,[185] as it has in the Senate, but to what degree? The parties may well be too set in their ways for radical adaptation. One American scholar believed that his country's political parties could not adapt to the introduction of a parliamentary system — 'it is probably too late now; we may have passed the point of no return'[186] — and the same may be true here. Could Australia afford to take the risk that party discipline would not relax appreciably upon the introduction of an American presidency? If that occurred, the resulting hybrid mutant would no longer resemble its American parent, and would combine the worst features of both systems. Such an Australian president would enjoy greater power than an American president or Australian prime minister, and would be far less accountable than either. He would combine the former's power over the executive branch with the latter's control over the legislature. Moreover, an executive president would, in any event, enjoy one significant advantage denied his American model — freedom from restraint by a Bill of Rights.

In sum, Australian republicans contemplating radical institutional change would do well to remember that

History . . . counsels caution toward even well-motivated fundamental reforms of the system's messy architecture: whether in the form of constitutional amendments or institutional changes. *They seldom work out the way we hope and anticipate.*[187]

Chapter 6
The States

As was noted earlier, the advent of an Australian republic need not, and is unlikely to, have any significant effect on Australia's federal system. An Australian republic will continue to include both the Commonwealth and States and, possibly, Commonwealth territories. Consequently, two questions arise: 'Must the Commonwealth and all States become republics simultaneously?' and 'Need all States adopt the same form of republican government?'

REPUBLICAN COMMONWEALTH/MONARCHICAL STATE?

Politically speaking, the prospect of an Australian republic would be much brighter if the advent of republican government at the Commonwealth level did not pre-empt the decision of State governments, but left them free to decide for themselves whether and when to follow the Commonwealth into republicanism. If republican government at the Commonwealth level necessitates republican government at the State level as well, State governments favouring retention of the present monarchical form of government could be expected to oppose, and even obstruct, Commonwealth republican proposals even more stridently than they would if the States remained free to make their own decisions in their own time. Moreover, it is at least arguable that the people of each State (but not gerrymandered State governmental organs) should be free to determine for themselves the appropriate form of State government, rather than have one thrust upon them, possibly against their wishes, by the people of other States voting in a referendum under section 128 of the Commonwealth Constitution.

Is a combination of Commonwealth republican government with monarchical government in some or all of the States either theoretically or practically feasible?

As 'Queen of Australia',[1] the Queen is head of state of 'Australia', a notional entity comprising seven polities: the Commonwealth and the six States. If she ceased to be head of state of any of those seven polities, she would no longer, in fact, be Queen of 'Australia', although there is no legal reason why she could not continue to describe herself by that title. Hence, when the Commonwealth becomes a republic, there will, *in fact*, no longer be a Queen of 'Australia', but there is no legal reason why the former Queen of Australia could not continue to act as head of state of any of the other Australian polities, i.e. the States. (Likewise, if one of the States chose to become a republic before the Commonwealth, the former Queen of Australia could continue to act as head of state of the Commonwealth and the other five States.) In that event, it would probably be preferable for the Queen's title to reflect reality, so that the head of state of New South Wales would no longer be the 'Queen of Australia', but the 'Queen of New South Wales', the Head of State of Victoria would be the 'Queen of Victoria', and so on.[2] This change of title would not effect any change in the *real* position of the Queen. Indeed, it would more accurately reflect reality, especially upon removal of the anomaly whereby State governments communicate with their head of state through the British Foreign and Commonwealth Secretary, rather than with the Queen directly or through her private secretary, as does the Commonwealth government; once that anomaly is removed, the Queen's role as head of state of the Australian States will become more readily apparent. (Moreover, 'the Crown in right of the Commonwealth', 'the Crown in right of New South Wales', 'the Crown in right of Victoria', etc. have always been recognized as separate juristic persons — namely, the Commonwealth, New South Wales and Victorian governments — which can, and do, enter into agreements with one another, sue one another in the courts, and so on.[3])

Hence, with all respect, the late Daniel O'Connell's opinion — shared by a Premier of Queensland[4] — that 'it is *impossible* to have a republic in one level of power and a monarchy in another'[5] is incorrect. But, even if a republican Commonwealth is theoretically compatible with monarchical States, is such a combination practically feasible?

Several commentators, including James Wilson, an American 'founding father' and one of the first Supreme Court justices, have thought not.[6] Senator Gareth Evans, for example, has remarked that 'it would be hardly plausible to have a republic at one level of government and a monarchy at one or more of the others'.[7] Indeed, the constitution of virtually every federal republic, including the United States, Switzerland, West Germany, Austria, India, Mexico, Argentina and Brazil, imposes a republican form of government on its constituent States as well.[8]

However, it is submitted that the infeasibility of combining (probably only temporarily in any event) republican government at the federal level with the retention of monarchical forms by some or all of the States has been exaggerated. A federal republic with State monarchies is, indeed, anomalous, but hardly more so than many of the present and long-standing features of State constitutions (pending the severance of 'imperial links'), which result, at least in theory, in Australia comprising an independent national government together with six British colonies. These features include the States' continuing incapacity to enact legislation repugnant to British legislation applying therein by paramount force (a disability from which the Commonwealth and all Canadian legislatures, federal and provincial, were freed by the Statute of Westminster 1931 (U.K.)) and State governments' continuing inability to communicate with the Queen either directly or through the Commonwealth Governor-General, instead of via the medium of a foreign government.

In sum, legally and — by and large — practically, the advent of republican government at the Commonwealth level need not be deferred until all States are willing to abandon monarchical forms.

FORM OF REPUBLICAN GOVERNMENT

Australian governments, like those of Canada and New Zealand, were modelled on that at Westminster. Hence, they are similar in essentials, although there are also significant differences among them. Queensland, for instance, has a unicameral legislature, and the Commonwealth and some States (New South Wales, Victoria and South Australia) have procedures for resolving deadlocks between the legislative houses, while the others do not. The similar form of all Australian governments is undoubtedly convenient for politicians and the public, who might experience difficulty in operating and dealing with different governmental structures at the federal and State levels. There is, however, no legal reason why the national and State governments need adopt the same form of republican government. The Commonwealth, for instance, could retain its present 'Washminster' structure,[9] while one or more States might follow the American model or some variant thereof. Would such a combination be wise or even practical?

In virtually all federal republics the form of State or provincial government resembles that of the national government: national and State governments both adopt either a 'parliamentary' executive, or an 'executive presidency', or some variant thereof, as in Switzerland. Thus, in federal republics with an executive presidency — the United States, Mexico, Argentina, Brazil and Nigeria (under its 1979 Constitution) — State governmental structures mirror those of the national government. The structure of Swiss cantonal governments also resembles that of the national government, although one significant difference between them is that cantonal governments are elected directly by the people, whereas the national government is chosen by the federal parliament.[10]

Differences between the national and State governments tend to be greater in federal republics where the form of executive at both levels is essentially 'parliamentary', as it is in India, Austria and West Germany. Only in India do the two levels of government parallel one another to the extent that both are headed by a separate, largely ceremonial officer — the president of India at the national level, and State governors appointed by the president.[11] In Austria and West Germany, on the other hand, the principal structural difference between the two levels of government is the absence of any *Land* equivalent of the national President. But there are other significant differences as well between the national and *Land* governments.

The most significant difference in Austria is the manner in which the governments are selected: the national government is appointed and dismissed by the federal president,[12] while *Land* governments are elected by the *Land* legislature (the *Landtag*), the members of the government other than the chief minister (the *Landeshauptmann*) being elected by proportional representation.[13] Both the national and *Land* governments must retain the confidence of their respective legislatures (at the federal level, only of the lower house — the *Nationalrat*).[14]

The West German national and *Land* governments resemble one another more closely than their Austrian counterparts. The principal difference between the two levels of West German government is the absence of a head of state at the *Land* level and the consequences thereof for the operation of *Land* government. Thus, while the federal chancellor is elected by the lower house of the federal parliament (the *Bundestag*) 'upon the proposal of the Federal President',[15] the chief minister of *Land* governments (the *Ministerpräsident*) is simply elected by the *Land* legislature (the *Landtag*).[16] Similarly, federal ministers are appointed and dismissed by the federal president 'upon the proposal of the Federal Chancellor',[17] whereas *Land* ministers are generally appointed and dismissed by the *Land* chief minister, subject to ratification by the *Landtag*.[18] As in Austria, West German governments at both levels cannot retain office if they lose the confidence of their respective legislatures — at the federal level and in Bavaria (the only *Land* with two legislative houses), if they lose the confidence of the lower House.[19]

If the Commonwealth and any States opt for republican government with a 'parliamentary executive' along the lines of current Australian governments, should they follow India in appointing a separate head of state at the State level or emulate Austria and West Germany which lack such an officer? Even apart from the expense in maintaining the Government House in each State capital, there seems little need for a separate State head of state. Australian State constitutions could, like those of Germany and Austria, eliminate the necessity for an officer to operate the machinery of responsible government by enacting detailed provisions to cover most situations. For example, West German constitutions at both levels of government provide that the legislature should be dissolved in the event that it cannot agree upon a chief minister within the stipulated time. But, while in that event, dissolution of the (federal) *Bundestag* is effected by the president,[20] in several *Länder* dissolution of the legislature occurs automatically, pursuant to their constitutions.[21] Moreover, a *Landtag* can resolve to dissolve itself at any time.[22] Furthermore, insofar as it is still considered necessary or desirable to retain some officer to operate the machinery of responsible government, that function could be performed by the speaker of the lower house, as it is in Sweden, and in some respects (by the *Landtag* president) in German and Austrian *Länder*.[23]

If, however, the States decided to retain a separate head of state there is no reason why the same person could not act as head of more than one State, thereby enabling expenses to be shared. Indeed, a 1956 amendment to the Indian Constitution specifically authorized the sharing of State governors: 'nothing . . . shall prevent the appointment of the same person as Governor of two or more States'.[24]

Finally, apart from the consideration of convenience to politicians and the general public, already noted, there is no reason why the form and structure of State republican governments need resemble those of the Commonwealth or the other States. This was also the view of Sir Kenneth Wheare.

It would not do to state absolutely that a union between states of different regimes is impossible to work. Much depends on the regime. American states and Canadian provinces differ in political institutions. The former have the non-parliamentary executive, the latter the parliamentary executive. Yet it is conceivable that the two systems could find a place in the same union. For they are fundamentally at one — they are founded on the democratic principles of free election, free criticism and representative institutions.[25]

Indeed, in view of the novelty, for Australia, of republican government and the potential dislocation of its governmental organs, especially if the American model of republican government were favoured, there is much to be said for using a State (voluntarily) as a 'social laboratory'[26] or 'insulated chamber'[27] — guinea pig, if you will — in which to assess the effects of the Australian political, constitutional and cultural environment — especially the party system — upon the American system before imposing it upon the whole nation. In this way, necessary adjustments can be made, or the whole experiment even abandoned, before the entire population is subjected to it. As Justice Brandeis wisely observed,

It is one of the happy incidents of the federal system that a single courageous State may, if its citizens choose, serve as a laboratory; and try novel social and economic experiments without risk to the rest of the country.[28]

Chapter 7
The President

It was submitted in chapter 5 that an Australian republic would be well-advised to retain Australia's present system of responsible parliamentary government (albeit with improvements), and should substitute a largely ceremonial head of state for the Queen and the Governor-General. The following chapter suggested that the States should emulate West Germany and Austria among federal republics, rather than India, by dispensing with a separate head of state at the State level.

This chapter examines briefly some of the principal considerations to be taken into account in establishing an Australian presidency. Table 7.1 setting out the position of the president in eight republics with responsible parliamentary government (three of them federations — India, West Germany and Austria) should provide useful background information enabling detailed reference to other republican constitutions to be kept to a minimum.

ELECTION

In view of the current method of selecting our *de facto* heads of state — the Governor-General and State governors — inevitably the first question to arise will be whether the president should simply be chosen in the same way, that is by appointment by the government. In effect, then, the only change would be the elimination of the monarchy and renaming the Governor-General 'president'. Although the exercise of 'reserve powers' by an elected head of state is easier to accept, probably making their exercise more likely — which would be undesirable — it is submitted that the presidency of an Australian republic must be elective. It would demean the office at its inception, and contradict the democratic and egalitarian motivation inevitably accompanying the establishment of a republic if the new head of state were merely the old appointive Governor-General under a new name. As Donald Horne has argued,

Whatever method is chosen, in a democracy it would seem to be of essential symbolic significance that the legitimacy of even a purely ceremonial figure should come from the people, either by direct election, or by an election among those who have themselves been elected by the people.[1]

Once it is decided that the presidency should be elective it is vitally important to select the method of election very carefully. The method chosen should be that best calculated to combine and reconcile two fundamental objectives. First, the method of election should minimize as much as possible the political polarization attending the election to ensure that the electoral process does not prejudice the president's political neutrality, and the public's perception of it, once he or she takes office. Obviously the method of election should facilitate rather than hamper the president's role as a national symbol — the representative of the entire nation, not merely some groups or parties within it. Secondly, while the electoral method should ensure that his appointment has wide public support, it definitely should not enable the president to claim a popular mandate superior to the government's. The last thing an Australian republic needs is a duplication of the ruinous internecine struggles between African heads of state and their prime ministers which have done so much damage to democracy on that continent.[2]

These considerations suggest the following conclusions.

Direct Popular Election

Notwithstanding the apparently successful popularly elected presidencies of Ireland, Austria and Iceland, neither objective would be advanced by direct popular election of the president. As Carl Friedrich and Robert Guttman concluded in 1954,

Direct election gives the Head of State political authority even without express constitutional provision. It also tends to make him a partisan and though the purpose of direct election is to provide an embodiment of the federation, it destroys that air of neutrality that both the ceremonial functions in any federation and the specific powers under a Parliamentary system demand . . .[3]

Moreover, direct presidential election would be rather costly, a not unimportant consideration in a country which already faces frequent federal, State and local elections, not to mention the occasional half-Senate election. The expense would be greater still if the States decided to retain separate elective heads of state.

The experience of the Fifth French Republic demonstrates clearly how significantly presidential authority is enhanced by direct popular election. Under the original 1958 Constitution, the president was elected by an Electoral College of 81 764 members, comprising the members of both houses of parliament (who, sitting together as a 'Congress' at Versailles had elected the presidents of the Third and Fourth Republics) together with representatives of local government.[4] While at its inception, the Fifth Republic was considered a 'hybrid', combining elements of an executive presidency with parliamentary responsible government,[5] it effectively ceased to be 'hybrid' and became predominantly presidential after October 1962 when the

Table 7.1   Some Non-executive Presidents

Country	Method of election	Minimum age	Term of office	Eligible for re-election for consecutive term?
Austria**	Popular	35 years	6 years	Yes. Only once
Federal Republic of Germany**	Federal Convention (members of lower house of federal parliament together with equal number of *Land* representatives)	40 years	5 years	Yes. Only once
Iceland*	Popular	35 years	4 years	Yes
India**	Electoral College (federal parliament plus State Legislative Assemblies)	35 years	5 years	Yes
Ireland**	Popular	35 years	7 years	Yes. Only once — even non-consecutively

How removable	Politically responsible to legislature?	Eligible for membership of legislature?	Principal `reserve powers'	Vice-president?
By the federal Constitutional Court at the instance of a $\frac{2}{3}$ majority at a joint sitting of both houses of federal parliament	No — but can be removed by referendum called by a joint sitting of both houses of federal parliament	No	Appointment and dismissal of federal chancellor and dismissal of the entire federal ministry	No
By the federal Constitutional Court on impeachment by $\frac{2}{3}$ majority of either house of federal parliament	No	No	Appointment of federal chancellor and dissolution of lower house of federal parliament (in very limited circumstances)	No
Referendum called by $\frac{3}{4}$ majority of parliament (Althing)	No	No	Much like those of the U.K. Queen	No
As in Ireland	No	No	Essentially those of the U.K. Queen	Yes
By $\frac{2}{3}$ absolute majority of either house of parliament upon impeachment by $\frac{2}{3}$ absolute majority of the other house	No	No	1. Refuse to dissolve lower house of parliament on advice from prime minister who has lost its confidence 2. Convene a meeting of parliament 3. Refer Bills to Supreme Court to review constitutionality	No

Table 7.1 Some Non-executive Presidents (*cont'd*)

Country	Method of election	Minimum age	Term of office	Eligible for re-election for consecutive term?
Israel*	Parliament (Knesset)	—	5 years	Yes. Only once
Italy**	Electoral College (parliament sitting jointly with regional representatives)	50 years	7 years	Yes
Trinidad and Tobago**	Both houses of parliament in joint session	35 years	5 years	Yes

  * Unicameral parliament
 ** Bicameral parliament

Constitution was amended (by referendum) to provide for direct popular election of the president. As Vincent Wright has noted, that change greatly augmented presidential authority, although it 'conferred no new functions, privileges or prerogatives upon the Presidency'.[6]

The political significance of the October 1962 reform cannot be overestimated, for it completely upset, in favour of the President, the uneasy and ambiguous balance established in the 1958 Constitution. As President de Gaulle claimed in his January 1964 press conference, 'we behave in such a way that power . . . emanates directly from the people, which implies that the Head of State, elected by the nation, must be the source and holder of power . . . that is what was made clear by the last referendum'.[7]

Among Australian commentators, Brian Buckley has favoured direct popular election of a largely ceremonial president (and a vice-president),[8] but others, such as Geoffrey Sawer, have seen the danger that 'a President of restricted powers . . . would probably try to exceed [them] if directly elected'.[9] Professor Sawer is undoubtedly correct. The proper balance of authority between president and prime minister would be gravely threatened, if not severely distorted, were

How removable	Politically responsible to legislature?	Eligible for membership of legislature?	Principal 'reserve powers'	Vice-president?
Parliament by $\frac{3}{4}$ majority	No	No	Allowing popularly-elected prime minister to dissolve Opposition-controlled Knesset	No
By Constitutional Court upon impeachment	No	No	Appointment of prime minister	No
By $\frac{2}{3}$ absolute majority of both houses of parliament in joint session after considering report of judicial tribunal	No	No	Appointment of prime minister, leader of the opposition, and 9 of the 31 senators	No

a directly elected president to co-exist with a prime minister unable to claim such a direct popular mandate.

Electoral College

Most non-executive presidents are elected by some type of electoral college. The 'hybrid' president of Finland[10] and even the archetypal executive president, that of the United States, are elected by popularly elected electoral colleges. But electoral colleges are usually not directly elected as such and comprise instead the members of both houses of parliament in joint session (as in Trinidad and Tobago, and the Third and Fourth French Republics) or the members of parliament sitting together with representatives of the States (as in India and West Germany (lower house of the national parliament only)) or local government authorities (as in Italy and France (1958)). If, as was urged above, direct popular election of the president be rejected, the realistic alternative methods for electing an Australian president essentially boil down to two: election either by the Commonwealth parliament alone — probably by a joint sitting of both houses, perhaps with a two-thirds or even a three-quarters majority — or by an electoral college comprising the members of the Commonwealth parliament together with representatives of the States and perhaps, although un-likely, local government.

Commonwealth Parliament

If the States decided to retain separate local heads of state so that, at least in the exercise of governmental functions, the national president was head of state only of the Commonwealth, logic might suggest that the president should be elected by the Commonwealth parliament alone, probably in the manner described above. Such a course was indeed recommended by the General Constitutional Commission of Papua New Guinea (not a federation) in 1983 and a committee of the Canadian Bar Association in 1978, which excluded the Canadian Senate from the presidential electoral process because its members are appointed by the government, not elected.[11]

However, it is submitted that, for several reasons, it may be unwise to exclude the States from direct participation in presidential elections, whether or not they retain separate heads of state — and this issue is, of course, complicated by the fact that the States may not be uniform on the question whether or not to retain a separate local head of state. (The Senate cannot realistically be regarded as a mouthpiece of the States, whether or not senators 'represent' them.)

First, the president's electors should reflect his constituency. Since he or she should be a symbol representing the entire nation, not just the Commonwealth, the States, and perhaps local government also, should participate in his or her election. Secondly, because State opposition to the establishment of a republic may be appeased some-what if the States have a voice in the president's election, this electoral method can be justified on the ground of political expediency. But it can, in any event, be argued that it would only be fair to allow State participation in presidential elections if republican government were imposed upon the States via section 128 of the Commonwealth Constitution — possibly, in some cases, against the wishes of a majority of their electors.

State Participation

For the reasons already mentioned, it is submitted that the most appropriate form of electoral college is one modelled on West German lines, comprising the members of the House of Representatives and an equal number of State representatives selected by proportional representation.[12] (India's electoral college is broadly similar but includes the elected members of the national upper house of parliament as well. For reasons of political expediency, the members of the Australian Senate may also have to be included.)

TERM OF OFFICE

At this stage of the republican debate it would be premature to enunciate definite views on questions such as the President's minimum age, term of office, or eligibility for re-election. However, it may be appropriate to mention briefly the present writer's views on these questions.

It is suggested that no minimum age (other than the age of majority) need be prescribed, although of the eight republics included in table 7.1 only Israel has adopted that position. The Governor-General's usual term of five years appears unobjectionable, and could well be retained for the president. Five years (a reduction of one year from the current term of the Governor-General) was recommended recently by Papua New Guinea's General Constitutional Commission.[13] Finally, there appears to be no good reason why a non-executive head of state should not be eligible for re-election indefinitely.

REMOVAL

At present the Governor-General, who is appointed by the Queen on the advice of the Commonwealth prime minister, holds office, pursuant to section 2 of the Constitution, 'during the Queen's pleasure'. This means, presumably, that he is subject to removal or 'recall' (a gentler expression deriving from the era when Governors-General returned to Britain on the expiry of their term of office) at any time, and that such recall is effected in the same manner as his appointment — on the advice of the Commonwealth prime minister. No Australian Governor-General has been recalled, but that fate befell the Governor-General of the Irish Free State in October 1932 and Governors-General have been recalled more recently in the Caribbean — in Grenada in 1974 and St Kitts in 1981.[14]

Sir John Kerr's failure in October–November 1975 adequately to warn Prime Minister Whitlam that he contemplated dismissing the government was apparently motivated, at least in part, by his apprehension that Mr Whitlam's reaction to such a warning might be to request the Queen to recall him. (As is to be expected on any question involving those events, opinion is divided on the question whether Sir John Kerr's principal concern was a selfish desire to retain his office or a statesmanlike resolve to prevent the Queen's involvement in the crisis.[15]) Several Australian commentators have argued that the Governor-General's tenure should be put on a more secure footing, so that this distraction does not influence future exercises of the 'reserve powers'.[16] A republican constitution should satisfy that concern because the president will inevitably enjoy a fixed term of office, subject to earlier termination only in the event of his resignation, death, incapacity or misconduct.[17]

Misconduct

The major democratic republics evince considerable diversity as to the severity of the misconduct for which the president is removable. In general, however, they can be grouped into three broad categories.

The first group, including India and Austria provide for presidential removal for violation of the Constitution (although Austria also provides for removal by a popular referendum).[18]

The second group remove their president for a wide range of offences, ranging from 'high treason' (France), 'high treason or treason' (Finland) and 'high treason or breaches of the Constitution' (Italy) to 'wilful violation of [the Constitution] or any other federal law' (West Germany), 'treason, bribery, or other high crimes and misdemeanours' (the United States) and 'intentional violation of the Constitution, treason, bribery, misconduct or corruption involving the abuse of the powers of his office, or any offence under any law, involving moral turpitude' (Sri Lanka).[19]

The final group do not confine the misconduct to criminal activity and include charges wide enough to allow for removal on political grounds — no doubt only in an extreme case. These provisions range from removal for wilful violation of the Constitution or behaving 'in such a way as to bring [the presidency] into hatred, ridicule or contempt' or 'in a way that endangers the security of the State' (Trinidad and Tobago), to misbehaviour rendering the president 'unfit to continue in office' (Ireland) and 'conduct unbecoming his status as President' (Israel). Austria and Iceland authorize presidential removal by popular referendum, without specifying any constitutional grounds.[20]

It is submitted that Australia's grounds for presidential removal ought to fall within the second category because, quite simply, the first category is too narrow and the third is too wide because it could expose the president to removal on merely political grounds. A relatively wide formulation within the second category would be appropriate and Sri Lanka's provision may serve as a useful general model. 'Misconduct' probably includes activities that are not criminal but that is appropriate so that behaviour such as persistent political bias, or even habitual drunkenness while performing official duties, might constitute a ground for removal.[21]

Tribunal

Democratic republics also prescribe diverse procedures for determining whether the grounds for presidential removal have been satisfied. In all of them the initiative for presidential removal lies with the legislature or one house thereof. Thereafter, apart from Austria and Iceland, which authorize presidential removal by a popular referendum called by parliament, the constitutionally prescribed procedures fall, once again, into three broad categories.

In the first group, which includes the United States, Ireland, India, Israel and France, the removal process is confined within the legislature. In the United States, Ireland and India the president is impeached by one house (the House of Representatives in the United States, either house in Ireland and India) and tried by the other. A conviction is recorded only if two-thirds of the members of that house concur. (A two-thirds absolute majority is necessary in India and Ireland; a two-thirds simple majority suffices in the United States.) The Israeli president is removed by a three-quarters majority vote in the unicameral Knesset, and the French president upon conviction by a 'High Court of Justice' comprising members of parliament elected, in equal numbers, by both houses of parliament.

In the second group, which includes Austria, West Germany, Italy and Finland, the president is tried by a judicial body — the Constitutional Court in the first three, the Supreme Court in Finland.

The third group, including Sri Lanka and Trinidad and Tobago, combine elements of the other two, as, indeed, does the United States to a very limited degree in that the chief justice presides when the Senate tries the president upon impeachment by the House of Representatives.

The procedures in Sri Lanka and Trinidad and Tobago are very similar and comprise the following steps:

1. Parliament decides by a two-thirds absolute majority to refer the question of presidential misconduct to the specified judicial body. The Sri Lankan parliament is unicameral; the two houses of the Trinidad and Tobago parliament meet in joint session.

2. The judicial body investigates the charge and reports back to parliament. In Sri Lanka this task is performed by the Supreme Court; in Trinidad and Tobago by 'the Chief Justice and four other Judges appointed by him, being as far as practicable the most senior Judges'.

3. Parliament considers the judicial report, and can remove the president by a resolution passed by a two-thirds absolute majority. In Trinidad and Tobago the houses meet in joint session.

The only significant difference in the removal procedures of the two countries is that an adverse decision by the judicial body (the Supreme Court) is necessary for presidential removal in Sri Lanka, but appears not to be in Trinidad and Tobago.

Which, if any, of these three models should Australia adopt?

The third model has much to commend it.[22] First, the head of state must ultimately be answerable to the people, and parliament is the appropriate forum for enforcing this accountability. Hence, the final decision to remove the president should be taken by parliament. Secondly, the task of dispassionately ascertaining facts and determining presidential culpability is not one to which legislatures are particularly suited. Rather, that function is best left to judges, who are widely perceived as politically neutral, and whose professional lives are devoted to tasks such as ascertaining facts, assessing credibility, and determining guilt. Moreover, as President Nixon noted when resigning in August 1974, a presidential trial would greatly disrupt parliament's usual business for lengthy periods.

It is submitted that the task of trying the president upon impeachment ought not to be entrusted to a regular court, but rather a specially constituted panel of judges, comprising the State chief justices or their nominees, and presided over by the chief justice of the High Court or one of his colleagues nominated by him. The task should not be entrusted to the High Court itself because that court may well be called upon to review questions arising out of the president's impeachment and trial. Moreover, a specially constituted judicial tribunal would be easier to reconcile with the rigorous separation of powers notions expounded in the Boilermakers' case.[23]

Interim President

Finally, what should happen in the event of the president's resignation, removal from office, death or disability while in office?

In most republics with non-executive presidencies the interim president in such circumstances is the presiding officer of parliament (Israel) or its upper house (Italy, West Germany, and Trinidad and Tobago). In Ireland and Iceland that function is performed by a commission comprising the chief justice together with the presidents of the two houses of parliament (Ireland) or the speaker of parliament and the prime minister (Iceland). In Austria the federal chancellor is interim president for twenty days; thereafter the function devolves upon a committee comprising the three presidents of the lower house of parliament. Among non-executive presidencies, only India has a vice-president, the usual successor in executive presidencies — although not in France and Sri Lanka where the interim presidents are, respectively, the president of the Senate and the prime minister.

It is submitted that in Australia either the speaker of the House of Representatives or the president of the Senate would be a suitable interim president. However, if the States retain separate heads of state, it may be appropriate to continue the present practice whereby the senior State governor becomes administrator of the Commonwealth in the absence of the Governor-General.[24]

POWERS

Probably the most important of all the 'machinery of government' questions to arise upon the establishment of a republic is the power to be conferred upon the head of state.

Severance of the links joining the (*de facto*) Australian heads of state to the monarchy would, in itself, significantly affect the republican head of state's effective power even if it formally remained the same as the Governor-General's. Because the Queen would cease to be the formal head of state, there would no longer be any reason for equating the 'reserve powers' of the Australian head of state with those of the head of state of Britain rather than, say, of India, Ireland, Italy or West Germany. In other words, the declaration of the Imperial Conference of 1926 that the (*de facto*) Australian head of state occupied 'in all essential respects the same position in relation to the administration of public affairs . . . as is held by . . . the King in Great Britain'[25] would be rendered obsolete.

Furthermore, the establishment of a republic would remove a vital influence restraining the exercise of 'reserve powers': fear of damaging and, therefore, endangering the monarchy. Henceforth, abuse of power by the head of state would threaten his tenure and might even bring the presidency into disrepute but the future of the republic is unlikely to be jeopardized. In this respect, republics are more resilient than monarchies — or at least perceive themselves to be. Fear of republicanism is a pervasive concern of monarchies and greatly restrains their heads of state; but few republics fear monarchy, especially when, as in Australia, there is no obvious monarch-in-waiting.

Hence, unlike their monarchical counterparts of the 1890s, the framers of Australia's republican constitution will not be able to vest powers in the head of state on the assumption that they will be read against a background of the conventions of the British monarchy. Unlike their forebears, they will be obliged to spell out those powers in detail.

What powers, then, should be conferred upon the republican head of state?

It is submitted that the powers conferred upon Australia's republican head or heads of state should definitely not exceed those of the Governor-General and State governors. As noted in chapter 3, this means that, in practical terms, the only matter on which they could exercise independent judgment is the selection of the chief minister.[26] In that event, the position of the Australian head or heads of state would be essentially the same as that of most of the republics included in table 7.1 in this chapter.

However, while some commentators have argued that a non-executive head of state needs wider reserve powers to protect the constitution and the people from the government,[27] others would confine the head of state to formal and ceremonial functions only, believing that he should have no reserve power whatever.[28] Gough Whitlam, for example, claims that '[e]xperience has shown that a Head of State who is anything more than an ornament is a menace.'[29] There is, indeed, much to be said for removing from the head of state even the power to select the chief minister,[30] and leaving that task to the lower house of parliament, as in Ireland, West Germany, Japan and Papua New Guinea.[31] If that occurred, the head of state could still exert 'influence', like the presidents listed in table 7.1, and exercise Bagehot's three rights: to be consulted, to encourage, and to warn — publicly if necessary.

The effectiveness of presidential influence on the government and the community would, of course, depend upon a host of variable factors, including the personality, health and party affiliation of the president and his chief minister, their perceptions (and those of the public) of his proper role, and the current political situation. The presidency of Sandro Pertini of Italy (1978–85), for instance, demonstrated clearly that even a non-executive head of state need not be a mere figurehead, rubber-stamp, or marionette in the hands of the prime minister.[32]

ROYAL PREROGATIVES

As governments of the Queen, Australian governments — Commonwealth and/or State — possess the powers ('executive prerogatives'), proprietary rights, privileges and immunities which are part of the inherited 'royal prerogative' or common law powers, rights, privileges and immunities of the English Crown.[33] The executive prerogatives include the power to execute treaties, declare war, make peace, coin money, incorporate bodies by royal charter, pardon offenders, and confer honours. The Crown's proprietary rights include entitlement to the royal metals, royal fish, treasure trove, escheat, and ownership of the foreshore, and of the seabed and subsoil, and maybe even of the sea, within territorial limits. Finally, the Crown's immunities and preferences include entitlement to be paid in preference to other creditors, freedom from distress for rent, and immunity from the ordinary process of the courts, including discovery of documents, interrogatories, and costs.[34]

Upon the inauguration of a republic, Australian governments would, of course, cease to be governments of the Queen, with the consequence that, at least in theory, the prerogative powers, rights, privileges and immunities of the Crown would cease to apply to them. As Andrew Inglis Clark noted in 1905,

[I]f the Commonwealth of Australia had been established as an independent nation, and if the Constitution had provided for the election of a President, or any other supreme depositary of executive authority in the Commonwealth in substitution for the British Crown, such depositary of the executive powers of the Commonwealth would have possessed only such executive powers and functions as the Constitution of the Commonwealth and the laws of the Parliament of the Commonwealth would have expressly conferred upon him; and none of the powers of the British Crown which are included in the designation of royal prerogative would have attached to him without an express grant of it by the Constitution or the laws of the Commonwealth.[35]

Accordingly, if the prerogatives of the Crown are to be inherited by a republican Australia, express constitutional provision should be made to that effect, as was done in Ireland.[36]

Chapter 8
Constitutional Amendment

Consideration must now be given to the question whether abolition of the monarchy is constitutionally possible in Australia and, if it is, the appropriate means for accomplishing it. Because different legal issues are involved, amendment of the Commonwealth and State constitutions will be considered separately.

COMMONWEALTH CONSTITUTION

The extent of constitutional amendment necessary to implement republican government at the Commonwealth level depends, of course, upon the form of government chosen. As already noted,[1] all that would be required to achieve republican government modelled on the present form of responsible government would be

1. to substitute new 'machinery' provisions — specifying the president's qualifications, mode of election, term of office, method of removal and salary (and, if thought appropriate, similar 'machinery' for a vice-president) — in lieu of the current 'machinery' provisions relating to the Queen and the Governor-General (sections 2–4 and 126);

2. to remove obsolete provisions dealing with reservation of Bills and disallowance of legislation (sections 58–60 and 74); and

3. to substitute 'president' for 'Queen' or 'Governor-General' wherever appropriate in the rest of the Constitution.

These amendments could all be implemented pursuant to section 128 of the Commonwealth Constitution, which (impliedly) authorizes unrestricted amendment of the Commonwealth Constitution.[2] Pursuant to that provision, a proposed constitutional amendment must first be passed by an absolute majority of both houses of the Commonwealth parliament (or twice — with a three-month interval — by either house with an absolute majority), and must then be submitted to referendum and approved by a double majority: an overall majority of Australian electors (including those in the territories) and a majority of the electors in four States. Finally, the proposed amendment must be assented to by the Governor-General. Since this power is not a 'reserve power', the Governor-General could not, as has somewhat fancifully been hypothesized,[3] lawfully decline to follow ministerial advice to assent to constitutional amendments introducing a republic which had been approved at a referendum.[4]

Since responsible government is implied in the Commonwealth Constitution — especially in sections 62–64 — that system could not be abandoned in favour of an American-style executive presidency without a constitutional amendment.[5] Such an amendment could undoubtedly be accomplished under section 128, as Quick and Garran noted in 1901:

[The Constitution] could certainly be amended by remodelling the Executive Department, abolishing what is known as Responsible Government, and introducing a new system, such as that which prevails in Switzerland, according to which the administration of the public departments is placed in the hands of officers elected by the Federal Legislature.[6]

However, were Australia to adopt an executive presidency for the Commonwealth, uncertainty as to the adaptability of that form of government to a political environment shaped by a different political structure (responsible monarchical government) would make it appropriate to allow alteration of the new governmental structure to be effected by a procedure less stringent than that prescribed in section 128. Since the structure of the Commonwealth executive is of only marginal concern to the States, it would be appropriate to amend section 128 to allow this aspect of the Commonwealth Constitution to be altered with the approval only of an overall majority of Australian electors (thereby dispensing with any requirement that a majority of electors in four, or even fewer, States must also approve). Indeed, it might even be thought expedient to leave amendment of these provisions, perhaps in the alternative, to the Commonwealth parliament, possibly with two-thirds majorities in both houses. A model for such a provision is section 44 of the Constitution Act 1982 (U.K.), which authorizes the Canadian parliament (by simple majorities in both houses) to 'make laws amending the Constitution of Canada in relation to the executive government of Canada or the Senate and House of Commons.'[7]

Since it has, occasionally, been suggested that the preamble to the Commonwealth of Australia Constitution Act 1900 (U.K.) constitutes an impediment to abolition of the monarchy,[8] some reference to that question is apposite.

The preamble recites that the people of Australia (except Western Australia) 'have agreed to unite in one indissoluble Federal Commonwealth *under the Crown of the United Kingdom* . . ., and under the Constitution hereby established'.[9] Section 128 of the Constitution (which is contained in section 9 of the Commonwealth of Australia Constitution Act) (impliedly) authorizes amendment of 'this Constitution', which *prima facie* would not include the preamble and the nine sections — the 'covering clauses' — of the Constitution Act.

(Section 8 of the Statute of Westminster 1931 (U.K.) impliedly confirms this distinction by referring to both 'the Constitution' and 'the Constitution Act' of the Commonwealth.) Is the preamble's reference to the Crown, then, an impediment to abolition of the monarchy? It is submitted that it is not, for several reasons.

First, the preamble is not, and does not purport to be, prescriptive; it merely recites, as a historical fact, the intention of the people of Australia to create a federal monarchy. As Dr Wynes remarked,

it is clear that, when all is said and done, the preamble at the most is only a recital of a present (i.e., as in 1900) intention. But in any event the insertion of an express reference to amendment in the Constitution itself must surely operate as a qualification upon the mere recital of the reasons for its creation.[10]

Hence, the preamble's reference to 'the Crown of the United Kingdom' does not limit the power of the parliament and people of the Commonwealth to abolish the monarchy pursuant to section 128. Nor does it require Australia to remain a member of the Commonwealth of Nations of which the British monarch is 'head'.[11]

Other references to the Queen in the covering clauses likewise constitute no impediment to abolition of the monarchy in Australia. Covering clause 2, for example, which provides that 'The provisions of this Act referring to the Queen shall extend to Her Majesty's heirs and successors in the sovereignty of the United Kingdom', cannot be regarded as requiring, even impliedly, that Australia retain the British monarch as its head of state.[12] And covering clause 3's provision that 'the Queen may, at any time after the proclamation [of the Commonwealth — which occurred on 17 September 1900], appoint a Governor-General for the Commonwealth' clearly authorized only appointment of the first Governor-General, which occurred on 21 September 1900. Covering clause 3 did not authorize the Queen to appoint his successors: that power was (impliedly) conferred by section 2 of the Constitution,[13] which is clearly subject to amendment pursuant to section 128.

Secondly, even if the preamble and/or covering clause 2 be regarded as prescriptive and as requiring, at least by implication, that Australia remain a monarchy, does the section 128 amendment power extend to the amendment or repeal of the covering clauses? While, admittedly, most commentators — including Sir Robert Garran, H. B. Higgins, Professors Sawer and Harrison Moore and Dr Wynes — have denied the power,[14] it is submitted that the preferable interpretation of section 128 is that it *does* authorize amendment or repeal of the covering clauses. Denial of the power is based upon a literal interpretation of the term 'this Constitution' in section 128 (which *prima facie* would not include the covering clauses) but it is submitted that a more purposive view of the power, which takes into account its framers' intentions, leads to the opposite conclusion. Thus, Sir Samuel Griffith told the 1891 Sydney Convention, whose early version of section 128 also included the term 'this Constitution', that he

certainly agree[d] with those who have said that after the establishment of a federal constitution in Australia there should be no necessity to refer to the British Parliament to do anything for Australia, either in changing a constitution or in anything else. I think the constitution will be by no means an adequate one for the purpose for which it is to be designed if we shall have occasion to refer to the Parliament of the United Kingdom to do anything for us.[15]

If the covering clauses cannot be amended or repealed pursuant to section 128, only the United Kingdom parliament could amend or repeal them.[16] Yet, as early as 1913, the Privy Council recognized that the Australian framers had succeeded in their intention to avoid the necessity to come to London for constitutional amendments like their Canadian colleagues.

No doubt the Act of 1900 contains large powers of moulding the Constitution. Those who framed it intended to give Australia the largest capacity of dealing with her own affairs, and the Imperial statute enables her to act without coming to the mother Parliament.[17]

Only one High Court justice has commented directly on the question whether section 128 extends to the amendment or repeal of the covering clauses. In *China Ocean Shipping Co.* v. *South Australia*, Justice Murphy held that the Commonwealth of Australia Constitution Act 'is capable of amendment by the procedure in s.128 which involves the Australian people, without reference to the United Kingdom.'[18] This opinion is shared by Professors Enid Campbell and R. D. Lumb, the latter remarking that

the covering clauses of the Constitution are so intertwined with the Constitution as a whole or sections of it that they may be regarded as part of its fabric. Therefore in relation to the content of those sections, which have not ceased to operate or are not subject to specific Commonwealth legislative powers, the processes of section 128 must be followed if any change affecting them is to be made.[19]

While endorsing this conclusion, the present writer would prefer to base the extension of section 128 to the preamble and the covering clauses upon the view that, when interpreted in light of the framers' intention to avoid the necessity of petitioning Westminster for any constitutional amendment, the term 'this Constitution' in section 128 includes the entire Constitution Act, and not merely the contents of section 9 thereof. With all respect to those who have seen the matter differently, the alternative interpretation seems unduly pedantic for so fundamental and apparently unlimited a power as one of constitutional amendment by national referendum.

Thirdly, even if (a) the preamble and/or covering clause 2 were regarded as prescriptive and (b) section 128 does not authorize direct amendment or repeal of the Constitution Act, it need not necessarily follow that any requirement that Australia retain the monarchy, derived (at the most, by implication) from the preamble and covering clause 2, would limit or impair the power to abolish the monarchy and establish a republic pursuant to section 128. At least since 3 September 1939, when the Commonwealth acquired the power to enact legislation repugnant to imperial legislation applying in Australia by paramount force (such as the Constitution Act),[20] constitutional amendments pursuant to section 128 have enjoyed a legal status *equal* to that of the preamble and covering clauses,[21] in which case any inconsistency between them should be resolved in favour of the constitutional amendment pursuant to the principle that a later law prevails over an inconsistent earlier one.[22] In other words, even if section 128 does not authorize *direct* amendment or repeal of the preamble and covering clauses, it is at least arguable that they can be amended or repealed *indirectly* pursuant to the power conferred by that section.[23] Reasoning along similar lines presumably underlies Senator Gareth Evans's opinion that

You could not change, by local referendum, that part of our constitutional system which is embodied in the United Kingdom law and the covering clause [*sic*] of the Constitution, but you could certainly *displace* that law as it operates in Australia. And once the monarchy was abolished in Australia there would simply be no scope for any purported overriding United Kingdom law to operate.[24]

Finally, need the United Kingdom parliament be involved in the establishment of an Australian republic, as it was in the 'patriation' of the Canadian Constitution in 1982? A request to that parliament to pass legislation to enable the Commonwealth to abolish the monarchy at the Commonwealth level can be envisaged in two situations.

1. It might be thought wise to seek such legislation 'from an abundance of caution' as a supplement to constitutional amendment under section 128, lest (contrary to the views expressed above) that power be held insufficient to overcome some implied requirement of monarchy imposed by the preamble and/or covering clauses.[25]

2. The Commonwealth government might seek such legislation in order to avoid submitting the proposal to a referendum under section 128 — no doubt because it feared that it would fail to secure the necessary level of support.

Three questions arise. Would the British parliament have the power to enact such legislation? By what means could the Commonwealth 'request and consent'[26] to such legislation? And how would the British government and parliament respond to such a request?

British Parliament's Power

It is arguable that section 128 of the Commonwealth Constitution is a 'manner and form' provision whereby the British parliament defined the 'legislature' capable of amending the Commonwealth Constitution or, in the language of A. V. Dicey, abdicated its power to amend that document.[27] Consequently, the British parliament would lack power to enact any amendment which could be implemented pursuant to section 128.[28] Although not unattractive, because it essentially represents the practical position regarding British intervention, recognized by Quick and Garran in 1901[29], this proposition is nevertheless legally dubious. The opening words of section 128 — 'This Constitution shall not be altered except in the following manner:' — are simply too ambiguous to support the weight sought to be placed upon them. (By whom is the Constitution not to be altered?) More direct reference to the British parliament would surely be necessary if they were to constitute an abdication of its power as a matter of *law*, not merely convention. In any event, even if section 128 does limit the British parliament's power it would, of course, only affect Commonwealth requests in the second category, not those in the first, since if section 128 does not extend to the amendment or repeal of the preamble and covering clauses it could hardly impair the British parliament's power to deal with them.

One or two commentators have gone further, however, and, without relying specifically on section 128, have argued that the legal effect of Australia's political independence from the United Kingdom is that the British parliament simply lacks power to legislate for Australia. The most forceful proponent of this view is Justice Murphy, who has argued that the British parliament lost the power to legislate for Australia, Commonwealth and States, at the inauguration of the Commonwealth on 1 January 1901.

On the inauguration of the Commonwealth on 1 January 1901, British hegemony over the Australian colonies ended and the Commonwealth of Australia emerged as an independent sovereign nation in the community of nations. From then, the British Parliament had no legislative authority over Australia. The authority for the Australian Constitution then and now is its acceptance by the Australian people. Any continuing authority over the Australian people by the British Parliament would be inconsistent with Australia's sovereignty; Australia would not be a legitimate member of the community of nations. The notion that the States of Australia are still colonies subject to the legislative authority of the British Parliament is absurdly incompatible with their status as constituent parts of the Commonwealth of Australia. . . .

The British Parliament can pass a law to regulate rights and liabilities between persons in Australia or anywhere else. This law would be perfectly valid in Britain and would be given effect to by British courts as far as they could. In Australia or elsewhere (apart from those places controlled by Britain, such as Hong Kong and other colonies), it would be of no legal effect, except to the extent that those countries allowed it. To contend otherwise denies the sovereignty of other nations and attributes to the British Parliament some divine right to legislate for other peoples.[30]

(Justice Murphy's view that British legislative power over Australia terminated in 1901 has not been accepted by his colleagues, although they have not expressly rejected the possibility that it terminated at some later date.[31])

A less unorthodox view, similar to Justice Murphy's, has been espoused by Professor R. D. Lumb, who has argued that

> the rule that the Imperial Parliament had ultimate legal authority over the Australian federal system, even though it was never exercised in practice,[32] had, *for a certain period after 1900*, a superior status over the rule embodied in section 128 . . . .
>
> At some point of time, however, in the first fifty years of federation, this hierarchical relationship was reversed: the method of amendment based on the exercise of Imperial legislative power *disappeared* from the Australian rules of recognition of constitutional change. This disappearance or elimination . . . was the direct result of the development of dominion status reflected in various acts and events having constitutional significance, for example, the Balfour Declaration and the Statute of Westminster. At least it could be said that the process was complete by the time the Statute was adopted in Australia (1942).[33]

However, the argument that *legal* change has been effected by extra-legal means should be weighed with extreme caution, for it is a slippery slope leading to notions of extra-constitutional and emergency powers, revolutionary changes of *grundnorm* and even martial rule. Comparison with Canada, for which the British parliament legislated as recently as 1982 (the Canada Act 1982), suggests that the only tenable ground upon which to base any extinction of British power to amend the Commonwealth Constitution (unlike that of Canada — until 1982) is the argument, already noted, that section 128 of the Commonwealth Constitution constituted an 'abdication' of power, or a definition of the 'legislature' authorized to amend the Constitution. If that is so, the British parliament *never* possessed the power to amend the Commonwealth Constitution, as Justice Murphy has argued on wider grounds.[34] However, as noted earlier, it is doubtful that section 128 did constitute an abdication of power, and that section certainly could not have extinguished the British Parliament's power to amend those provisions of the Commonwealth of Australia Constitution Act 1900 (if any) not reached by section 128.

Petitioning Organ

A Commonwealth request to amend the Constitution and/or the preamble and covering clauses would be governed by section 4 of the Statute of Westminster 1931 (U.K.), which provides:

No Act of Parliament of the United Kingdom passed after the commencement of this Act shall extend, or be deemed to extend, to a Dominion as part of the law of that Dominion, unless it is expressly declared in that Act that that Dominion has requested, and consented to, the enactment thereof.[35]

Section 9(3) of the Statute, which took effect in Australia on 3 September 1939,[36] provides that 'In the application of this Act to the Commonwealth of Australia the request and consent referred to in section 4 shall mean the request and consent of the Parliament and Government of the Commonwealth.' What is the meaning of 'the Parliament . . . of the Commonwealth' in section 9(3)? Can it be argued that, at least insofar as constitutional amendments capable of implementation pursuant to section 128 are concerned, that term includes the 'legislature' prescribed by section 128? Geoffrey Marshall has argued that it can.

On the view that the effective basic norm of the constitution is an Australian one, the necessity (if it exists) for procuring legislative action at Westminster may be regarded in the same light as the majority and referendum requirements of section 128 — namely, as part of the definition of the way in which for this purpose 'the Commonwealth Parliament' must function . . . . 'Parliament and Government of the Commonwealth' is intended by the Statute of Westminster to mean those entities functioning in terms of the Australian constitution. It would seem, therefore, to be improper for constitutional amendment to be obtained in Britain by any request from the federal government and Parliament which is not authorized by the procedure laid down in section 128 of the Commonwealth constitution for carrying through an amendment in Australia. Any request not made in this way would not be a request of the Parliament of the Commonwealth functioning as the constitution requires.[37]

With all respect, this argument is unpersuasive for several reasons. First, Dr Marshall's argument is based upon the erroneous assumption that an Act requesting the United Kingdom to amend the Constitution can be equated with a law which itself effects such an amendment. Section 128 refers to a 'proposed law for the alteration' of the Constitution; upon receiving the royal assent, such a law effects a constitutional amendment. But nothing is effected by the royal assent to a proposed law requesting the United Kingdom to enact legislation. Hence, the two types of proposed law can hardly be equated.

Secondly, section 1 of the Commonwealth Constitution (enacted by the British parliament) provides that the Queen, the Senate and the House of Representatives constitute a body 'hereinafter called . . . "The Parliament of the Commonwealth"', and it is reasonable to suppose that the identical term in the Statute of Westminster (also enacted by the British parliament) was intended to refer to the same body. Finally, although the body constituted by section 128, including the electors of Australia, is clearly an *Australian* 'legislature', it is neither a *Commonwealth* legislature nor a *'parliament'*. Not every legislative body is a 'parliament'.[38] Hence, the 'Parliament of the Commonwealth' in section 9(3) of the Statute of Westminster is the Commonwealth Parliament defined in section 1 of the Constitution.

British Response

Since Britain is disinterested, if not uninterested, in Australia's internal affairs, its response to a Commonwealth request to enact legislation to amend or repeal the preamble and/or covering clauses to facilitate the advent of an Australian republic is likely to be grounded upon three constitutional principles.

1.   The British parliament should not intervene — and should not even be requested to do so — unless, constitutionally speaking, there is no alternative manner in which the proposed constitutional changes can be effected.

Following discussions with British ministers, including the Prime Minister, Prime Minister Gough Whitlam reported in May 1973 that 'the United Kingdom would wish . . . that whatever can be done in and by Australia should be done in and by Australia herself.'[39] This British attitude is certain to remain constant, since it follows from its 'general position in relation to Australian constitutional problems, . . . that they [are] essentially matters for resolution *by Australians in Australia*'.[40] The British government and parliament would, accordingly, be most reluctant to become involved in constitutional amendment which could be effected pursuant to section 128 of the Commonwealth Constitution.

2.   The British parliament will be willing to enact legislation on matters concerning only the Commonwealth (and not the States) at the sole request of the Commonwealth parliament and government. On such matters, the British parliament will not decline to act on account of the opposition of the Australian States or any of them.

This principle, in effect a corollary of section 9(2) of the Statute of Westminster 1931 (U.K.), has been recognized (albeit *obiter*) on several occasions. One of its earliest formulations was by the Joint Committee of the House of Commons and House of Lords which considered Western Australia's petition to secede from the Commonwealth. The Committee held that the federal division of powers in Australia

cannot be ignored in considering the application of the general constitutional principles governing the intervention in the affairs of any self-governing member of the British Empire. *It is clearly only at the request of the Government and Legislature primarily concerned that the Parliament of the United Kingdom can be entitled to legislate. In respect of matters appertaining to the Commonwealth, it could not so legislate without the request of the Commonwealth authorities*; in respect of matters appertaining to the sphere of State powers it could not so legislate without the request of the State authorities.[41]

Strictly interpreted, this observation merely notes that a Commonwealth request is *necessary* in regard to matters affecting only that polity; it does not expressly assert that a Commonwealth request would alone *suffice*, and that State consent might not also be required. However, subsequent British observations indicate clearly that State consent is not necessary in regard to matters affecting only the Commonwealth. In November 1980 the British Foreign and Commonwealth Office noted that 'the UK authorities would be unlikely to question a validly made request for UK legislation from the Commonwealth Government and Parliament on any matter which affected only the Commonwealth of Australia.'[42] Indeed, the House of Commons Foreign Affairs Committee appeared (*obiter*) to confine even further the situations in which Canadian provincial consent would be required. It argued that the British parliament 'retains the role of deciding whether or not a request for amendment or patriation of the BNA Acts conveys the clearly expressed wish of *Canada as a whole*, bearing in mind the federal nature of that community's constitutional system',[43] and added that: '*In all ordinary circumstances, the request of the Canadian Government and Parliament will suffice* to convey that wish.'[44]

Moreover, further support for the second principle can be derived by analogy from the conventions governing advice to the Queen: 'The Queen will act on the advice of Commonwealth Ministers in matters of exclusively Commonwealth concern, and on the advice of State Ministers in matters of exclusively State concern.'[45]

3. The British parliament will enact legislation on matters concerning both the Commonwealth and the States (or some of them) only if both the Commonwealth and the relevant States concur in requesting it to do so.

This principle, like the previous one, has been recognized (*obiter*) on several occasions. It is clearly implied in the previously quoted remarks of the Joint House of Commons–House of Lords Committee in 1935,[46] which noted that it would be contrary to constitutional convention for the British parliament to legislate on State matters without State consent — a proposition since endorsed by the Supreme Court of Victoria[47] — and added that the Commonwealth would lack '*locus standi*', to seek British amendment of a State constitution.[48] More recently, the House of Commons Committee which considered the 'patriation' of the Canadian Constitution in 1980–81 argued that the presence of an amendment power (section 128) in the Commonwealth Constitution, unlike that of (pre-patriation) Canada, enabled the British parliament to draw a vital distinction between the two countries when requested to amend their constitutions. In the case of Australia, the British parliament should insist upon a unanimity of all concerned governments which might not be required in the case of Canada. (And, in fact, the Canada Act 1982 (U.K.) was enacted over the objections of Quebec.)

[T]he fact that the Constitution of the Commonwealth of Australia embodies 'a procedure for amendment which enables the Australian Constitution to be remodelled in Australia' without involving the Westminster Parliament[49] . . . may be thought of as significant because it means that the UK authorities can insist . . . on *unanimous* governmental concurrence in requests from Australia which *affect any constitutional interest beyond the interests of the government or legislature making the request*; and this insistence on unanimity will not result in constitutional paralysis of the Australian community. This often-stated requirement of unanimity will not frustrate what the Joint Committee of 1935 called the 'clearly expressed wish of the Australian people as a whole', since on almost all matters there is available to the Australian people an alternative and workable procedure for giving effect to their clearly expressed wishes without involving the UK. The same cannot be said of Canada.[50]

Once again, this principle derives support from the analogous principle allegedly governing advice to the Queen. Cheryl Saunders and Ewart Smith, following D. P. O'Connell, advised the Australian Constitutional Convention that 'The Queen will not act on matters which affect both the States and the Commonwealth unless all governments are in agreement.'[51]

Applying these principles, how would the British parliament respond to a Commonwealth request that it amend or repeal the preamble and/or covering clauses to facilitate abolition of the Australian monarchy? If the United Kingdom were requested to abolish the monarchy at both Commonwealth and State levels, the consent of the relevant States would be necessary pursuant to the third principle. But, following the second principle, a Commonwealth request to abolish the monarchy only at the Commonwealth level should suffice, and State consent ought not to be required, since the subject of the request is a matter which concerns only the Commonwealth.[52]

STATE CONSTITUTIONS

If the issues raised by abolition of the monarchy at the Commonwealth level appear complex, they fairly pale into insignificance beside those involved in establishing republican government in the States. The present, moreover, is not the ideal time to consider the legal issues involved because the British legislation expected to sever imperial links in early 1986 will inevitably affect State constituent power by empowering the States to legislate repugnantly to imperial legislation applying therein by paramount force (except, of course, the Commonwealth of Australia Constitution Act 1900).

Present impediments to the introduction of State republican government derive from two sources, although some States face only the first.

1.   Abolition of the monarchy would be repugnant to imperial legislation applying by paramount force in all States. These Acts provide for disallowance of state legislation by the Queen, assent, non-assent and reservation of Bills by State governors, and the issue of royal instructions to governors in regard thereto.[53] Because the States presently lack power to enact legislation repugnant to imperial legislation applying to them by paramount force (recognized by section 2 of the Colonial Laws Validity Act 1865 (U.K.)[54]), State legislatures cannot remove the monarchy from the State governmental structure.[55] Nor can it be argued that a State's 'full Power', under section 5 of the Colonial Laws Validity Act 1865 (U.K.), 'to make Laws respecting the Constitution . . . of [its] Legislature' enables it to eliminate the Crown therefrom, an argument Justice Isaacs rejected in 1917.

[T]he word 'legislature' in this connection is not intended to include the Crown. . . . When power is given to a colonial legislature to alter the constitution of the legislature, that must be read subject to the fundamental conception that, consistently with the very nature of our constitution as an Empire, the Crown is not included in the ambit of such a power.[56]

2.   The constitutions of three States — Victoria, Queensland and Western Australia — entrench the office of Governor by a 'manner' provision which is, itself, likewise entrenched.[57] The Victorian Constitution, in effect, requires a Bill altering the position of the Crown or the governor to be passed by an absolute majority in both houses of parliament; the Queensland Constitution requires a Bill altering or abolishing the office of governor to be approved by the electors at a referendum; and the Western Australian Constitution requires such a Bill to be approved by both an absolute majority in both houses and a referendum of electors.[58]

The constitutions of New South Wales, South Australia and Tasmania do not contain any relevant 'manner and form' provisions. Hence, subject only to repugnant imperial legislation, their legislatures could abolish or alter the office of governor.[59] But a State governor would not be entitled to assent to a Bill abolishing the Crown (i.e. removing it from the State governmental structure) or the office of governor. A combination of imperial legislation and royal Instructions require such Bills to be reserved for the Queen's 'pleasure' (i.e. consideration). The Australian States Constitution Act 1907 (U.K.) section 1(1)(b) requires a governor to reserve every Bill which 'affects the salary of the Governor'; a Bill abolishing the office of governor must, inevitably, affect his salary. The royal Instructions require a Governor to reserve 'Any Bill of an extraordinary nature and importance, whereby [the Queen's] prerogative . . . may be prejudiced'[60], which would surely include a Bill removing the Crown from the State governmental structure. Moreover, in any event, State governors enjoy a general discretion to reserve any Bill for the Queen's consideration.

Reservation and disallowance (which has long been obsolete[61]) do not, in reality, detract from State independence, because the Queen's power to assent to reserved Bills (and her theoretical power to disallow State Acts) is exercised on State advice[62], albeit currently still anomalously conveyed to her through the British Foreign and Commonwealth Secretary. (This anomaly will be terminated with the severing of imperial links in 1986.) But, in the unlikely event that a State sought to introduce republican government before the Commonwealth did, it is possible that the Commonwealth government might seek to interfere in the State legislative process by requesting the Queen (or the British government to advise the Queen) not to assent to a reserved Bill or, perhaps, even to disallow a State Act assented to by the governor.[63]

The response of the British government and the Queen to such Commonwealth intervention would probably depend upon their decision as to whether the nature of a State's government (whether to be a monarchy or a republic) was a matter which concerned only that State, or whether it was also of concern to the Commonwealth and, perhaps, other States as well. If it were regarded as a matter of concern only to that State, the State government's advice should be acceded to.[64] Moreover, even if there were no clear answer to the question whether the Commonwealth had an interest in the matter, if the Commonwealth's sole, or perhaps principal, objection were that the proposed State legislation would be invalid, the Queen would be well-advised to assent to it and leave the question of its validity to the courts.

Finally, it is submitted that State responsible government is not imposed by imperial legislation, so that, apart from the position of the Crown, a State's conversion from responsible government to an American-style executive would not be repugnant to imperial legislation applying therein by paramount force.[65]

Imperial Legislation

Detailed examination of the current avenues for repealing imperial legislation preventing the States adopting republican government is unwarranted because the States themselves will soon be empowered to repeal such legislation. (Indeed the British parliament itself will probably repeal most of it in 1986 in its legislation severing 'residual constitutional links' between the United Kingdom and the States.) However, it is appropriate to comment briefly upon the current position, if only because the Commonwealth may wish to impose republican government upon an unwilling State.

Section 128

As is argued below, State constitutions can be amended pursuant to section 128 of the Commonwealth Constitution.[66] Since the legislature constituted by section 128 can legislate repugnantly to imperial legislation applying in Australia by paramount force,[67] the United Kingdom legislation impeding State adoption of republican government could be amended or repealed by a constitutional amendment under section 128.

Section 51(xxxviii)

Although there has, as yet, been no significant judicial pronouncement on the ambit of section 51(xxxviii) of the Commonwealth Constitution, that provision would appear to authorize the Commonwealth parliament (with State consent) to amend or repeal imperial legislation on subjects otherwise outside Commonwealth power which applies in the States by paramount force. Section 51(xxxviii) authorizes the Commonwealth parliament, subject to the Constitution, to make laws with respect to

The exercise within the Commonwealth, at the request or with the concurrence of the Parliaments of all the States directly concerned, of any power which can at the establishment of this Constitution be exercised only by the Parliament of the United Kingdom . . .

The power to amend or repeal imperial legislation applying in the States by paramount force is one which at the establishment of the Commonwealth was exercisable only by the United Kingdom parliament. Hence, it falls within section 51(xxxviii), and is exercisable by the Commonwealth parliament with the consent of the relevant State or States.[68] Since a State's governmental structure concerns only that State, and is not of direct concern to any other State, pursuant to this power the Commonwealth could, with that State's consent, amend or repeal the imperial legislation impeding State adoption of republican government insofar as it applied in that State.

There is, however, a possible impediment to the exercise of power under section 51(xxxviii) — section 106 of the Commonwealth Constitution, which provides: 'The Constitution of each State of the Commonwealth shall, subject to this Constitution, continue as at the establishment of the Commonwealth, . . . until altered in accordance with the Constitution of the State.' Two aspects of section 106 remain uncertain in view of the dearth of judicial comment thereon. First, since both section 51 and section 106 are expressly 'subject to this Constitution' prima facie each appears to be subject to the other. Which provision prevails? Can State constitutions be amended under section 51 powers, or is section 106 an express prohibition limiting the Commonwealth's section 51 powers? Secondly, exactly what constitutes a State's 'Constitution' within section 106? As Justice Evatt inquired (but did not answer) in 1932, does it include 'every provision found in the *Constitution Act* of a State, or only those provisions or terms, wherever found, which really define and describe the framework and scheme of its government?'[69]

The latter question need not be resolved here, because amendment or repeal of the position of the Crown and the role of the Queen and the governor would surely fall within even the narrower meaning of a State's 'Constitution',[70] the interpretation preferred by the Senate Standing Committee on Constitutional and Legal Affairs in 1985.[71]

Opinion is more divided on the first question — whether section 106 is subject to section 51 or vice versa — and respectable arguments can be marshalled on both sides,[72] as was demonstrated by the division of opinion in the Senate Standing Committee on Constitutional and Legal Affairs.[73] The view that section 106 limits the Commonwealth's power under section 51 derived support recently from a rather unexpected quarter — Justice Deane, who remarked that

subject to the Constitution and *to the State Constitutions which it protects*, the Commonwealth Parliament possesses legislative competence to preclude or exclude from Australia and from Australian law the direct operation of the laws, executive actions and judicial decisions of any other country including the United Kingdom.[74]

With all respect, however, the present writer finds the converse arguments more persuasive. As Leslie Zines has pointed out,

Once the general approach of the *Engineers'* case[75] is accepted, the only way to treat s.106 as a limitation on Commonwealth power is by the artificial reading down of s.106 [to preserve the structures of the State constitutions as distinct from State legislative and judicial powers] . . . .

From a textual viewpoint the phrase 'subject to this Constitution' in s.106 should be taken as referring to all other provisions in the Constitution, including federal powers, that necessarily alter the operation of the State's Constitution and not as reserving any powers or immunities to the States. The similar phrase in s.51 should be construed as a reference to all those provisions that are expressed as a restriction of Commonwealth powers . . .[76]

Hence, it is submitted that section 106 does not restrict the Commonwealth parliament's powers under section 51. Moreover, the necessary concurrence of State parliaments to an exercise of power under section 51(xxxviii) would clearly render inapplicable any argument that legislation enacted thereunder contravened any implied prohibition against Commonwealth laws which discriminate against the States or any of them, or impair their capacity to function as governments.[77]

Section 51(xxix)

Arguably, a further possible source of power pursuant to which the Commonwealth parliament could repeal, but not amend,[78] imperial legislation applying in the States by paramount force is section 51(xxix), which confers power to make laws with respect to 'External affairs'.

However, the High Court was equally divided on the question in the only case in which this aspect of the 'external affairs' power was considered. The three justices who held that the power authorized the Commonwealth parliament to repeal such imperial legislation — Justices Mason, Murphy and Deane — argued simply that the power to regulate Australia's relations with other countries — conferred by the 'external affairs' power — includes power to '[preclude] the direct operation within Australia of a law of another country'.[79] Their reasoning was expounded clearly by Justice Deane.

The question of the extent to which legislative enactments, judicial decisions or executive actions of one independent and sovereign nation should be permitted, merely of their own force, to operate or possess local authority within another is plainly a matter which directly concerns the relations between the two .... To the extent to which [United Kingdom statutes] operate directly within Australia by virtue of their character as laws of the Parliament of the United Kingdom, their operation must, at the present time, be seen as a matter concerning the relations between Australia and the United Kingdom ....

Once the conclusion is reached that the extent to which an Act of the Parliament of the United Kingdom should, of its own force ... operate or continue to operate within Australia is a matter concerning the relations between those two countries, it follows that a law repealing such a local operation of a United Kingdom Act is a law ... with respect to 'external affairs'.[80]

It is submitted, however, that this reasoning is unpersuasive. Because the United Kingdom parliament presently still retains power under Australian law to legislate for Australia (a proposition denied by Justice Murphy, but not by Justice Mason and (at least explicitly) by Justice Deane[81]), United Kingdom legislation applying in Australia by paramount force[82] is not 'foreign' law but as much the domestic law of the State as legislation enacted by the State parliament. (Justice Mason's attempt to circumvent this fatal flaw in his argument by reference to multiple-subject characterization is, with respect, altogether too glib.[83]) Hence, the argument that the Commonwealth parliament's undoubted power to exclude foreign legislative, executive and judicial acts from Australia includes power to exclude British legislation applying here by paramount force is, with respect, unconvincing. As Chief Justice Gibbs explained:

I find it impossible to say that an Act which forms part of the whole body of the law of New South Wales is something external to Australia.

The fact that the source of the Act was external to Australia does not, in my opinion, alter the position. It is true that relations between Australia and the United Kingdom may properly be described as external affairs. However, in repealing an Act which is part of the law of an Australian State the Commonwealth Parliament is not legislating with respect to its relations with the United Kingdom. It is legislating with respect to the law of an Australian State. The future exercise by the United Kingdom Parliament of its powers in relation to Australia might, I would agree, be described as an external affair . . . .

There is no analogy between an Act of the Commonwealth Parliament which repeals an Act of the United Kingdom Parliament which is in force as part of the law of a State and an Act of the Commonwealth Parliament which, for example, forbids an Australian citizen to comply in Australia with the law of another country which purports to extend to Australia but which could operate in Australia, if at all, only as a law of that foreign country. An Act which denies recognition to a foreign law which purports to affect things done in Australia, but which is not part of the law of Australia, is a law with respect to external affairs. An Act which changes the law in force in Australia is not.[84]

It is, therefore, submitted that the 'external affairs' power does not authorize the Commonwealth parliament to repeal the imperial legislation impeding the States' transition to republican government.

British Legislation

It can confidently be predicted that by the time the States seriously contemplate abandoning monarchical government they will have long possessed the power to amend or repeal British legislation presently still applying in the States by paramount force. Hence, detailed examination of the British parliament's role in amending or repealing such legislation is unwarranted.

However, an Australian request for British legislation to facilitate the implementation of State republican government is conceivable in several situations, even after the States acquire power to amend or repeal British legislation themselves. First, once the State parliaments are empowered to repeal (erstwhile paramount force) British legislation, State monarchists can be expected to advocate entrenchment of the monarchy by the imposition of a rigorous 'manner and form' for the enactment of legislation repealing the British legislation currently entrenching the Crown; for example, by requiring the Bill's approval by the electors at a referendum. In that event, it is quite conceivable that the State government and/or parliament (as usually constituted) might seek to bypass that 'manner and form' provision by requesting the British parliament to repeal the locally entrenched British legislation, much as the Commonwealth parliament might, conceivably, request British amendment of the Commonwealth Constitution in order to circumvent the rigours of section 128. Secondly, the Commonwealth parliament might request British legislation to facilitate the introduction of State republican government.

British Response

Pursuant to the first principle noted earlier, the British parliament would probably refuse to intervene if the relevant legislation could be enacted by an Australian legislature.[85] Since the States themselves will by then be empowered to amend or repeal British legislation applying to them, there would be no need for British legislative intervention. Hence, none would be forthcoming. Moreover, even apart from State legislation, the British parliament would probably decline to act because the amendment or repeal of British legislation extending to the States could be effected pursuant to section 128 of the Commonwealth Constitution[86] — although the applicability of that provision is unlikely to be endorsed unanimously.

If the British parliament were prepared to intervene, it is submitted that it would act pursuant to a fourth principle, the corollary of the second noted above[87]: the request and consent of the State (or States) directly affected is both a necessary and a sufficient pre-condition for the enactment of legislation which concerns only that State (or those States).

This principle has received wide recognition. It was embodied in section 9(2) of the Statute of Westminster 1931 (U.K.), and was clearly endorsed by the Joint House of Commons–House of Lords Committee on Western Australian Secession, which held (a) that 'in respect of matters appertaining to the sphere of State powers' the British parliament could not (as a matter of convention) 'legislate without the request of the State authorities',[88] and (b) that the Commonwealth would lack '*locus standi*' to seek British amendment of a State constitution.[89] More recently, the Full Court of the Victorian Supreme Court has argued that

it cannot be doubted that in these times the Parliament at Westminster would not legislate so as to affect the law in operation in an Australian State except at the request of and with the consent of the State concerned. Indeed, *even the request or the consent of the Parliament and Government of the Commonwealth would be irrelevant so far as a matter within the authority of the States of Australia is concerned.*[90]

This principle has, moreover, been recognized by the British government. During the debate on 'patriation' of the Canadian Constitution, the British Foreign and Commonwealth Office advised a House of Commons committee that

To the extent that the Australian States remain self-governing dependencies of the British Crown,[91] the UK authorities would consider a request from a State for UK legislation on any matter which affected no other Australian State and/or the Commonwealth of Australia. Should this condition not be met, the UK authorities would wish to be assured that the request met with the agreement of all parties concerned in Australia before considering the question of UK legislation.[92]

However, notwithstanding its wide endorsement, this fourth principle has been criticized on the ground that it is based upon the (admittedly) erroneous notion that 'there are specific heads of power granted or reserved to the States'.[93] The same fallacy is said to underpin section 9 of the Statute of Westminster 1931 (U.K.).[94]

Insofar as the fourth principle is based upon the 'heresy' of 'reserved State powers' it is, of course, unsupportable. But it is submitted that the concept of 'matters exclusively of State concern' should not be interpreted in a legalistic way, but rather as a practical question, and is not necessarily one of fixed and unchanging content.[95] For present purposes, it is necessary only to consider whether the implementation of State republican government is likely to fall within the fourth principle. If section 106 of the Commonwealth Constitution were interpreted as a limitation on Commonwealth legislative power, it clearly would fall within that principle, but it was argued above that section 106 should not be so interpreted.

Former Commonwealth Solicitor-General Sir Maurice Byers has argued that it cannot be said that amendment of State constitutions is a matter which does not concern the Commonwealth.[96] While it is undoubtedly correct that it cannot be stated in abstract that adoption of State republican government could *never* concern the Commonwealth — it is, for example, conceivable that that question could involve (*inter alia*) the Commonwealth's 'external affairs' power[97] — that issue is at least *unlikely* to be of direct concern to the Commonwealth. (The functions imposed on State governors by sections 7, 12, 15 and 21 of the Commonwealth Constitution in regard to the machinery for electing Senators, in which they act as 'the Constitutional Head of the State',[98] is surely insufficient to give the Commonwealth a direct interest in the form of State government. Even if these constitutional provisions were not amended, upon the advent of State republican government these functions of the State governors would obviously devolve upon the new 'Constitutional Head of the State', whatever his title.[99]) In any event, if at the relevant time the Commonwealth is not directly concerned, the fourth principle would apply.

Finally, it is submitted that the structure of a State's government is not a matter that directly concerns any other State.

'Manner and Form' Provisions

Section 128

Undoubtedly the most interesting and controversial issue regarding the amendment of State constitutions is the question whether they can be amended pursuant to section 128 of the Commonwealth Constitution. Such an amendment could be initiated (politically) by a State government in order to circumvent an inconvenient State constitutional provision imposing a rigorous 'manner and form' for constitutional amendment. But the section 128 procedure could also be employed by the Commonwealth, by which it must legally be initiated, in order to impose republican government upon an unwilling State. That contingency is, indeed, quite possible, if not probable, because the Commonwealth is likely to take the view that, for legal and/or practical reasons, the institution of republican government should occur simultaneously in all Australian governments notwithstanding the likely opposition thereto of some State governments.

Section 128 of the Commonwealth Constitution authorizes (impliedly) amendment of 'this Constitution'. Hence, State constitutions are subject to amendment pursuant to that provision only if they are part of the Commonwealth Constitution. Are they?

The Commonwealth Constitution contains no express provision on this question, and is not concerned with the structure of State governments. However, section 106 of that Constitution provides that 'The Constitution of each State . . . shall, subject to this Constitution, continue as at the establishment of the Commonwealth . . . until altered in accordance with the Constitution of the State.' Although it has been argued, especially by Chief Justice Barwick and Justice Murphy, that section 106 is the source of authority of State constitutions,[100] that view is questionable.[101] But, even if State constitutions do not legally derive from the Commonwealth Constitution, it is submitted that they are incorporated within it by virtue of section 106. As Quick and Garran wrote in 1901:

By the force of the legislative mandate that 'the Constitution of each State of the Commonwealth shall, subject to this Constitution, continue as at the establishment of the Commonwealth' it may be argued that the Constitution of the States are incorporated into the new Constitution, and should be read as if they formed parts or chapters of the new Constitution. The whole of the details of State Government and Federal Government may be considered as constituting one grand scheme provided by and elaborated in the Federal Constitution; a scheme in which the new national elements are blended harmoniously with the old provincial elements, thus producing a national plan of government having a Federal structure.[102]

Hence, State constitutions can be amended pursuant to section 128 because that provision (impliedly) authorizes amendment of section 106 wherein they are incorporated. Once again, Quick and Garran expressed this clearly: 'Nor is the scope of the amending power restricted to the structure and functions of the Federal Government; *it extends to the structure and functions of the Governments of the States.*'[103]

Republican government could, therefore, be introduced into a State by a referendum under section 128,[104] even against the wishes of the electors of that State. But such an exercise of the amendment power would be politically most unwise. As Geoffrey Sawer has argued,

It is a reasonable *political* inference from s.106 and from the course of Australian history that the Commonwealth should not intervene in State constitutional questions except to the extent that the enlargement of Commonwealth competence and the changing of Commonwealth-State interrelations pursuant to s.128 necessarily does so.[105]

Section 51(xxxviii)

Can a State parliament as usually constituted circumvent a State 'manner and form' provision governing amendment of the State constitution by requesting Commonwealth legislation pursuant to section 51 (xxxviii) of the Commonwealth Constitution, either to amend the State constitution or to empower the State parliament as usually constituted to do so notwithstanding its non-compliance with the 'manner and form' provision?

In view of the dearth of authority on this intriguing question, a brief summary should suffice.

1.   A State parliament could anticipate such an attempt to circumvent its 'manner and form' provision by subjecting a State Bill requesting or consenting to Commonwealth legislation under section 51(xxxviii) to the same, or even a different, 'manner and form' provision. The present 'manner and form' provisions for constitutional amendment in Western Australia and Queensland appear to be wide enough to extend to such a Bill because they apply to any Bill which 'expressly or impliedly *in any way affects*' certain constitutional provisions, including those dealing with the Crown, the governor, and constitutional amendment.[106]

2.   The power to amend State constitutional provisions entrenched by a local 'manner and form' provision was not one which in 1901 was exercisable 'only by the Parliament of the United Kingdom'; such provisions could be amended not only by the United Kingdom parliament but also by the State legislature complying, or constituted in accordance, with the 'manner and form' provision. Hence, section 51 (xxxviii) does not empower the Commonwealth parliament to amend those provisions.

3.   But the position is different in the case of Commonwealth legislation empowering a State parliament as usually constituted to disregard a 'manner and form' provision — even one falling outside section 5 of the Colonial Laws Validity Act 1865 (U.K.), provided that such legislation binds (as the present writer submits is the case) the State parliament as usually constituted — because in 1901 such legislation could have been enacted only by the United Kingdom parliament. The Commonwealth parliament could, therefore, enact such legislation pursuant to section 51(xxxviii).[107]

Chapter 9
Arguments for Retaining Monarchy

[A] republican form of government, in which the executive assumes independence of the trusteeship of the Crown, leads straight along the path to Tea Pot Dome, Watergate or Mulder and the Sanjay motor factory, and, possibly to Idi Amin or worse . . .

Lord Hailsham[1]

As was pointed out in chapter 2, it is not this book's purpose to debate the pros and cons of monarchy vs. republicanism. Instead, the book assumes that sooner or later Australia will wish to become a republic, and discusses the principal constitutional and governmental issues involved in that decision. But, having examined the principal reasons likely to motivate Australians in choosing republican government, the book would be incomplete and rather lopsided if it omitted to note the countervailing considerations likely to motivate opposition to that transition. Moreover, having considered one side of the question, fairness if nothing else would warrant examination of the other.

This chapter endeavours, accordingly, to outline the principal considerations likely to motivate those advocating retention of the monarchy — or, as some would prefer to express it, the 'governor-generalate'.

WHY CHANGE SOMETHING WHICH WORKS?

This is probably the most effective argument in the monarchists' armoury. A republic, they argue, will bring people no material benefit[2] — their lives are not affected one iota by substituting an elected president for an appointed Governor-General — so why tamper with an institution which works and, indeed, works well? Why waste time and public resources on such a trivial issue when other, far more important, issues cry out for public attention?[3] Whether or not it be derided as 'conservative' (for many not a term of derision at all), 'inertial', 'defence of the status quo', or whatever, this reasoning is undeniably the monarchists' great counter-argument, the great hurdle facing republicans. As Frederic Harrison noted in 1872, 'the serious arguments for monarchy all resolve themselves into this — that it is there',[4] a judgement vindicated by Geoffrey Kirk's warning a century later:

A republic may be a logical form of state organization; but it would be a wanton act to destroy an institution which is woven into the history of the country without being very sure that the alternative would make for greater unity and cohesion.[5]

These remarks concerned Britain. To what extent the monarchy is 'woven into the history' of Australia is debatable, but undoubtedly much less so than in Britain.

Indeed many defenders of the monarchy forgo Kirk's restraint. While few go as far as Lord Hailsham in threatening Teapot Dome, Watergate and Idi Amin as inevitable concomitants of a republic, the *in terrorem* argument is a favourite of monarchists. At its gentlest, they warn of the 'pain and divisiveness' abolition of the monarchy would bring,[6] but Lord Hailsham is not alone at the other end of the spectrum. The late Daniel O'Connell, who regarded South Africa as an ostensible parliamentary democracy which had 'avoided the locking up or . . . serious intimidation of opposition party leaders',[7] argued along lines similar to Lord Hailsham's:

A struggle over the corpse of Monarchy for distribution of the spoils of power would hardly safeguard the Australian heritage of liberty. There are not all that many obstacles to Australia becoming in the next century another Argentina. Fidelity to institutions is one of them.[8]

UNIFYING AND STABILIZING INFLUENCE

A claim frequently made for the Crown is that it unites all citizens — people of all races, classes, religions, occupations, and ethnic background — in a common allegiance to one rather ordinary person, whose succession was completely uncontroversial and free from chicanery, since it was decreed by the accident of birth. This supposedly unites and stabilizes the nation. As Robert Ball observed in the rather purple prose endemic to extreme monarchists,[9] the 'image of the Crown' is 'the archetype, the straight line, which gives us our national identity and provides the cohesion without which our affairs would fall apart in chaos and confusion.'[10] Sir Garfield Barwick has argued, more prosaically, that the Crown's unifying force is especially needed in Australia with its federal system, ethnic diversity, and divisive political and industrial relations.

[T]he presence of a head of state untouched by any of these . . . divisive factors can have an important effect on our progress towards national unity. In the monarch we have a head of state who is quite apart from party politics but who can form in her person a rallying point for us all, affording us one of the very few symbols of unity which modern life has so far left us.[11]

However, there are, of course, vociferous dissenters who maintain that the monarchy is, in fact, divisive,[12] and was certainly not a stabilizing influence in 1975.[13] Moreover, while the Crown is undeniably a 'symbol', as monarchists never tire of reminding us, the important question is: of what is it symbolic? It certainly symbolizes hereditary wealth and privilege, and maybe even English or British history. But surely it does not symbolize Australia. Even moderate monarchists must balk at Sir Garfield Barwick's claim that 'the more frequent appearance in Australia' of the Queen and members of the Royal Family 'may well do much to aid the popular appreciation of the monarchy in Australia as an *Australian* component of our constitutional independence.'[14]

POLITICAL NEUTRALITY

Much is made of the Crown's alleged political neutrality and, at least since the reign of George V, the monarch's reputation for evenhandedness has been well deserved. (On the other hand, no one could accuse Queen Victoria of evenhandedness in her relations with Disraeli and Gladstone.) The Queen's role as a politically neutral national symbol has led some monarchists to make extreme claims. Lord Hailsham — by no means at his most cogent when discussing monarchy — has argued, for example, that 'The Crown is a trustee for the Constitution on behalf of the Sovereign people',[15] but he overlooked the fact that the monarchy is jeopardized whenever the Queen or her representative seeks to exercise any of a trustee's powers. The only safe way to demonstrate political neutrality is to follow ministerial advice; once the Crown exercises independent judgement it will, in Asquith's apt phrase, inevitably 'become the football of contending factions.'[16]

But, even if the Queen is politically neutral in the sense that she is evenhanded in her relations with the two main political parties and their leaders, it can be argued that the monarchy is not neutral from a 'social' perspective. Despite some overstatement, Colin Macinnes's observations in this regard contain much sense.

The fact, surely, is that a monarchy, as it is hereditary, is by essence a conservative institution, and because of its possessions, a capitalist one. Since the vast majority of our people in whatever party are equally conservative and wedded to capitalism (whether they call themselves Conservative, Labour or whatever), the fiction of the monarchy being 'non-political' can be maintained without great strain. *But to suggest that our constitutional monarchy is by its nature 'non-political' is absurd.*[17]

Defenders of monarchy argue that, as long as the Queen behaves in a politically disinterested manner, her personal political predilections, which she presumably has like everyone else, can remain completely private. But the same cannot be said for an elected president, who will be associated with the political party to which he or she belonged, or which sponsored his or her election. In short, 'Can a head of state who emerges from an electoral struggle be "above the battle"?', as Sir Garfield Barwick inquired rhetorically.[18] Sir Robert Menzies, likewise, argued that 'the notion of a non-political President periodically elected by popular vote, after an election campaign, is a contradiction in terms.'[19]

There is indeed merit in these arguments, and republicans should consider them carefully in framing suitable machinery for electing (or appointing) a president. The recent experience of Italy and West Germany suggests that republics succeed, at least occasionally, in electing presidents who are popular, respected, and widely perceived to be politically neutral. This is more likely to occur when their nomination is supported by several parties, as occurred in the elections of President Richard von Weizsäcker of West Germany in May 1984 and Francesco Cossiga of Italy in June 1985. On the other hand, several Australian Governors-General — McKell, Casey and Hasluck — were widely perceived as partisan at the time of their appointment, however unwarranted that imputation turned out to be.

APPEAL TO THE IMAGINATION

The exaggerated and almost hysterical panegyrics of some of the monarchy's staunchest defenders[20] reflect the underlying truth that the fundamental appeal of monarchy is emotional. The basic attachment to monarchy is sentimental; it supposedly inspires, and appeals to, man's imagination. Republicanism may be more rational, monarchists frequently concede, but it is basically boring. Monarchy is interesting, exciting, glamorous. No one has expressed this observation more cogently than Walter Bagehot.

To state the matter shortly, royalty is a government in which the attention of the nation is concentrated on one person doing interesting actions. A Republic is a government in which that attention is divided between many, who are all doing uninteresting actions. Accordingly, so long as the human heart is strong and the human reason weak, royalty will be strong because it appeals to diffused feeling, and Republics weak because they appeal to the understanding.[21]

Even an American statesman like Fisher Ames (1758–1808) is reputed to have remarked that 'A monarchy is a merchantman which sails well, but will sometimes strike on a rock, and go to the bottom; a republic is a raft which will never sink, but then your feet are always in the water.'[22]

Observers of monarchy have made much of its 'mystery' and 'mystique', with Bagehot claiming that 'Its mystery is its life.'[23] It has even been maintained with some cogency that monarchy serves a very useful purpose in providing a healthy release for emotions which might otherwise find more dangerous outlets. Thus, Richard Crossman argued that 'Monarchy, in fact, is a deeply rooted national myth which canalizes and purges the emotions of a mass democracy exposed to mass media in an irreligious age.'[24] So much may be accepted as at least partially accurate — although unprovable — but the historicity of Crossman's further observations is more doubtful.

[I]n terms of siphoning off dangerous emotions, the monarchy has enormous value, as you realize if you consider the Weimar Republic. The Germans are tremendously susceptible to myth and legend. If they had been allowed a constitutional monarchy, they might well have been able to prevent the coming of Hitler.

It was because the Nazis were able to capture the emotions which are siphoned off into a monarchy, and to concentrate them against the regime, that they won.[25]

Because this monarchical argument is based upon emotion rather than logic, republicans cannot 'rebut' it and should not even try to do so. Fulminating about such alleged 'emotional retardation'[26] is pointless; it will never convert a committed monarchist and is probably counterproductive. Their only sensible response can be that we really have a 'governor-generalate', not a monarchy. Our Queen is British, if not English, and, as Donald Horne has wryly noted, 'People who feel their lives need vicarious glamour from the monarchy will still be able to read about Queen Elizabeth in the *Women's Weekly*.'[27]

Notes

Abbreviations of Periodicals Cited

A.C.	Appeal Cases (U.K.)
A.I.R.	All India Reporter
A.L.J.	Australian Law Journal
A.L.R.	Australian Law Reports
A.Q.	Australian Quarterly
Adel. L. Rev.	Adelaide Law Review
Aust. Mining and Petroleum L.J.	Australian Mining and Petroleum Law Journal
C.L.R.	Commonwealth Law Reports
Colum. J. of Law and Social Probs.	Columbia Journal of Law and Social Problems
Current Affairs Bull.	Current Affairs Bulletin
F.L. Rev.	Federal Law Review
Geo. Wash. L. Rev.	George Washington Law Review
Hist. Stud.	Historical Studies
J. of Politics	Journal of Politics
J.R.A.H.S.	Journal of the Royal Australian Historical Society
L.Q.R.	Law Quarterly Review
Law Institute J.	Law Institute Journal (Victoria)
M.U.L.R.	Melbourne University Law Review
P.N.G.L.R.	Papua New Guinea Law Reports
Parl. Affs.	Parliamentary Affairs
Pol. Q.	Political Quarterly
Pol. Sc. Q.	Political Science Quarterly
Rev. of Politics	Review of Politics
S.A.	South African Law Reports
S.A.S.R.	South Australian State Reports
S.C.R.	Supreme Court Reports (Canada)
Tas. L.R.	Tasmanian Law Reports
Tas. U.L. Rev.	Tasmanian University Law Review
U.N.S.W.L.J.	University of New South Wales Law Journal
U.S.	United States Reports
V.R.	Victorian Reports
W.A.R.	Western Australian Reports
West Indian L.J.	West Indian Law Journal

1   A 'Republic'

1. The Commonwealth of Australia Constitution Act 1900 (U.K.) preamble (the people of the colonies had 'agreed to unite in one indissoluble Federal Commonwealth under the Crown of the *United Kingdom of Great Britain and Ireland'*), covering clause 2 ('The provisions of this Act referring to the Queen shall extend to Her Majesty's heirs and successors in the sovereignty of the *United Kingdom.*') (emphasis added).Technically, the Queen is, of course, the 'Queen of Australia' (Royal Style and Titles Act 1973 (C'th) section 2), as Sir Garfield Barwick has emphasized: G. Barwick, *The Monarchy in an Independent Australia* (Sir Robert Menzies Lecture Trust, Monash University, 1982), 4–5, 7, 11–12, 19, 20.

2. E.g., J. D. Lang, *Freedom and Independence for the Golden Lands of Australia* (London, 1852), 63–5; J. D. Lang, *The Coming Event! or Freedom and Independence for the Seven United Provinces of Australia* (Sydney, 1870), 295–301. Some of the leaders at the Eureka Stockade (Ballarat, 3 December 1854) were republicans.

3. See B. Mansfield, 'The Background to Radical Republicanism in New South Wales in the Eighteen-Eighties' (1953) 5 *Hist.Stud.* 338, 340, 348.

4. See *infra*, this chapter, 'The Prospects for a Republic' (pp. 12–17).

5. See *Republican Australia?* (G. Dutton ed., Melbourne, 1977), 210–15.

6. G. Winterton, 'Modern Republicanism' (1992) 6 *Legislative Studies*, No.2, 24. See also P. Pettit, 'Republican Themes', ibid., 29.

7. W. M. Wiecek, *The Guarantee Clause of the U.S. Constitution* (Ithaca, N.Y., 1972), 17. Likewise, ibid., 14: 'By 1787 most Americans considered a monarchy incompatible with the republican ideal'.

8. See *infra* note 30.

9. See, e.g., F. W. Maitland, 'The Crown as Corporation' (1901) 17 *L.Q.R.* 131, 136–7, reprinted in 3 *The Collected Papers of Frederic William Maitland* (H.A.L. Fisher ed., Cambridge, 1911), 244, 253–4; C. H. McIlwain, 'Some Illustrations of the Influence of Unchanged Names for Changing Institutions', in *Interpretations of Modern Legal Philosophies: Essays in Honor of Roscoe Pound* (P. Sayre ed., New York, 1947, repr. Littleton, Colo., 1981), 484, 488.

10. See *infra*, text accompanying notes 17–24.

11. See, e.g., Dr Johnson's *A Dictionary of the English Language*, first published in 1755, which defined a 'republick' primarily as a 'commonwealth; state in which the power is lodged in more than one', and a 'republican' as 'one who thinks a commonwealth without monarchy the best government'.

12. Montesquieu, in 1748, defined 'republican government' as 'that in which the body, or only a part of the people, is possessed of the supreme power'. The former he called a 'democracy' and the latter an 'aristocracy': 1 *The Spirit of the Laws* (T. Nugent transl., New York, 1949), 8.

13. See W. P. Adams, 'Republicanism in Political Rhetoric Before 1776' (1970) 85 *Pol. Sc. Q.* 397; W. P. Adams, *The First American Constitutions* (R. and R. Kimber transl., Chapel Hill, 1980), 100–1, 106–12.

14. F. D. Wormuth, *The Origins of Modern Constitutionalism* (New York, 1949), 90.

15. M. J. C. Vile, *Constitutionalism and the Separation of Powers* (Oxford, 1967), 37–9. From about 1660 to 1750 the prevailing theory was one of

a 'balanced constitution': ibid., 53–4, 98–9. See also C. C. Weston, *English Constitutional Theory and the House of Lords 1556–1832* (London, 1965); S. Pargellis, 'The Theory of Balanced Government', in *The Constitution Reconsidered* (C. Read ed., New York, rev. ed., 1968), 37; G. S. Wood, *The Creation of the American Republic, 1776–1787* (Chapel Hill, 1969), ch. VI ('Mixed Government and Bicameralism').

16. 18 June 1642, reprinted in J. P. Kenyon, *The Stuart Constitution 1603–1688* (Cambridge, 1966), 21–3.

17. J. G. A. Pocock, *The Machiavellian Moment* (Princeton, 1975), 363.

18. See, e.g., F. Harrison, 'The Monarchy' (1872) 11 *Fortnightly Review* (N.S.) 613, 614, 616, 619, 621, 636, 637, 638, 641; John Adams, *Novanglus: or, A History of the Dispute With America, From its Origin, in 1754, to the Present Time* (1774), in 4 *The Works of John Adams* (C. F. Adams ed., Boston, 1851, repr. New York, 1971), 106; John Adams, *A Defence of the Constitutions of Government of the United States of America,* vol. 1 (1787), in ibid., 462. See also Charles James Fox, 29 *The Parliamentary History of England* (London, 1817), 414 (House of Commons, 11 May 1791), quoted *infra* note 31. Thomas Paine called the House of Commons 'the republican part in the constitution': *Common Sense* (I. Kramnick ed., Harmondsworth, 1976, orig. publ. 1776), 81 (and see also ibid., 69). For James Madison, 'one republican branch only, combined with a hereditary aristocracy and monarchy' did not make England a republic: *The Federalist* (J. E. Cooke ed., Middletown, Conn., 1961), 251 (No.39). See also P. Peterson, 'The Meaning of Republicanism in *The Federalist*' (1979) 9 *Publius*, No. 2, 43, 47.

19. E.g., Harrison, *supra* note 18 at 618.

20. E.g., ibid., 625, 628; W. Bagehot, *The English Constitution* (R. H. S. Crossman ed., London, 1963, orig. publ. 1867), 266 note 1 (and see ibid., 262).

21. E.g., Letters from John Adams to Roger Sherman, 17 and 18 July 1789, in 6 *The Works of John Adams* (C. F. Adams ed., Boston, 1851, repr. New York, 1971), 428, 429. See also John Adams, *A Defence of the Constitutions, supra* note 18 at 558, chs III ('Monarchical or Regal Republics') and IX ('Ancient Monarchical Republics').

22. E.g., Harrison, *supra* note 18 at 614, 619. See also John Adams, *A Defence of the Constitutions, supra* note 18, chs. II ('Aristocratic Republics') and VIII ('Ancient Aristocratical Republics').

23. B. Crick, *Basic Forms of Government* (London, 1973), 56.

24. E.g., H. Evans, 'Proposals for Constitutional Change in Australia' (1982) 63 *The Parliamentarian* 151, 152; H. Evans, 'Questioning the Tyranny' 27 *Quadrant*, No. 4, 70, 71 (April 1983); G. S. Reid, 'Introduction', in *Parliament & Bureaucracy* (J. R. Nethercote, ed., Sydney, 1982), 1, 12.

25. *Pace* Frank MacKinnon, who has argued that 'republic' is not the opposite of 'monarchy' and, hence, that 'A constitutional monarchy can thus be a republic too, because its government is actually carried on, not by the sovereign, but by and through the people's representatives in the name of the people.': F. MacKinnon, *The Crown in Canada* (Calgary, 1976), 18–19.

26. *The Federalist, supra* note 18 at 251 (No. 39). Justice James Wilson's definition of republican government was 'one constructed on this principle, that the Supreme Power resides in the body of the people.': *Chisholm* v. *Georgia* (1793) 2 U.S. (2 Dall.) 419, 457.

27. Letter to John Adams, 20 July 1789, in 6 *The Works of John Adams, supra* note 21 at 437 (emphasis in original). See also Peterson, *supra* note 18 at 46–7.

28. See Letter from Thomas Jefferson to John Taylor, 28 May 1816, in 11 *The Works of Thomas Jefferson* (P. L. Ford ed., New York, 1905), 529; Letter from James Madison to Thomas Jefferson, 24 October 1787, in 12 *The Papers of Thomas Jefferson* (J. P. Boyd ed., Princeton, 1955), 276–9. On 'democracy', see B. Bailyn, *The Ideological Origins of the American Revolution* (Cambridge, Mass., 1967), 282 ff.

29. *The Federalist, supra* note 18 at 84 (No. 14). See, similarly, ibid., 62 (No. 10, Madison); and see also ibid., 427–8 (No. 63, Madison); W. C. Jarvis, *The Republican; or, A Series of Essays on the Principles and Policy of Free States* (Pittsfield, Mass., 1820, repr. New York, 1974), 79; R. W. Shoemaker, '"Democracy" and "Republic" as Understood in Late Eighteenth Century America' (1966) 41 *American Speech* 83; Wood, *supra* note 15 at 222–3; Wiecek, *supra* note 7 at 18–19; Adams, *First American Constitutions, supra* note 13 at 113–17.

30. See C. M. Walsh, *The Political Science of John Adams* (New York, 1915, repr. Freeport, N.Y., 1969), 27–34; Wood, *supra* note 15 at 48, 585–6; Bailyn, *supra* note 28 at 282–3 note 50. See also Wiecek, *supra* note 7 at 12–13, 17ff.

31. Letter to Samuel Adams, 18 October 1790, in 6 *Works, supra* note 21 at 415 (emphasis added). Cf. Charles James Fox, cited *supra* note 18: republican governments were those 'where the *res publica* was the universal principle, and the people, as under our constitution, had *considerable weight* in the government.' (emphasis added).

32. Letter from Samuel Adams to John Adams, 20 November 1790, in 6 *Works, supra* note 21 at 420–1 (emphasis in original).

33. See Peterson, *supra* note 18 at 47 note 9. On the speed with which Americans embraced republicanism, see Wood, *supra* note 15 at 91, 92–3. See also P. Maier, *From Resistance to Revolution* (New York, 1972), 272 (including note 2).

34. Wood, *supra* note 15 at 205–6, 236–8. See also Wiecek *supra* note 7 at 22.

35. D. Horne, 'The Case for a Republic', in *Republican Australia?* (G. Dutton ed., Melbourne, 1977), 7, 8.

36. D. P. O'Connell, 'Monarchy or Republic?', in *Republican Australia?* (G. Dutton ed., Melbourne, 1977), 23, 23–4. See also ibid., 39, 42.

37. Ibid., 25, 32.

38. Ibid., 33.

39. *Infra*, ch. 8.

40. Cf. correspondence, (1981) 55 *A.L.J.* 360 (Byers), 701 (Saunders and Smith), 763 (Galligan), 829 (Finnis), 893 (Griffin), (1982) 56 *A.L.J.* 316 (Byers); C. Harders, 'Conventions Associated with the Australian Constitution: The Effect of the Events of 1973–1975 Relating to References and Appeals to the Privy Council' (1982) 56 *A.L.J.* 132.

41. O'Connell, *supra* note 36 at 31.

42. D. P. O'Connell, 'Canada, Australia, Constitutional Reform and the Crown' (1979) 60 *The Parliamentarian* 5, 10. Accord, O'Connell, *supra* note 36 at 29: 'Commonwealth veto of State functions . . . through capture of the Royal prerogative'.

43. D. Dawson, 'The Constitution — Major Overhaul or Simple Tune-up?' (1984) 14 *M.U.L.R.* 353, 353–4.

44. See Senator Gareth Evans, 'God Save the Queen? — Australia as a Republic' (unpublished address to Counterpoint Forum, Murdoch University, 29 September 1982), 3.

45. Cf. Government of Canada, Hon. Jean Chrétien, Minister of Justice, *The Role of the United Kingdom in the Amendment of the Canadian Constitution*, Background Paper (March 1981), paras 7–9, 50, 78–81.

46. Evans, *supra* note 44 at 3; E. G. Whitlam, *The Whitlam Government 1972–1975* (Ringwood, Vic., 1985), 147. See also Z. Cowen, 'The Constitutional Aspects', in *Republican Australia?* (G. Dutton ed., Melbourne, 1977), 44, 56. Cf. Papua New Guinea, General Constitutional Commission, *Final Report* (Port Moresby, 1983), p. 93 (advocating that a republican Papua New Guinea remain in the Commonwealth); Canadian Bar Association, Committee on the Constitution, *Towards a New Canada* (1978), 34 (advocating that a republican Canada remain in the Commonwealth).

47. See N. Mansergh, *Survey of British Commonwealth Affairs: Problems of Wartime Co-operation and Post-War Change 1939–52* (London, 1958), 249–56 on the circumstances surrounding the London Declaration.

48. Papua New Guinea (hereafter 'PNG') Constitution section 88.

49. See G. Winterton, *Parliament, the Executive and the Governor-General* (Melbourne, 1983), 98–101. However, many constitutional scholars would deny parliament this power: see the views noted in ibid., 99, 287 note 47; G. Lindell, Book Review (of ibid.) (1983) 6 *U.N.S.W.L.J.* 261, 267–8.

50. For the details, see C. Cunneen, *Kings' Men, Australia's Governors-General from Hopetoun to Isaacs* (Sydney, 1983), 173–82.

51. Cf. E. McWhinney, *Canada and the Constitution 1979–82: Patriation and the Charter of Rights* (Toronto, 1982), 131.

52. *Official Report of the National Australasian Convention Debates* (Sydney, 1891), 572. For Sir George Grey's views, see ibid., 138, 561–4.

53. Manifesto of the People's Federal Convention (Bathurst, January 1897), in *Proceedings of the People's Federal Convention at Bathurst, November 1896* (Sydney, 1897), 190, reprinted in C. M. H. Clark, *Select Documents in Australian History 1851–1900* (Sydney, 1955), 505.

54. See Cunneen, *supra* note 50 at 144–7, 150, 161–3, 168.

55. *Official Report of the National Australasian Convention Debates* (Adelaide, 1897), 24.

56. See D. Horne, *His Excellency's Pleasure* (Melbourne, 1977); L. J. M. Cooray, *Conventions, the Australian Constitution and the Future* (Sydney, 1979), ch. 1.

57. D. Solomon, *Elect the Governor-General!* (Melbourne, 1976), 40–1.

58. C. A. Hughes, 'Machinery of Government', in *Australian Politics. A*

Fifth Reader (H. Meyer and H. Nelson eds, Melbourne, 1980), 188, 189. (However, it should be noted that French ministers are not eligible for parliamentary membership.)

59. Solomon, *supra* note 57 at 44.
60. See Hughes, *supra* note 58 at 189–90.
61. Solomon, *supra* note 57 at vii; accord 40, 51.
62. See Winterton, *supra* note 49 at 4–5, 76, 77–8, 80.
63. J. Quick and R. R. Garran, *The Annotated Constitution of the Australian Commonwealth* (Sydney, 1901, repr, Sydney, 1976), 706–7. Such an amendment could be accomplished under section 128: ibid., 989.
64. See J. McMillan, G. Evans and H. Storey, *Australia's Constitution: Time for Change?* (Sydney, 1983), 223.
65. Sections 58, 59, 60 and 74 para. 3. The Melbourne (1975) and Hobart (1976) sessions of the Australian Constitutional Convention recommended the repeal of section 59 (disallowance) as an 'outmoded and expended' provision, and the Adelaide (1983) session concurred, and also recommended repeal of references to reservation of bills in sections 58 and 74, in which case section 60 would go as well. These provisions would have been repealed had the government proceeded with the Constitution Alteration (Removal of Outmoded and Expended Provisions) Bill 1983 (C'th), which was passed by the Senate on 13 October 1983.
66. See *supra*, text accompanying notes 62 and 63.
67. See G. Sawer, *Federation Under Strain* (Melbourne, 1977), 188, 198; Evans, *supra* note 44 at 6; E. G. Whitlam, *The Truth of the Matter* (2nd ed., Ringwood, Vic., 1983), 184.
68. See PNG Constitution sections 82 and 138; Papua New Guinea Government, *Proposals on Constitutional Principles and Explanatory Notes* (Port Moresby, August 1974), ch. 7, Part A (p. 26).
69. Papua New Guinea, *Final Report of the Constitutional Planning Committee* (1974), Part 1, ch. 7, paras 3–15.
70. See Irish Constitution articles 13.1.1° and 28.10; Federal Republic of Germany (hereafter 'FRG') Basic Law articles 63 and 67; Swedish Constitution ch. 6, articles 2, 3 and 5; PNG Constitution section 142. (Sweden and Papua New Guinea are monarchies.)
71. Swedish Constitution ch. 6, articles 2–5, noted in McMillan, Evans and Storey, *supra* note 64 at 190.
72. See Swedish Constitution ch. 3, article 4, and ch. 6, article 5.
73. E.g., Lord Hailsham of St Marylebone, *Hamlyn Revisited: The British Legal System Today* (London, 1983), 26.
74. O'Connell, *supra* note 36 at 36.
75. D. Dunstan, 'The State, the Governors and the Crown', in *Republican Australia?* (G. Dutton ed., Melbourne, 1977), 202, 204–5, 208.
76. Whitlam, *supra* note 67 at 184.
77. Dunstan, *supra* note 75 at 202–3, adopted by Barwick, *supra* note 1 at 17–18. See also E. A. Forsey, *The Royal Power of Dissolution of Parliament in the British Commonwealth* (Toronto, 1943), 7, 259; E. A. Forsey, *Freedom and Order* (Toronto, 1974), 29–31, 48–9.
78. Winterton, *supra* note 49 at 155; Sawer, *supra* note 67 at 188.
79. Cf. Irish Constitution article 13.8; Italian Constitution article 90; Icelandic Constitution article 11; Greek Constitution article 49.

80. PNG Constitution sections 28, 142 (5)(b) and (6)(a), and 144 (4)(b)(ii). See also *State* v. *Independent Tribunal, ex parte Sasakila* [1976] P.N.G.L.R. 491.

81. PNG, *Final Report of the Constitutional Planning Committee, supra* note 69, ch. 7, para. 11.

82. Ibid., ch. 7, paras 7, 8, 10, 12 and 13. However, the Committee's principal objection to a separate head of state appears to have been its incompatibility with Papua New Guinean notions of government: ibid., ch. 7, paras 4, 6, 9 and 10.

83. See D. Horne, *Power From the People. A New Australian Constitution?* (Victorian Fabian Society Pamphlet No. 32, October 1977), 18.

84. Ibid.

85. For the results of section 128 referenda, see McMillan, Evans and Storey, *supra* note 64, ch. 2; *House of Representatives Practice* (J. A. Pettifer ed., Canberra, 1981), 738.

86. Sources: McMillan, Evans and Storey, *supra* note 64 at 178; *Sun Herald* (Sydney), 4 February 1979, p. 38; *Herald* (Melbourne), 25 September 1982; *Bulletin*, 22 February 1983, p. 47; *Bulletin*, 8 May 1984, p. 32; *Age*, 3 March 1986, p. 3; Morgan Gallup Polls Nos. 934 (1953), 1914 and 1917 (1966), 2044 (1968), 2156 (1969), 211 (1970), 238 and 18 (1973).

87. But cf. the results of 'the Australian Social Barometer': the percentage of affirmative responses to the statement 'Australia should become a republic, independent of England' were

November 1972	53%
May 1973	48%
January 1974	40%
December 1974	39%

R. Wilson, 'How Fast is Australia Changing?' in *Australian Politics. A Fourth Reader* (H. Mayer and H. Nelson eds, Melbourne, 1976), 59, 60. These figures no doubt reflect the early euphoria and subsequent disillusionment of the Whitlam era.

88. *Republican Australia?, supra* note 5 at 212. But cf. the lower figure (43 per cent) for non-British European migrants given in Solomon, *supra* note 57 at 69.

89. *Republican Australia?, supra* note 5 at 211. In December 1978 the figures were men 37 per cent, women 25 per cent: *Sun Herald* (Sydney), 4 February 1979, p. 38.

90. *Republican Australia?, supra* note 5 at 212.

91. Ibid., 211.

92. Ibid., 212.

93. Ibid. But cf. the lower figure for Labor voters (40 per cent) given in Solomon, *supra* note 57 at 69.

94. This is the view of many commentators: e.g., Sir Ninian Stephen, Press Conference, *Sydney Morning Herald*, 15 January 1982, p. 4; Sir Zelman Cowen, *supra* note 46 at 59; O'Connell, *supra* note 36 at 24; Solomon, *supra* note 57 at 69; McMillan, Evans and Storey, *supra* note 64 at 375 (no republic by 1988); S. Jobson, 'The Cultural Implications of a Republic', in *Republican Australia?* (G. Dutton ed., Melbourne, 1977), 166–7.

95. Senator Gareth Evans has estimated that almost half the Australian popu-

lation is ethnically non-British (excluding the Irish), comprising about 25 per cent Irish and 23 per cent who are neither British nor Irish: Evans, *supra* note 44 at 10.

96. Ibid., 12.
97. Sawer, *supra* note 67 at 197.
98. See Evans, *supra* note 44 at 13–14; M. Grattan, 'Republican Victory at Labor Conference', *Age*, 28 July 1981, p. 3.
99. Patrick White, 'A Democratic Australian Republic', in *Republican Australia?* (G. Dutton ed., Melbourne, 1977), 197, 201.

2 Reasons for Becoming a Republic

1. See, e.g., R. J. L. Hawke, *The Resolution of Conflict* (1979 Boyer Lectures, Sydney, 1979), 22; G. Evans, 'God Save the Queen? — Australia as a Republic' (unpublished address to Counterpoint Forum, Murdoch University, 29 September 1982), 9–10; G. Dutton, 'Preface', in *Republican Australia?* (G. Dutton ed., Melbourne, 1977), vii; D. Horne, 'The Queen as Queen of Australia', in *The Queen* (Harmondsworth, 1977), 29, 41; F. Arena, 'Clinging to Britannia's Apron Strings', *Weekend Australian Magazine*, 25–26 June 1983, p. 14; B. Buckley, *Dawning of a Republic* (Sydney, 1979), 11; P. Coleman, 'The Phoney Debate', in *Australia and the Monarchy* (G. Dutton ed., Melbourne, 1966), 171, 180. See also *infra*, notes 7 and 8.
2. Royal Style and Titles Act 1973 (C'th) section 2.
3. The Commonwealth of Australia Constitution Act 1900 (U.K.) covering clause 2, quoted *supra*, chapter 1 note 1.
4. G. Barwick, *The Monarchy in an Independent Australia* (Sir Robert Menzies Lecture Trust, Monash University, 1982), 12.
5. But apparently not invariably: in late 1976 the British government (contrary to the wishes of the Queensland government) reportedly advised the Queen not to reappoint Sir Colin Hannah as Governor of Queensland: C. A. Hughes, *The Government of Queensland* (St Lucia, 1980), 195–6; J. I. Fajgenbaum and P. J. Hanks, *Australian Constitutional Law* (2nd ed. by P. J. Hanks, Sydney, 1980), 350.
6. The practice whereby a British minister advises the Queen on State matters has been widely condemned as an 'anachronistic [survival] from the colonial period . . . [having] little or no bearing on the theory or practice of Australian government': P. Hasluck, *The Office of Governor-General* (Melbourne, 1979), 27 note 1. Accord Z. Cowen, *The Virginia Lectures* (University of Virginia, March–April 1983) (Sir Robert Menzies Memorial Trust, Canberra, 1984), 15; Z. Cowen, 'The Constitutional Aspects', in *Republican Australia?* (G. Dutton ed., Melbourne, 1977), 44, 53–54; Barwick, *supra* note 4 at 5–6; D. Dunstan, 'The State, the Governors and the Crown', in *Republican Australia?*, *supra*, 202, 208, 209. Upon the severance of 'residual constitutional links' with the United Kingdom (to be effected in 1986), State governments will no longer advise the Queen through a British minister. Like the Commonwealth prime minister, State premiers will communicate directly with the Queen.
7. D. Horne, 'Republican Australia', in *Australia and the Monarchy* (G. Dutton ed., Melbourne, 1966), 86, 88.

8. C. Howard, *The Constitution, Power and Politics* (Melbourne, 1980), 118.

9. Barwick, *supra* note 4 at 20.

10. See, e.g., chapter 1 note 2.

11. E.g. Papua New Guinea, General Constitutional Commission, *Final Report* (Port Moresby, 1983), p. 93; Canadian Bar Association, Committee on the Constitution, *Towards a New Canada* (1978), 34. (There was some adverse reaction to this report: see E. McWhinney, *Quebec and the Constitution 1960–1978* (Toronto, 1979), 121.)

12. D. Horne, *Power From the People. A New Australian Constitution?* (Victorian Fabian Society Pamphlet No. 32, October 1977), 17. Donald Horne adds: 'And maintenance of the symbolism of the monarchy maintains an affirmation of infantility, of honor [*sic*] through subservience, that helps sustain generally servile attitudes in matters of foreign policy, defence, economic policy and cultural life': ibid., 17–18. This is highly questionable.

13. See P. Smark, 'Queen Plays the Arab Card', *Age*, 28 March 1984, p. 9.

14. *Australian*, 29 March 1984, p. 8.

15. *Age*, 30 March 1984, p. 12.

16. Senator Gareth Evans, Senate, *Weekly Hansard*, 29 March 1984, p. 875.

17. Senator Gareth Evans, Senate, *Weekly Hansard*, 7 May 1984, p. 1633 (emphasis added).

18. The Queen's visit to the United States and the United Nations in 1957 demonstrated the possible transformations of role on a single royal tour. See H. Duncan Hall, *Commonwealth* (London, 1971), 879–81 ('The Visit of the Queen of the United Kingdom, the Queen of Canada and the Head of the Commonwealth, to the United States and the United Nations, 1957').

19. Or a Commonwealth monarchy with its own monarch (such as Malaysia, Tonga or Swaziland) or, presumably, a monarchy or republic outside the Commonwealth.

20. Cf. Anthony Low, Letter, *Times*, 11 February 1984, p. 9; H. V. Hodson, 'Crown and Commonwealth' (1984) *Round Table*, No. 292, 354, 359.

21. See Editorial, 'Queen and Commonwealth', *Times*, 6 February 1984, p. 15; C. Douglas-Home, 'Crown and Commonwealth' (1984) *Round Table*, No. 292, 360, 365–66; Lord Blake, Letter, *Times*, 20 February 1984, p. 11. See also Enoch Powell, 'What Commonwealth?', *Times*, 26 January 1984, p. 12, and Letter, *Times*, 23 February 1984, p. 13.

22. See Duncan Hall, cited *supra* note 18.

23. Book Review, *Weekend Australian Magazine*, 2–3 July 1983, p. 14.

24. However, the Australian Constitutional Convention has endorsed as a 'convention of the Constitution' the proposition that the Governor-General should be an Australian citizen: *Official Record of Debates of the Australian Constitutional Convention* (Adelaide, 1983), 319 (item 5).

25. Noted by Cowen, *The Virginia Lectures*, *supra* note 6 at 15.

26. See, e.g., A. Wynn, 'The Republicans Are Coming!' in *Republican Australia?* (G. Dutton ed., Melbourne, 1977), 172, 177–8.

27. T. Paine, *Rights of Man* (H. Collins ed., Harmondsworth, 1969), 138 (emphasis in original); accord: ibid., 198.

28. Ibid., 198 (emphasis added).
29. T. Paine, *Common Sense* (I. Kramnick ed., Harmondsworth, 1976), 76.
30. Paine, *supra* note 27 at 144.
31. Ibid., 194 (emphasis added).
32. Kramnick, 'Editor's Introduction', in Paine, *supra* note 29 at 8–9, 29–30; P. S. Foner, 'Introduction', in 1 *The Complete Writings of Thomas Paine* (P. S. Foner ed., New York, 1945), xiii–xvii, 2; W. P. Adams, *The First American Constitutions* (R. and R. Kimber transl., Chapel Hill, 1980), 104, 106.
33. Ibid., 26; G. S. Wood, *The Creation of the American Republic, 1776–1787* (Chapel Hill, 1969), 92–3.
34. Letter from John Adams to James Madison, 17 June 1817, in 10 *The Works of John Adams* (C. F. Adams ed., Boston, 1856, repr. New York, 1971), 267, 268.
35. See the Maryland Declaration of Rights 1776 article 40 (3 F. N. Thorpe, *The Federal and State Constitutions, Colonial Charters, and Other Organic Laws* (Washington D. C., 1909), 1690), and the North Carolina Declaration of Rights 1776 article 22 (5 ibid., 2788). Cf. the Georgia Constitution 1777 article 11 (no person holding a title of nobility entitled to vote or hold public office): 2 ibid., 780.
36. Article VI: '. . . nor shall the united states in congress assembled, or any of them, grant any title of nobility.' C. C. Tansill, *Documents Illustrative of the Formation of the Union of the American States* (Washington D.C., 1927), 29.
37. Article I section 9(8): 'No title of nobility shall be granted by the United States'.
38. *The Federalist* (J. E. Cooke ed., Middletown, Conn., 1961), 577–8 (No. 84). See also ibid., 253 (No. 39, Madison).
39. See B. Mansfield, 'The Background to Radical Republicanism in New South Wales in the Eighteen-Eighties' (1953) 5 *Hist. Stud.* 338, 342–3.
40. Ibid., 343 (emphasis added).
41. *Supra*, chapter 1, 'The Meaning of "Republic"' (pp. 2–4).
42. See W. P. Adams, 'Republicanism in Political Rhetoric Before 1776' (1970) 85 *Pol. Sc. Q.* 397, 420; Adams, *supra* note 32 at 26, 127.
43. *Supra* note 38 at 251 (No. 39).
44. 1 G. T. Curtis, *Constitutional History of the United States* (New York, 1889), 612.
45. E.g., the Constitutions of France article 3 ('National sovereignty belongs to the people'), Ireland article 6 ('All powers of government, legislative, executive and judicial, derive, under God, from the people, whose right it is to designate the rulers of the State') and Italy article 1 ('Sovereignty belongs to the people'). Cf. the preambles to the constitutions of the United States ('We, the People of the United States . . . do ordain and establish this Constitution') and India ('We, the People of India . . . do hereby adopt, enact and give to ourselves this Constitution.').
46. Japanese Constitution article 1 ('The Emperor shall be the symbol of the State and of the unity of the people, deriving his position from the will of the people *with whom resides sovereign power.*') (emphasis added), and Swedish Constitution ch. 1, article 1 ('All public power in Sweden emanates from the people.').

47. Curtis, quoted *supra*, text accompanying note 44.
48. E.g., P. Worsthorne, 'The case for the Monarchy', in *The Queen* (Harmondsworth, 1977), 165, 166–74.
49. See Evans, *supra* note 1 at 8.
50. 1 *Democracy in America* (P. Bradley ed., New York, 1945; orig. publ. 1835), 435–6. See also P. Peterson, 'The Meaning of Republicanism in *The Federalist*' (1979) 9 *Publius*, No. 2, 43, 72.
51. F. Grimke, *The Nature and Tendency of Free Institutions* (J. W. Ward ed., Cambridge, Mass., 1968; orig. publ. 1848), 260.
52. D. Horne, 'A Case for A Republic', in *Republican Australia?* (G. Dutton ed., Melbourne, 1977), 7, 22. See also Evans, *supra* note 1 at 10–11.
53. E.g., Howard, *supra* note 8 at 93, 98, 100–1, 139.
54. For some details, see G. Winterton, *Parliament, the Executive and the Governor-General* (Melbourne, 1983), 246–7 note 2.
55. See, e.g., D. P. O'Connell, 'Monarchy or Republic?', in *Republican Australia?* (G. Dutton ed., Melbourne, 1977), 23; J. Bjelke-Petersen, 'Australian Federalism: A Queensland View', in *Australian Federalism: Future Tense* (A. Patience and J. Scott eds, Melbourne, 1983), 63, 71.
56. See *supra*, chapter 1, text accompanying notes 40–42.
57. D. Dawson, 'The Constitution — Major Overhaul or Simple Tune-up?' (1984) 14 *M.U.L.R.* 353.
58. See the letter of 17 November 1975 from the Queen's Private Secretary to Speaker Scholes, in G. Sawer, *Federation Under Strain* (Melbourne, 1977), 211.
59. See, e.g., E. G. Whitlam, *The Truth of the Matter* (2nd ed., Ringwood, Vic., 1983), 185; E. G. Whitlam, *The Whitlam Government 1972–1975* (Ringwood, Vic., 1985), 130. See also Horne, *supra* note 12 at 21.
60. Buckley, *supra* note 1 at 16.
61. G. Freudenberg, *A Certain Grandeur* (Melbourne, 1978; orig. publ. 1977), 400.
62. He dismissed the Prime Minister under section 64 para. 2 of the Constitution.
63. See Whitlam, *supra* note 59 at ch. 12; J. McClelland, 'Republican Australia — A Labor View', in *Republican Australia?* (G. Dutton ed., Melbourne, 1977), 132, 134, 139, 141; J. McClelland, 'We can't afford irritants like the Governor-General and the Senate', *National Times*, 16–21 February 1976, p. 18.
64. A point frequently noted: see, e.g., O'Connell, *supra* note 55 at 35; Cowen, 'The Constitutional Aspects', *supra* note 6 at 51; Evans, *supra* note 1 at 5; D. A. Low, 'Wearing the Crown: New Reflections on the Dismissal 1975' (1984) 19 *Politics* 18, 23; Z. Cowen, 'The Office of Governor-General' (1985) 114 *Daedalus*, No. 1, 127, 146; Sir Harry Gibbs, 'Some Thoughts on the Australian Constitution' (unpublished address at All Nations Club, Sydney, 21 November 1985), 6, quoted in *Sydney Morning Herald*, 22 November 1985, p. 17.
65. See Winterton, *supra* note 54 at 150. On the other hand, a republican head of state would no longer enjoy the aura of 'royal legitimacy', such as it is: see R. Lucy, *The Australian Form of Government* (Melbourne, 1985), 17.

66. This question is discussed *infra*, chapter 7.
67. B. Grant, *The Australian Dilemma* (Sydney, 1983), 50.
68. For Speaker Scholes's letter of 12 November 1975 to the Queen, see Whitlam, *supra* note 59 at 175–6.
69. See D. Horne, *Death of The Lucky Country* (Ringwood, Vic., 1976), 54; Howard, *supra* note 8 at 67, 77, 78 ('governor-generalship'). See also Whitlam, *supra* note 59 at 183, 185.
70. See Howard, *supra* note 8 at 69, 72, 79, 81, 83; Horne, *supra* note 1 at 38–9.
71. Cf. Winterton, *supra* note 54 at 155–6.

3   The Crown in Australian Government

1. See *supra*, chapter 2, note 6 and accompanying text.
2. On the appointment of governors and Governors-General, see G. Winterton, *Parliament, the Executive and the Governor-General* (Melbourne, 1983), 17–20; *Official Record of Debates of the Australian Constitutional Convention* (Adelaide, 1983), 319; D. P. O'Connell, 'Monarchy or Republic?', in *Republican Australia?* (G. Dutton ed., Melbourne, 1977), 23, 39. But see *supra*, chapter 2 note 5 (the 1976 'Hannah affair').
3. See the Commonwealth Constitution section 59; the Australian Constitutions Act 1842 (U.K.) section 32; the Australian Constitutions Act 1850 (U.K.) section 12; the New South Wales Constitution Act 1855 (U.K.) section 3; the Victoria Constitution Act 1855 (U.K.) section 3; the Constitution Act 1867 (Qd.) section 13; the Western Australia Constitution Act 1890 (U.K.) section 2.
4. H. R. Anderson, 'The Constitutional Framework', in *The Government of the Australian States* (S. R. Davis ed., Melbourne, 1960), 3, 6.
5. In 1975, 1976 and 1983: see Winterton, *supra* note 2 at 218 note 186; *Official Record of Debates of the Australian Constitutional Convention* (Adelaide, 1983), 321.
6. See clause 7 of the Bill (repealing section 59).
7. See the Australian States Constitution Act 1907 (U.K.) section 1; the Constitution Act 1867 (Qd.) section 11B; the Constitution Act 1889 (W.A.) section 51(1); R. D. Lumb, *The Constitutions of the Australian States* (4th ed., St Lucia, 1977), 71–2, 130–1.
8. See the Australian Constitutions Act 1842 (U.K.) section 31, and the provisions of the other five Acts cited, *supra* note 3.
9. See the Commonwealth Constitution section 58. For recent examples, see Winterton, *supra* note 2 at 218 note 185.
10. The Commonwealth Constitution section 74 para. 3.
11. See *Official Record of Debates of the Australian Constitutional Convention* (Adelaide, 1983), 319, 320 (items 1, 2, 10 and 28); Lumb, *supra* note 7 at 72 note 48; C. Saunders and E. Smith, *A Paper . . . Identifying the Conventions Associated with the Commonwealth Constitution* (Australian Constitutional Convention, Standing Committee D, 1980), 6, 12–13. (This paper is Appendix G to Standing Committee D's Fourth Report in *Proceedings of the Australian Constitutional Convention* (Adelaide 1983), vol. 2.)

12. Clauses 6, 8 and 10.
13. See *Official Record of Debates of the Australian Constitutional Convention* (Adelaide, 1983), 321.
14. See the Constitution Act 1867 (Qd.) section 16; the Constitution Act 1934 (S.A.) section 75; the Constitution Act 1889 (W.A.) section 55.
15. See Winterton, *supra* note 2 at 22–6; *Official Record of Debates of the Australian Constitutional Convention* (Adelaide, 1983), 320 (item 11).
16. Reprinted in G. Sawer, *Federation Under Strain* (Melbourne, 1977), 211.
17. Letters Patent of 21 August 1984, in Commonwealth of Australia *Gazette*, No. S 334 (24 August 1984).
18. See the Constitution Act 1889 (W.A.) section 51(1).
19. *Official Record of Debates of the Australian Constitutional Convention* (Adelaide, 1983), 319 (items 1 and 2).
20. See Saunders and Smith, *supra* note 11 at 12–13.
21. The closest is the provision that the governor is to be the Queen's representative in the State: the Constitution Act 1975 (Vic.) section 6; the Constitution Act 1889 (W.A.) section 50(1).
22. For a good description of the role of a State governor, see R. S. Parker, *The Government of New South Wales* (St Lucia, 1978), 171–86.
23. This is as true for the States as for the Commonwealth, notwithstanding a provision in the governors' royal Instructions allowing him to act 'in opposition to the opinion of the [Executive] Council' (but he must report his action and reasons to the Queen without delay) 'if in any case he shall see sufficient cause to dissent' therefrom (although he is, in general, to be 'guided by the advice of the Executive Council'). See, e.g., clause VI of the Queensland Governor's Royal Instructions (1925), in Lumb, *supra* note 7 at 130. A virtually identical provision appears in the royal Instructions of the other States' governors. This clause is obsolete: ibid., 74 note 65; M. C. Harris and J. R. Crawford. '"The Powers and Authorities Vested in Him": The Discretionary Authority of State Governors and the Power of Dissolution' (1969) 3 *Adel. L. Rev.* 303, 312–15. The High Court has recognized that State governors must act in accordance with ministerial advice: *F.A.I. Insurances Ltd.* v. *Winneke* (1982) 151 C.L.R. 342, 349 (Gibbs C. J.), 355–6 (Stephen J.), 364–6 (Mason J.), 373 (Murphy J.), 382–3 (Aickin J.), 396–7, 400–1 (Wilson J.), 414–16 (Brennan J.). The clause of the royal Instructions mentioned above was noted by Mason, Wilson and Brennan JJ. (ibid., 365, 396–7, 415).
24. See W. Bagehot, *The English Constitution* (London and Glasgow, 1963; orig. publ. 1867), 111: '[T]he sovereign has, under a constitutional monarchy such as ours, three rights — the right to be consulted, the right to encourage, the right to warn. And a king of great sense and sagacity would want no others.' Bagehot's observation was endorsed by Wilson J. in *F.A.I. Insurances Ltd.* v. *Winneke* (1982) 151 C.L.R. 342, 401. But see the comments of Murphy and Aickin JJ. (ibid., 373, 383) noted in Winterton, *supra* note 2 at 325 note 75. Professor R. S. Parker has remarked that, although they have Bagehot's three rights, 'there is not a great deal of evidence of N.S.W. governors playing the part of counsellor and confidant to their ministers to the extent attributed to British sovereigns since Victoria's time.': *supra* note 22 at 172.

25. P. Hasluck, *The Office of Governor-General* (Melbourne, 1979), 17-20, 38-42, endorsed by Sir John Kerr, 'The Governor-Generalship in Australia' (1975) 17 *J. of the Indian Law Institute* 1, 3-5. Sir Zelman Cowen also has recently emphasized the Governor-General's constructive role in ensuring regularity in government, especially in the proceedings of the Federal Executive Council: Z. Cowen, 'The Office of Governor-General' (1985) 114 *Daedalus*, No. 1, 127, 141-2. (This issue was also published as a book, *Australia: The Daedalus Symposium* (S. R. Graubard ed., Sydney, 1985).) See also J. Kerr, *Matters for Judgment* (Melbourne, 1978), 229-30 (justiciable matters should be left to the courts). For some vice-regal exercises of the 'right to warn', see C. Lloyd and A. Clark, *Kerr's King Hit!* (Sydney, 1976), 62-3; P. Howson, *The Life of Politics: The Howson Diaries* (D. Aitkin ed., Ringwood, Vic., 1984), 288, 851.

Professor Colin Howard rightly criticized some of Sir Paul Hasluck's more controversial assertions of power: see F. Brenchley, 'Hasluck Claim: An Active Watchdog at Yarralumla', *National Times*, 27 November-2 December 1972, pp. 1, 8, reprinted in *National Times*, 19-25 April 1981, p. 32. However, many commentators appear to accept that the Governor-General can properly defer matters brought to the Executive Council in order to ensure that they accord with government policy: see Kerr, *Matters for Judgment, supra*, at 228-9; Sawer, *supra* note 16 at 104; Lloyd and Clark, *supra*, at 64. Professor H. V. Emy appears to go too far in asserting that 'The Governor-General is responsible for checking that the advice tendered to him is *cabinet advice.*': *The Politics of Australian Democracy* (2nd ed., Melbourne, 1978), 157 (emphasis added). Professor Geoffrey Sawer has noted that 'Very little of the business of Cabinet goes to the Executive Council, and hardly any of the business of the Executive Council goes to Cabinet.': 'Cabinet Secrecy-Limits of the Law', *Canberra Times*, 10 August 1983, p. 2.

26. The Acts Interpretation Act 1901 (C'th) section 16A; the Interpretation Act 1897 (N.S.W.) section 15(ii); the Acts Interpretation Act 1915 (S.A.) section 23; the Interpretation Act 1918 (W.A.) section 23; the Acts Interpretation Act 1931 (Tas.) section 43(1).

27. This sentence states the realistic position, but a pedant may argue that even a reserve power can only be exercised on ministerial 'advice' because some minister must always take responsibility (to parliament) for the vice-regal exercise of power — even if the viceroy has to change ministers to ensure this. This doctrine of *ex post facto* responsibility is a sham, and should be discarded: see Sawer, *supra* note 16 at 143-4; Winterton, *supra* note 2 at 197-8 note 12.

28. Most commentators appear to believe that the restraints on the Governor-General's exercise of a reserve power have the status merely of 'conventions of the Constitution', whereas the better view is that they are implied provisions of the Commonwealth Constitution: see Winterton, *supra* note 2 at 124-7, 128-9, 151; C. Howard, *Australian Federal Constitutional Law* (3rd ed., Sydney, 1985), 117, 123, 137. For the purposes of the current work, the restraints will be treated as conventions, which is clearly their correct status in the United Kingdom and, probably, the Australian States.

29. The authors are Professor Geoffrey Sawer, Professor (now Justice) Ryan (two papers), Geoffrey Lindell and the present writer. Standing Committee D considered the papers of Professors Sawer and Ryan and drafted a list of 'practices' to be recognized by the Adelaide Convention. After a brief debate at the Convention, they were referred to the Standing Committee for further study, followed by consideration by the Brisbane Convention in July–August 1985 which adopted eighteen 'principles' (appended to this chapter).

30. For some of the literature, see Winterton, *supra* note 2 at 196 note 12; G. Marshall, *Constitutional Conventions* (Oxford, 1984), chs 2 and 3.

31. See the Commonwealth Constitution sections 5, 28, 57, 62, and 64; Lumb, *supra* note 7 at 72 (State provisions).

32. See Winterton, *supra* note 2 at 154–5.

33. *Report of the Imperial Conference, 1926* (Cmd. 2768), 16.

34. See G. Marshall and G. C. Moodie, *Some Problems of the Constitution* (5th ed., London, 1971), 41.

35. See, e.g., Lumb, *supra* note 7 at 77; A. C. Castles, 'Limitations on the Autonomy of the Australian States' [1962] *Public Law* 175, 179–82.

36. *Report, supra* note 33 at 16.

37. See D. Dunstan, 'The State, the Governors and the Crown', in *Republican Australia?* (G. Dutton ed., Melbourne, 1977), 202, 208. (See also *supra*, chapter 2 note 6.) Yet Premier Dunstan noted that '[t]he Governors see themselves as delegates not only of the Queen, but of that foreign government to which they refer for advice.': ibid., 207.

38. See, e.g., the Queensland Royal Instructions clauses VII and VIII, in Lumb, *supra* note 7 at 130–1. (The governor must reserve Bills inconsistent with British (presumably) treaties or prejudicing British trade and shipping and, in considering whether to grant a pardon which might directly affect the interests of the British Empire, the governor must 'take those interests specially into his own personal consideration' in conjunction with ministerial advice.)

39. E. A. Forsey, *The Royal Power of Dissolution of Parliament in the British Commonwealth* (Toronto, 1943, repr. Toronto, 1968), 5; accord Harris and Crawford, *supra* note 23 at 317–19.

40. H. V. Evatt, *The King and His Dominion Governors* (2nd ed., London, 1967), 216.

41. J. I. Fajgenbaum and P. J. Hanks, *Australian Constitutional Law* (2nd ed. by P. J. Hanks, Sydney, 1980), 351.

42. Parker, *supra* note 22 at 182.

43. E. Forsey, *Freedom and Order* (Toronto, 1974), 60.

44. See, e.g., Winterton, *supra* note 2 at 7; *Re Resolution to Amend the Constitution* [1981] 1 S.C.R. 753, 857–8, 878.

45. Ibid., 882.

46. Harris and Crawford, *supra* note 23 at 305–07, 319; V. Bogdanor, *Multi-party Politics and the Constitution* (Cambridge, 1983), 104–05, 108–12. But cf. the comment of six judges of the Supreme Court of Canada: 'it is a fundamental requirement of the constitution that if the opposition obtains a majority at the polls, the government must tender its resignation *forthwith*.': *Re Resolution to Amend the Constitution* [1981] 1 S.C.R. 753, 878 (emphasis added).

47. Bogdanor, *supra* note 46 at 109–10 (emphasis in original).
48. See ibid., 95–7, 104–5.
49. For a good discussion of the various situations that can arise after a general election, see R. Brazier, 'Choosing A Prime Minister' [1982] *Public Law* 395, 397–403.
50. See Bogdanor, *supra* note 46 at 110–12.
51. See ibid., 152–9, 164–6.
52. For the statistics of the election results, see C. A. Hughes and B. D. Graham, *A Handbook of Australian Government and Politics 1890–1964* (Canberra, 1968); C. A. Hughes, *A Handbook of Australian Government and Politics 1965–1974* (Canberra, 1977).
53. As proposed in Winterton, *supra* note 2 at 157; D. Horne, E. Thompson, D. Jaensch and K. Turner, *Changing the System* (APSA Monograph No. 25, 1981), 17; and Brazier, *supra* note 49 at 410–11 (but it is not clear why Brazier recommends that the House of Commons vote by secret ballot). One commentator has remarked of Brazier's proposal that: 'It seems safe to predict . . . that such a novel and adventurous constitutional expedient will not in fact be adopted.': Marshall, *supra* note 30 at 33–4.
54. See Irish Constitution article 13.1.1°; FRG Basic Law article 63; Japanese Constitution article 6; PNG Constitution section 142(2).
55. D. P. O'Brien, 'The Powers of the Governor-General to Dissolve the Houses of Parliament' (unpublished LL.M. thesis, Australian National University, 1982), 378; for a fuller quotation, see *infra*, text accompanying note 119.
56. For a recent discussion, see Brazier, *supra* note 49 at 403–08.
57. See ibid., 407.
58. S. Encel, *Cabinet Government in Australia* (2nd ed., Melbourne, 1974), 163.
59. If the deputy leadership of the party were vacant, the senior minister would be the appropriate interim prime minister.
60. This assertion is questionable, although it may strictly be correct that the Governor-General, Lord Gowrie, decided to commission Page before Page interviewed him. Page's account in his autobiography is unclear on this point, concentrating instead on his advice that his commission should be unqualified: E. Page, *Truant Surgeon* (Sydney, 1963), 268–9. Page also omits to mention that he and Hughes telephoned Sir John Latham, Chief Justice of the High Court, to seek his advice. Latham recommended that Page advise the Governor-General to appoint him interim Prime Minister: see J. G. Latham, Book Review (of *Truant Surgeon*) (1963) 7 *Quadrant*, No. 4, 82–3.
61. 159 *Commonwealth Parliamentary Debates* 15 (20 April 1939) (emphasis added).
62. See A. Reid, *The Power Struggle* (Sydney, 1969), 116–17, 130. McEwen had undertaken to step down as soon as the new Liberal leader was elected.
63. See ibid., 25–30.
64. See ibid.
65. See ibid., 22–3, 25–6, 105, 107, 122, 131, 152; Howson, *supra* note 25 at 365, 366.

66. See Reid, *supra* note 62 at 22–30, 102–04.
67. See ibid., 103–4 (seeking, while Governor-General, to patch up the McEwen-McMahon feud), an account corroborated by McEwen in the *Australian*, 20 January 1969, p. 1; Howson, *supra* note 25 at 36, 420, 491, 560, 567–8, 570–1, 573, 585, 586, 588, 593, 645–6 (after retirement as Governor-General, involved in moves to depose Gorton from the prime ministership).
68. Reid, *supra* note 62 at 103. (Of course, during Casey's term of office, 1965–69, all governments were of only one 'political complexion'.) Reid also notes that nine days before Holt died, Casey, apparently with the Prime Minister's consent, had discussed the McEwen–McMahon feud with the latter, and 'advised McMahon that his difficulties with McEwen could affect the stability of the coalition and hence the stability of the Government. He had told McMahon that he, as Governor-General, must be concerned about the maintenance of stable government in Australia.': ibid.
69. D. Aitkin, 'Political Review' (1969) 41 *Australian Quarterly*, No. 1, 68.
70. Ibid., 69.
71. See statement quoted *supra*, text accompanying note 61.
72. See Page, *supra* note 60 at 270–8; C. Edwards, *Bruce of Melbourne: Man of Two Worlds* (London, 1965), 264–6.
73. See Reid, *supra* note 62 at 113, 117–18, 121, 134, 144–6, 147–9, 153–5, 179, 198.
74. See ibid., 27, 117.
75. See, especially, William McMahon's comments, reported in Howson, *supra* note 25 at 367. See also Reid, *supra* note 62 at 102–09; L. F. Crisp, *Australian National Government* (5th ed., Melbourne, 1983), 410.
76. For the details, see: on Hughes: L. F. Fitzhardinge, *The Little Digger 1914–1952* (Sydney, 1979), 219ff.; E. Scott, *Australia During the War* (Sydney, 1936) (The Official History of Australia in the War of 1914–1918, vol. 11), ch. X; on Holman: H. V. Evatt, *Australian Labour Leader* (2nd ed., Sydney, 1942), 407ff.
77. See *Re Resolution to Amend the Constitution* [1981] 1 S.C.R. 753, 857–8, 878. For the eight Commonwealth resolutions of no-confidence in the government, see *House of Representatives Practice* (J. A. Pettifer ed., Canberra, 1981), 419–22.
78. See *Official Record of Debates of the Australian Constitutional Convention* (Adelaide 1983), 321 (item 32).
79. For an example, see 97 *Commonwealth Parliamentary Debates*, H. of R., 2930–2 (11 November 1975): 'That this House expresses its want of confidence in the Prime Minister [Malcolm Fraser] and requests the Speaker to immediately advise His Excellency, the Governor-General, to call the honourable member for Werriwa [Gough Whitlam] to form a government.'
80. See Marshall and Moodie, *supra* note 34 at 43–4.
81. See the authorities noted in the present writer's opinion on Practice 20(d) (referred to *supra* note 29): Australian Constitutional Convention 1984, Structure of Government Sub-Committee, *Report to Standing Committee* (August 1984), Appendix B, 28, 29.
82. See *Adegbenro* v. *Akintola* [1963] A.C. 614, 631 (P.C.); W. I. Jennings, *Cabinet Government* (3rd ed., Cambridge, 1959), 403–12.

83. *Adegbenro* v. *Akintola* [1963] A.C. 614, 631 per Viscount Radcliffe.
84. B. S. Markesinis, *The Theory and Practice of Dissolution of Parliament* (Cambridge, 1972), 115.
85. S. A. de Smith, *Constitutional and Administrative Law* (4th ed. by H. Street and R. Brazier, Harmondsworth, 1981), 124.
86. [1975–76] 2 *South Australian Parliamentary Debates* 1835, 1875.
87. 'Introduction', in Evatt, *supra* note 40 at xxxv.
88. *Ningkan* v. *Tun Abang Haji Openg* [1966] 2 *Malayan Law Journal* 187, 194 (Borneo H. C.).
89. Marshall, *supra* note 30 at 27, 28.
90. See *supra*, note 80 and accompanying text.
91. See E. G. Whitlam, *The Truth of the Matter* (2nd ed., Ringwood, Vic., 1983), 130 (reporting the view of a State governor who had formerly been Chief Justice); Jennings, *supra* note 82 at 412.
92. See the correspondence of 12–13 May 1932 between Governor Game and Premier Lang in A. S. Morrison, 'Dominions Office Correspondence on the New South Wales Constitutional Crisis 1930–1932' (1976) 61 *J.R.A.H.S.* 323, 342–3.
93. See Evatt, *supra* note 40 at 163, 173–4; J. M. Ward, 'The Dismissal', in *Jack Lang* (H. Radi and P. Spearritt eds, Sydney, 1977), 160, 170.
94. See Governor Game's letter of 2 July 1932, quoted in B. Foott, *Dismissal of a Premier* (Sydney, 1968), 223.
95. A. S. Morrison, 'Further Documents and Comment on the New South Wales Constitutional Crisis 1930–1932' (1982) 68 *J.R.A.H.S.* 122, 125–6.
96. Marshall, *supra* note 30 at 27 (emphasis added).
97. See Governor-General Kerr's Statement of 11 November 1975, in Sawer, *supra* note 16 at 207–10.
98. See Barwick C. J.'s letter of 10 November 1975, in ibid., 203–4.
99. G. Barwick, *Sir John Did His Duty* (Sydney, 1983), 5, 55, 66–7, 85, 94, 96, 99–100, 110, 114–15, 122, 124, 127.
100. See, e.g., Sawer, *supra* note 16, ch. 8, esp. at 160, 172; G. Winterton, 'The Third Man' (1984) 28 *Quadrant*, No. 4, 23–5; G. Evans, 'Repatriating the Debate' (1984) 28 *Quadrant*, No. 11, 76–7; J. A. Thomson, Book Review (1983) 6 *U.N.S.W.L.J.* 255, 255–6, and notes.
101. See the Constitution Act 1902 (N.S.W.) section 5A.
102. The principal authorities are marshalled in K. W. Ryan, *The Power of the Governor-General to Dissolve the House of Representatives and Both Houses of Parliament*, noted *supra* note 29, paras 22–42. (This paper is Appendix E to Standing Committee D's Fourth Report in *Proceedings of the Australian Constitutional Convention* (Adelaide, 1983), vol. 2.)
103. See especially Evatt, *supra* note 40, ch. VII; Forsey, *supra* note 39, chs V and VI; *The King-Byng Affair, 1926: A Question of Responsible Government* (R. Graham ed., Toronto, 1967).
104. See Forsey, *supra* note 39, ch. VII.
105. See Jennings, *supra* note 82 at 414–15, 424.
106. See Bogdanor, *supra* note 46 at 101–4, 159.
107. See E. Campbell, 'The Prerogative Power of Dissolution: Some Recent Tasmanian Precedents' [1961] *Public Law* 165; W. A. Townsley, *The Government of Tasmania* (St Lucia, 1976), 108–11; W. H. Craig, 'The

Governor's Reserve Powers in Relation to the Dissolution of the Tasmania House of Assembly' (1960) 1 *Tas.U.L.Rev.* 488.

108. Hasluck *supra* note 25 at 15–16.
109. Kerr, 'The Governor-Generalship in Australia', *supra* note 25 at 5–6.
110. Kerr, *Matters for Judgment, supra* note 25 at 403–15.
111. Markesinis, *supra* note 84 at 120; Ryan, *supra* note 102 at paras. 33–34; D. O'Brien, Letter to the Editor, *Age*, 30 July 1982, p. 12.
112. Sawer, *supra* note 16 at 156.
113. See Jennings, *supra* note 82 at 424, 425.
114. Marshall, *supra* note 30 at 38.
115. With respect, Professor Sawer adopts too liberal a standard in holding that 'a Governor may reject [advice to dissolve] if there is a *clear possibility* that an alternative Chief Minister could be found': *supra* note 16 at 155–6 (emphasis added). Dr Bogdanor's view is preferable: 'The Sovereign, if she is to take the risk of refusing a dissolution, must have a *cast-iron public guarantee* that a government can be formed commanding the confidence of the Commons.': *supra* note 46 at 161 (emphasis added).
116. Letter to the Editor, *Times*, 2 May 1950, in Markesinis, *supra* note 84 at 263; accord de Smith, *supra* note 85 at 126.
117. See O. Hood Phillips, *Constitutional and Administrative Law* (6th ed. by O. Hood Phillips and P. Jackson, London, 1978), 150–1; Ryan, *supra* note 102 at paras. 39–41.
118. E.g., the King-Byng crisis of 1926 in Canada.
119. O'Brien, *supra* note 55 at 377–8.
120. For provisions along these lines, see the government's Constitution Alteration (Fixed Term Parliaments) Bill 1983 (C'th) clause 2(2), and Haddon Storey M. L. C.'s Constitution (Reform) Bill 1983 (Vic.) clause 7. In both cases, the stipulated period was eight days.
121. Bogdanor, *supra* note 46 at 162.
122. See Marshall and Moodie, *supra* note 34 at 43–4; Forsey, *supra* note 39 at 260–1; Markesinis, *supra* note 84 at 120.
123. See the Constitution Act 1975 (Vic.) section 8(3), added by the Constitution (Duration of Parliament) Act 1984 (Vic.) section 4; the Constitution Act 1934 (S.A.) sections 28 and 28a, introduced by the Constitution Act Amendment Act 1985 (S.A.) section 4.
124. See the Commonwealth Constitution section 57, and the Constitution Act 1934 (S.A.) section 41.
125. See Forsey, *supra* note 39 at 270–1, doubted by Ryan, *supra* note 102 at paras. 7, 9 and 10.
126. See Markesinis, *supra* note 84 at 115, 120.
127. See the Commonwealth Constitution section 64 para. 3; Lumb, *supra* note 7 at 68–9. In the Commonwealth, Victoria and South Australia, a minister must become a member of parliament within three months.
128. See Winterton, *supra* note 2 at 79; Barwick, *supra* note 99 at 42, 45, 65.
129. *Report of the Royal Commission into the Constitution Act 1934 Tasmania* (Hobart, 1982), para. 5.77.
130. See the Constitution Act 1902 (N.S.W.) section 5A.
131. See the Commonwealth Constitution section 83; Lumb, *supra* note 7 at 69.

4 Types of Republic Government

1. Quoted in B. Stannard, 'The Quiet Man of Yarralumla', *Bulletin*, 12 February 1985, 62, 65.
2. See A. J. Wilson, *The Gaullist System in Asia* (London, 1980).
3. B. Grant, *The Australian Dilemma* (Sydney, 1983), 309.
4. V. Wright, *The Government and Politics of France* (2nd ed., London, 1983), 24.
5. Ibid., 130, 143.
6. Quoted in 1 D. Pickles, *The Government and Politics of France* (London, 1972), 142.
7. Quoted in W. G. Andrews, *Presidential Government in Gaullist France: A Study of Executive-Legislative Relations 1958–1974* (Albany, N.Y., 1982), 25; accord Edmond Michelet, quoted ibid., 32.
8. Andrews, *supra* note 7 at 28.
9. Ibid., 29.
10. Ibid., 30.
11. Wright, *supra* note 4 at 24–5 (emphasis added).
12. Pierre Viansson-Ponté, quoted in Pickles, *supra* note 6 at 131.
13. Ibid.
14. J. R. Frears, *France in the Giscard Presidency* (London, 1981), 37, 161, 212–13.
15. L. Derfler, *President & Parliament* (Boca Raton, Fla., 1983), 169.
16. Ibid., 189.
17. Quoted, ibid.
18. Pierre Viansson-Ponté, quoted ibid., 192.
19. See ibid. for a description.
20. Frears, *supra* note 14 at 30.
21. Ibid.
22. See ibid. 39; Derfler, *supra* note 15 at 233.
23. See the French Constitution article 5.
24. See S. E. Finer, *Comparative Government* (London, 1970), 321–4, 337–9; Pickles, *supra* note 6 at 116–22; Wright, *supra* note 4 at 35; Derfler, *supra* note 15 at 180, 183, 245–6.
25. See Frears, *supra* note 14 at 34; Derfler, *supra* note 15 at 178, 181.
26. Wright, *supra* note 4 at 25.
27. See ibid., 52–3; D. Geddes, 'Clinging on to power — if he can', *Times*, 4 March 1986, p. 12; Derfler, *supra* note 15 at 178, 205, 210, 223, 233; Frears, *supra* note 14 at 161, 211.
28. See ibid., 49, 211.
29. See ibid., 49.
30. See Wright, *supra* note 4, ch. 2; Derfler, *supra* note 15 at 210–11, 212–13, 221, 222; Frears, *supra* note 14 at 161, 166, 211; R. W. Johnson, 'By the Left, Slow March', *Times*, 29 December 1983, p. 8.
31. See Wright, *supra* note 4 at 54–8.
32. See Derfler, *supra* note 15 at 177, 178, 181, 183, 188–9; Finer, *supra* note 24 at 335ff.
33. Article 8.
34. Quoted in Andrews, *supra* note 7 at 18; accord Guy Mollet, quoted ibid., 29.
35. French Constitution article 21.
36. Ibid., article 20.

37. Derfler, *supra* note 15 at 185.
38. C. de Gaulle, *Memoirs of Hope* (transl. by T. Kilmartin, London, 1971), 274.
39. Ibid., 31–2.
40. Frears, *supra* note 14 at 33.
41. See *supra* note 30; 'Oil Scandal Blame for Giscard', *Times*, 22 November 1984, p. 6 (a parliamentary report held that former President Giscard d'Estaing had acted 'contrary to the Constitution' in not informing his Prime Minister, Jacques Chirac, of his project involving aerial search for oil).
42. See Derfler, *supra* note 15 at 224 (President Giscard d'Estaing). Contrast President de Gaulle's assertion that he never gave orders to officials over ministers' heads: *supra* note 38 at 274.
43. See Wright, *supra* note 4 at 29, 83, 85–6; Derfler, *supra* note 15 at 185, 208, 224, 227; Frears, *supra* note 14 at 38; E. N. Suleiman, *Politics, Power, and Bureaucracy in France* (Princeton, 1974), 360 (when appointed Prime Minister by President Pompidou in July 1972, Pierre Messmer's ministers, and even his principal advisers, were chosen for him by the Elysée).
44. French Constitution article 8.
45. Wright, *supra* note 4 at 77.
46. See ibid., 67; Derfler, *supra* note 15 at 223, 226; E. N. Suleiman, 'Presidential Government in France', in *Presidents and Prime Ministers* (R. Rose and E. N. Suleiman eds, Washington D.C., 1980), 94, 108, 109–10.
47. See de Gaulle, *supra* note 38 at 275.
48. Quoted in Frears, *supra* note 14 at 35.
49. Quoted in Derfler, *supra* note 15 at 209.
50. Frears, *supra* note 14 at 36.
51. Quoted in Wright, *supra* note 4 at 84.
52. Ibid., 43, 83.
53. Editorial, 'Enter the Dauphin', *Times*, 19 July 1984, p. 13.
54. See, e.g., Pickles, *supra* note 6 at 141–3; Wright, *supra* note 4 at 83, 145–6; Derfler, *supra* note 15 at 246.
55. Quoted in Pickles, *supra* note 6 at 142.
56. See 'Mitterrand toys with a change in the rules', *Economist*, 15 September 1984, p. 41.
57. See ibid.; A. Tillier, 'Mitterrand may cut his term', *Times*, 23 August 1984, p. 6; Derfler, *supra* note 15 at 211.
58. See Frears, *supra* note 14 at 160, 161.
59. See Wilson, *supra* note 2 at 45–7.
60. See the Constitution of Kiribati section 33 (2)(b) and (c).
61. See, e.g., D. Housego, 'Mitterrand: now the real battle has begun', *Financial Times*, 12 February 1985, p. 26.
62. See, e.g., ibid.; 'Boxed-in Mitterrand', *Economist*, 26 January 1985, p. 15; D. Housego, 'The trap France must avoid', *Financial Times*, 19 November 1984, p. 13 (reprinted, *Canberra Times*, 4 December 1984, p. 2); R. Joseph, 'Centre-right in France begins the long march back towards power', *Canberra Times*, 12 November 1984, p. 2; D. Geddes, 'Barre's refusal to serve with the left threatens fragile opposition accord', *Times*, 17 April 1985, p. 9; Editorial, 'France in 1986', *Times*, 13 May

1985, p. 13; 'The rule-book isn't much help', *Economist*, 11 January 1986, p. 37; Geddes, *supra* note 27; D. Geddes, 'France girds itself for conflict at the top', *Times*, 2 January 1986, p. 12.

63. See Housego, *supra* note 61; D. Geddes, 'Offer to "Cohabit" with Right', *Times*, 22 November 1985, p. 9.
64. See Wright, *supra* note 4 at 146.
65. See Pickles, *supra* note 6 at 369 note 107; Derfler, *supra* note 15 at 214.
66. See Pickles, *supra* note 6 at 142.
67. See the French Constitution article 12.
68. See Housego, *supra* note 62.
69. See Derfler, *supra* note 15 at 233, referring to Philippe Boucher in *Le Monde*, 5 December 1980 and others.
70. See the French Constitution articles 34 and 37.
71. Frears, *supra* note 14 at 161 (emphasis added).
72. Ibid., 32.
73. Ibid., 162, 165 (emphasis added).
74. Ibid., 209; accord ibid., 16, 30; Housego, *supra* note 61.
75. Finer, *supra* note 24 at 332 (emphasis in original); accord Derfler, *supra* note 15 at 175.
76. Finer, *supra* note 24 at 332.
77. See Frears, *supra* note 14 at 199; W. S. Livingston, 'Britain and America: The Institutionalization of Accountability' (1976) 38 *J. of Politics* 879, 894.
78. Quoted in Derfler, *supra* note 15 at 235.
79. Frears, *supra* note 14 at 214–15.

5   Parliamentary Executive or Executive Presidency?

1. *The Federalist* (J. E. Cooke ed., Middletown, Conn., 1961), 494 (No. 73). Accord ibid., 333 (No. 48, Madison): 'parchment barriers'.
2. See ibid., 333–6, 341 (Nos 48 and 49, Madison), 483, 494 (Nos 71 and 73, Hamilton); 2 M. Farrand, *The Records of the Federal Convention of 1787* (rev. ed., New Haven, 1937), 35, 74 (remarks of James Madison).
3. See M. J. C. Vile, *Constitutionalism and the Separation of Powers* (Oxford, 1967), ch. VI; G. S. Wood, *The Creation of the American Republic, 1776–1787* (Chapel Hill, 1969), 547–53.
4. *The Federalist, supra* note 1 at 323 (No. 47, Madison).
5. Ibid., 332, 349 (Nos 48 and 51). Accord 2 Farrand, *supra* note 2 at 77 (remarks of James Madison).
6. *The Federalist, supra* note 1 at 445 (No. 66). Accord ibid., 494 (No. 73, Hamilton).
7. R. E. Neustadt, *Presidential Power: The Politics of Leadership from FDR to Carter* (New York, 1980), 26 (emphasis in original).
8. *The Federalist, supra* note 1 at 522 (No. 78, Hamilton).
9. Ibid., 523.
10. For discussion of whether impeachment constitutes the only method of removing federal judges, see I. R. Kaufman, 'Chilling Judicial Independence' (1979) 88 *Yale L. J.* 681, 691–703 (Yes); Association of the Bar of the City of New York, Committee on Federal Legislation, *The Removal of Federal Judges Other than by Impeachment* (New York,

1 April 1977), 9ff. (Yes) (a precis of this report is published in (1977) 32 *Record of the Assoc. of the Bar of the City of N.Y.* 239); R. Berger, *Impeachment: The Constitutional Problems* (Cambridge, Mass., 1973), ch. IV (impeachment is not the sole method).

11. *Buckley* v. *Valeo* (1976) 424 U.S. 1.
12. *Myers* v. *United States* (1926) 272 U.S. 52.
13. J. L. Sundquist, *The Decline and Resurgence of Congress* (Washington D.C., 1981), 462.
14. W. S. Livingston, 'Britain and America: The Institutionalization of Accountability' (1976) 38 *J. of Politics* 879, 882.
15. P. Peterson, 'Separation of Powers and Checks and Balances: The Delicate Balance between Republican Liberty and Power', in *Taking the Constitution Seriously* (G. L. McDowell ed., Dubuque, Iowa, 1981), 193, 195.
16. See the United States Constitution article II section 2(1). The Twenty-Fifth Amendment section 4 (adopted in 1967) also refers to 'the principal officers of the executive departments'.
17. N. W. Polsby, 'Some Landmarks in Modern Presidential-Congressional Relations', in *Both Ends of the Avenue: The Presidency, the Executive Branch, and Congress in the 1980s* (A. King ed., Washington D.C., 1983), 1, 20 (emphasis in original). See also H. Heclo, 'One Executive Branch or Many?', ibid., 26ff.; ex-President Gerald Ford, 'Imperiled, Not Imperial', *Time*, 10 November 1980, 28.
18. Ibid., 29.
19. C. Rossiter, *The American Presidency* (2nd ed., New York, 1960), 15.
20. T. Engeman, 'Presidential Statesmanship and the Constitution: The Limits of Presidential Studies' (1982) 44 *Rev. of Politics* 266, 281.
21. T. C. Sorensen, *Watchmen in the Night: Presidential Accountability After Watergate* (Cambridge, Mass., 1975), 29.
22. Ibid., 72 (emphasis in original).
23. A. M. Schlesinger, Jr., *The Imperial Presidency* (Boston, 1973).
24. 'The Post-Watergate Presidency' (1974) 11 *Colum. J. of Law and Social Probs.* 11, 17.
25. Ibid., 19.
26. See, e.g., W. F. Mullen, *Presidential Power and Politics* (New York, 1976), 258ff.; G. E. Reedy, *The Twilight of the Presidency* (New York, 1970). Contrast ex-President Nixon, 'Needed: Clarity of Purpose', *Time*, 10 November 1980, 30, 35.
27. Rossiter, *supra* note 19 at 15–16.
28. P. B. Kurland, *Watergate and the Constitution* (Chicago, 1978), 153.
29. TRB (Richard Strout), 'Parliamentarianism', *New Republic*, 28 September 1974, p. 4. See also Mullen, *supra* note 26 at 262.
30. See A. M. Schlesinger, Jr., *The Imperial Presidency* (Popular Library ed., New York, 1974), 461–4 (epilogue to the work noted *supra*, note 23); A. Schlesinger, Jr., 'Parliamentary Government', *New Republic*, 31 August 1974, 13–15.
31. See, e.g., J. M. Burns, *The Power to Lead* (New York, 1984), 197–211, 237; L. N. Cutler, 'To Form a Government' (1980) 59 *Foreign Affairs* 126, especially 139ff.; W. Wilson, *Congressional Government* (Boston, 1885).

32. See Sundquist, *supra* note 13 at 464–7; Reedy, *supra* note 26 at 173.
33. See Sundquist, *supra* note 13 at 425, 439, 456–7.
34. See, e.g. ibid., 153, 441–57, 481.
35. See ibid., 445.
36. *Myers* v. *United States* (1926) 272 U.S. 52, 293 per Brandeis J.
37. N. W. Polsby, *Congress and the Presidency* (3rd ed., Englewood Cliffs, N. J., 1976), 191.
38. L. Henkin, *Foreign Affairs and the Constitution* (Mineola, N.Y., 1972), 33.
39. For this development, see Schlesinger, *supra* note 23.
40. L. W. Koenig, 'Historical Perspective: The Swings and Roundabouts of Presidential Power', in *The Tethered Presidency* (T. M. Franck ed., New York, 1981), 38, 43.
41. L. H. Tribe, *American Constitutional Law* (Mineola, N.Y., 1978), 157.
42. United States Constitution article II section 3.
43. See ibid., article I section 7(2) and (3).
44. Ibid., article I section 7(1).
45. Contrast the Commonwealth Constitution section 56.
46. J. F. Manley, 'Presidential Power and White House Lobbying' (1978) 93 *Pol. Sc. Q.* 255, 266.
47. See, e.g., J. L. Sundquist, Comment, in *Has the President Too Much Power?* (C. Roberts ed., New York, 1974), 112: 'I think the biggest trouble with our system . . . is the constant deadlock between the President and Congress in the legislative field . . . . Deadlock is the normal state of affairs.'; Cutler, *supra* note 31, especially at 126–8, 137 (but note ex-President Nixon's doubts, *supra* note 26 at 30); G. Hodgson, 'One lame duck after another', *Times*, 14 December 1983, p. 12; Sundquist, *supra* note 13 at 476–7. See also Burns, *supra* note 31 at 182–9.
48. Reedy, *supra* note 26 at 85.
49. See E. L. Davis, 'Congressional Liason: The People and the Institutions', in *Both Ends of the Avenue: The Presidency, the Executive Branch, and Congress in the 1980s* (A. King ed., Washington D.C., 1983), 59, 93–4.
50. Cutler, *supra* note 31 at 135.
51. Ford, *supra* note 17 at 28 (emphasis added).
52. See, e.g., M. P. Wattenberg, *The Decline of American Political Parties 1952–1980* (Cambridge, Mass., 1984); L. Morrow, 'The Decline of the Parties', *Time*, 20 November 1978, p. 43; Burns, *supra* note 31 *passim*; Sundquist, *supra* note 13 at 471–2, 474–6.
53. Sundquist, ibid., 427.
54. Ibid., 369.
55. Ibid.
56. See G. Easterbrook, 'What's Wrong With Congress?', *Atlantic*, December 1984, 57, 64, 70–9, 84.
57. See ibid., especially 71–2.
58. Ibid., 71.
59. See Burns, *supra* note 31 at 183; L. Fisher, *The Politics of Shared Power: Congress and the Executive* (Washington D.C., 1981), 61.
60. See Heclo, *supra* note 17 at 56.
61. Sundquist, *supra* note 13 at 425, 427 (emphasis added).

62. Ibid., 425 (emphasis added).
63. A few powers are vested in only one house: the power to impeach civil officers is vested in the House, and the power to try impeachments, confirm appointments, and ratify treaties is vested in the Senate.
64. See the United States Constitution articles I section 2(5) and II section 4.
65. See, e.g., T. Taylor, *Grand Inquest: The Story of Congressional Investigations* (New York, 1955).
66. However, Congress, or even one house thereof, could probably *force* a president to resign by refusing him supply. Since the speaker of the House of Representatives is next in line of succession after the vice-president, Congress, or either house, could, in effect, transfer the presidency to another political party by resolutely refusing supply. But it is almost impossible to envisage Congress contemplating this course unless the president and vice-president had committed impeachable offences, in which case impeachment would be the appropriate remedy. Indeed, congressional removal of the president and vice-president on purely political grounds is virtually inconceivable except in a situation close to civil war. Contrast Australia, 11 November 1975!
67. See 'Symposium on the Reuss Resolution: A Vote of No Confidence in the President' (1975) 43 *Geo. Wash. L. Rev.* 328ff.; Burns, *supra* note 31 at 197–8, 235–6, 237; J. L. Sundquist, 'Parliamentary Government and Ours', *New Republic*, 26 October 1974, 10; J. L. Sundquist, 'Needed: A Workable Check on the Presidency' (1973) 10 *Brookings Bulletin*, No. 4, 7, 11. See *contra* Schlesinger, 'Parliamentary Government', *supra* note 30.
68. See *Immigration and Naturalization Service* v. *Chadha* (1983) 462 U.S. 919.
69. See T. M. Franck and E. Weisband, *Foreign Policy by Congress* (New York, 1979), chs. 1 and 2; Koenig, *supra* note 40 at 58.
70. A. J. Groth, 'Britain and America: Some Requisites of Executive Leadership Compared' (1970) 85 *Pol. Sc. Q.* 217, 223.
71. Senator Monroney, quoted in Sundquist, *supra* note 13 at 325.
72. Representatives Bolling, Culver and others, quoted ibid., 324–5.
73. Ibid., 334–5.
74. Representative Frenzel, quoted ibid., 329.
75. See ibid., 332–40.
76. A 'long-time congressional assistant', quoted ibid., 336.
77. For an amusing example of bureaucratic nonsense under fire from Congress, see Polsby, *supra* note 37 at 168–9 (diplomat posted to London to maintain fluency in Chinese).
78. Sundquist, *supra* note 13 at 332–3.
79. Easterbrook, *supra* note 56 at 65.
80. See Sundquist, *supra* note 13 at 338.
81. Quoted ibid (unnamed).
82. D. Wass, *Government and the Governed*, BBC Reith Lectures 1983 (London, 1984), 33.
83. See R. F. Fenno, Jr, *The President's Cabinet* (Cambridge, Mass., 1963), 29. But, if true, Lincoln did not always treat his cabinet in such a cavalier manner: e.g., he abandoned his proposal to end the Civil War and pay the Confederate States $400 Million in government bonds as

compensation for the emancipation of their slaves if they abandoned their rebellion when the cabinet unanimously opposed it on 5 February 1865: see 4 C. Sandburg, *Abraham Lincoln: The War Years* (New York, 1939), 48.

84. See Livingston, *supra* note 14 at 885–6. This is well illustrated by Harry Hopkins's comparison of the behaviour of President Roosevelt and Prime Minister Churchill at the Newfoundland conference of August 1941: see 1 R. E. Sherwood, *The White House Papers of Harry L. Hopkins* (London, 1948), 362.

85. P. Weller, *First Among Equals: Prime Ministers in Westminster Systems* (Sydney, 1985), 122–3.

86. See ibid., 111, 123–4, 182–5; R. Lucy, *The Australian Form of Government* (Melbourne, 1985), 164–8.

87. Weller, *supra* note 85 at 124, 183, 196; P. Kelly, 'Hawke's competence the casualty', *Australian*, 8 February 1985, pp. 1, 2.

88. See Weller, *supra* note 85 at 124, 125–9; D. Butler, 'Ministerial Responsibility in Australia and Britain' (1973) 26 *Parl. Affs.* 403, 410–11, repeated in D. Butler, *The Canberra Model* (Melbourne, 1973), 58–9.

89. See, e.g., R. H. S. Crossman, 'Introduction', in W. Bagehot, *The English Constitution* (London, 1963), 49ff.; H. Berkeley, *The Power of the Prime Minister* (London, 1968), 21 ('disguised presidential rule on the part of the Prime Minister'), 24 ('unchecked presidential rule'), 76 ('the British Prime Minister is considerably more powerful in his own sphere than his American counterpart is in his'), 86–7, 118 ('the supra-presidential power of the Prime Minister'); F. W. G. Benemy, *The Elected Monarch* (London, 1965), ch. XV. However, it should be noted that many of these comments refer to the prime minister's overall power, and not specifically to his power within the executive branch. Richard Crossman, for example, told his Harvard audience in 1970 that 'It may be that I shall be able to show you that a Prime Minister exerts greater power than a President', but noted that the prime minister 'has not become in the least Presidential': *Inside View* (London, 1972), 27, 45 (published in the United States as *The Myths of Cabinet Government* (Cambridge, Mass., 1972), 6, 30).

90. See, e.g., Lord Blake, *The Office of Prime Minister* (London, 1975), 47–53; A. H. Brown, 'Prime Ministerial Power' [1968] *Public Law* 28, 96; G. W. Jones, 'The Prime Minister's Power' (1965) 18 *Parl. Affs.* 167; Weller, *supra* note 85 at 4ff; Lucy, *supra* note 86 at 171, 413 ('The Australian prime minister is not a presidential figure.').

91. Crossman, 'Introduction', *supra* note 89 at 49.

92. Quoted in Schlesinger, *supra* note 30 at 462–3. See also Harry Hopkins's report referred to *supra* note 84.

93. R. E. Neustadt, 'White House and Whitehall' (1966) *The Public Interest*, No. 2, 55, 66–8 (emphasis added).

94. Ibid., 65.

95. Ibid., 68.

96. See, e.g., J. P. Mackintosh, *The British Cabinet* (3rd ed., London, 1977), 428, 628 (quoting Lord Avon and Lord Butler); Brown, *supra* note 90 at 30–1; P. Norton, *The Constitution in Flux* (Oxford, 1982), 49; *supra* note 89.

97. Weller, *supra* note 85 at 201.

98. Ibid., 211, 210 respectively.
99. See the United States Constitution article I section 6(2).
100. See the Commonwealth Constitution section 64 para. 3; the Constitution Act 1975 (Vic.) section 51; the Constitution Act 1934 (S.A.) section 66(1); the Constitution Act 1934 (Tas) section 8B(1); R. D. Lumb, *The Constitutions of the Australian States* (4th ed., St Lucia, 1977), 68-9; R. S. Parker, *The Government of New South Wales* (St Lucia, 1978), 245.
101. The Constitution Act 1855-1856 (S.A.) section 32.
102. The Victorian and South Australian provisions (*supra* note 100) also provide for a three-month period of grace. The Tasmanian provision (*supra* note 100) does not.
103. See R. J. L. Hawke, *The Resolution of Conflict* (1979 Boyer Lectures, Sydney, 1979), 22-6, 31; D. Solomon, *Elect the Governor-General!* (Melbourne, 1976), 54-61, 72-5; J. McClelland, 'We can't afford irritants like the Governor-General and the Senate', *National Times*, 16-21 February 1976, 18, 19; D. Chipp, 'An Individual View', in *Republican Australia?* (G. Dutton ed., Melbourne, 1977), 142, 149-51, 153; D. Horne, 'Republican Australia', in *Australia and the Monarchy* (G. Dutton ed., Melbourne, 1966), 86, 102-3. Accord J. Hoskyns, 'Conservatism is Not Enough' (1984) 55 *Pol. Q.* 3, 12-15 (discussing the U.K.).
104. Hawke, *supra* note 103 at 23-4.
105. Ibid., 24.
106. As it is, e.g., by former Minister Gordon Bryant: G. M. Bryant, 'Our Parliament: What Is to be Done About It?' (1983) *Legislative Studies Newsletter*, No. 7, 18, 26, 28-9.
107. McClelland, *supra* note 103 at 19. See also the other proponents cited in note 103; J. McMillan, G. Evans and H. Storey, *Australia's Constitution: Time for Change?* (Sydney, 1983), 221-2.
108. House of Representatives: 21/82; Senate: 6/35.
109. R. Rose, 'British Government: The Job at the Top', in *Presidents and Prime Ministers* (R. Rose and E. N. Suleiman eds, Washington D.C., 1980), 1, 6 (table).
110. D. Horne, *Power From the People. A New Australian Constitution?* (Victorian Fabian Society Pamphlet No. 32, October 1977), 8.
111. Chipp, *supra* note 103 at 151 (emphasis in original).
112. See Weller, *supra* note 85 at 84 (table).
113. As it does in the United Kingdom also: Crossman, *Inside View, supra* note 89 at 46-7, 64 (*The Myths of Cabinet Government, supra* note 89 at 32, 53).
114. Lucy, *supra* note 86 at 136-7; Weller, *supra* note 85 at 43.
115. Accord W. C. Wentworth, 'Australia and the Monarchy — A Liberal View', in *Republican Australia?* (G. Dutton ed., Melbourne, 1977), 120, 121-2.
116. Wass, *supra* note 82 at 34.
117. Nevil Johnson, Letter to the Editor, *Times*, 17 October 1983, p. 13.
118. Chipp, *supra* note 103 at 150.
119. See H. Evans, 'Party Government versus Constitutional Government' (1984) 56 *A.Q.* 265, 273. See also three books by Philip Norton, *Dissension in the House of Commons 1945-74* (London, 1975), *Dissen-

sion in the House of Commons 1974–1979 (Oxford, 1980), and *Conservative Dissidents: Dissent within the Parliamentary Conservative Party 1970–74* (London, 1978).

120. H. Evans, 'Australia and the "Westminster System"' (1982) 50 *The Table* 48, 49.

121. 'Conversation with Sir Garfield Barwick' (1983) 57 *Law Institute J.* 1305, 1308; accord G. Barwick, 'Federalism in Australia — Its Origins, Its Operation and Its Future' (unpublished 1983 Edmund Barton Lecture, University of Sydney, 26 September 1983), 22.

122. Evans, *supra* note 119 at 265–6.

123. Ibid., 266.

124. H. Evans, 'Questioning the Tyranny' (1983) 27 *Quadrant*, No. 4, 70, 72.

125. Evans, *supra* note 119 at 276.

126. C. Howard, *The Constitution, Power and Politics* (Melbourne, 1980), 30.

127. Ibid., 90; accord ibid., 31.

128. K. J. Walker, 'Presidential Government — A Cure for Political Malaise?' (1969) 41 *A.Q.*, No. 3, 43, 44.

129. A. Rutherford and J. Hyde, 'Choosing the Lesser Evil', in *The Constitutional Challenge* (M. James ed., Sydney, 1982), 77, 79.

130. See G. S. Reid, 'The Westminster Model and Ministerial Responsibility' (1984) 61 *Current Affairs Bull.*, No. 1, 4, 11ff.

131. G. S. Reid, 'The Changing Political Framework' (1980) 24 *Quadrant*, Nos 1 and 2, 5, 7.

132. Letter to the Editor, *Times*, 3 August, 1977, p. 15. See also S. Encel, *Cabinet Government in Australia* (2nd ed., Melbourne, 1974), 107; Lucy, *supra* note 86 at 6, 9, 137, 144, 407 (ministers are primarily responsible to the governing party, not to the House of Representatives).

133. Crossman, *The Myths of Cabinet Government, supra* note 89 at 31 (emphasis in original). The second and fourth sentences were omitted from the British edition (*supra* note 89 at 46).

134. Butler, *supra* note 88 at 404, repeated in *The Canberra Model, supra* note 88 at 51 (emphasis added). See, similarly, Reid, *supra* note 130 at 11ff.

135. Groth, *supra* note 70 at 223 (emphasis added).

136. Ibid., 238.

137. Weller, *supra* note 85 at 177.

138. See the table in ibid., 170.

139. G. S. Reid, 'The Parliament in Theory and Practice', in *The Constitutional Challenge* (M. James ed., Sydney, 1982), 39, 49. For detailed statistics on House of Representatives sittings 1901–80, see *House of Representatives Practice* (J. A. Pettifer ed., Canberra, 1981), 744–5.

140. Rutherford and Hyde, *supra* note 129 at 87.

141. Based upon figures supplied by the clerical staff of the parliaments, whose assistance is gratefully acknowledged.

142. See G. Winterton, *Parliament, the Executive and the Governor-General* (Melbourne, 1983), 6–7, 79, 202 note 47.

143. For the relevant years, see *House of Representatives Practice, supra* note 139 at 748–50.

144. See M. Sexton, *Illusions of Power* (Sydney, 1979), chs 7 and 10.

145. See J. Uhr, 'The Australian Senate and Federalism: A Research Note' (unpublished paper presented at Third Federalism Project Conference, Research School of Social Sciences Department of Political Science, Australian National University, 10–11 February 1983), 3: 'remarkably free from party-political animosity.'; Senator David Hamer, 80 *Commonwealth Parliamentary Debates*, Senate, 232 (22 February 1979): 'rigid party attitudes melt away when a Senate committee is considering a particular problem, and there is a very general desire to get the best answer.'

146. D. J. Hamer, 'Towards a Valuable Senate', in *The Constitutional Challenge* (M. James ed., Sydney, 1982), 59, 64, 72 (emphasis added). Accord Senator Hamer, 80 *Commonwealth Parliamentary Debates*, Senate, 230ff. (22 February 1979). One commentator has called Hamer's proposal 'bizarre': R. Cullen, Book Review (1983) 14 *M.U.L.R.* 143, 145.

147. J. Gaul, *Sydney Morning Herald*, 11 November 1978, p. 12 (emphasis added). For an interesting case-study of government bargaining with individual Liberal senators regarding the content of legislation, see Lucy, *supra* note 86 at 216–22 (Freedom of Information Bill 1981).

148. E. Thompson, 'The "Washminster" Mutation', in *Responsible Government in Australia* (P. Weller and D. Jaensch eds, Richmond, Vic., 1980), 32. (Also published as 15 *Politics* No. 2.)

149. See *Samsher Singh* v. *Punjab* A.I.R. 1974 S.C. 2192, 2212 para. 104 per Krishna Iyer J.

150. B. M. Snedden, 'Ministers in Parliament — A Speaker's Eye View', in *Responsible Government in Australia, supra* note 148, 68, 75.

151. The present system whereby each State constitutes a single electorate is not constitutionally mandated: see the Commonwealth Constitution section 7 para. 1.

152. Uhr, *supra* note 145 at 6 (emphasis added). See also ibid., 10–11. Accord J. Quick and R. R. Garran, *The Annotated Constitution of the Australian Commonwealth* (Sydney, 1901, repr. Sydney, 1976), 189, 414, 421 ('The fact that new States are not entitled as of right to equal representation [in the Senate] shows that the system is not founded on a logical principle, but that it is a political compromise or contrivance regarded as one of the conditions precedent to the establishment of the Commonwealth.')

153. Wilson, *supra* note 31 at 284 (emphasis in original).

154. See Sundquist, *supra* note 13 at 424–6.

155. Cf. Wass, *supra* note 82 at 6–7.

156. See, e.g., Sorensen, *supra* note 21 at 83ff.; Livingston, *supra* note 14 at 882–3; Schlesinger, *supra* note 24 at 12–15, 18, 22; C. M. Hardin, *Presidential Power and Accountability* (Chicago, 1974).

157. Cf. H. N. Collins, 'What Shall we do with the Westminster Model?', in *Public Service Inquiries in Australia* (R. F. I. Smith and P. Weller eds, St Lucia, 1978), 360, 368.

158. See Peterson, *supra* note 15 at 193ff.

159. Livingston, *supra* note 14 at 882.

160. See Sundquist, 'Workable Check', *supra* note 67 at 7, 10.

161. See Hardin, *supra* note 156 at 12–14, ch. 2; Groth, *supra* note 70 at 217–18, 231–5; Schlesinger, *supra* note 23 at 389–90 (paperback ed.,

supra note 30 at 370–1); Reedy, *supra* note 26 at 86–7, 96–9, 134; E. J. Hughes, Comment in *Has the President Too Much Power?*, *supra* note 47 at 20: 'Isolation is the ultimate menace — the possible cancer — for any Presidency.'

162.   Cf. Wentworth, *supra* note 115 at 122–4; C. J. Friedrich and R. H. Guttman, 'The Federal Executive', in *Studies in Federalism* (R. R. Bowie and C. J. Friedrich eds, Boston, 1954), 63, 68.

163.   See *supra*, chapter 3, text accompanying notes 24 and 25.

164.   It should, however, be noted that some scholars maintain (incorrectly, in this writer's opinion) that the Commonwealth executive also enjoys a sphere of action independent from legislative control: see Winterton, *supra* note 142, ch. 5.

165.   See T. C. Sorensen, 'The Case for a Strong Presidency', in *Has the President Too Much Power?* (C. Roberts ed., New York, 1974), 24, 26–7; Sorensen, *supra* note 21 at 75–6; Mullen, *supra* note 26 at 254.

166.   Accord Schlesinger, *Imperial Presidency*, *supra* note 30 at 463–4, repeated in 'Parliamentary Government', *supra* note 30 at 15 (comparing Congress with the British parliament).

167.   J. A. G. Griffith, 'The Constitution and the Commons', in *Parliament and the Executive* (Royal Institute of Public Administration, London, 1982), 7 (emphasis added).

168.   P. Bowers, 'Whitlam Reflects on Whitlam', *Sydney Morning Herald*, 3 December 1982, p. 8. See, similarly, on the British prime minister, M. Shaw, 'The President and the Prime Minister' (1969) 50 *The Parliamentarian* 187, 196; Schlesinger, *supra* note 24 at 20.

169.   Indeed, Mr Whitlam expressly condemned the United States Senate for having 'made it impossible for the President to carry out his economic and diplomatic responsibilities': Bowers, *supra* note 168.

170.   To allay suspicions over his pardon of ex-President Nixon, President Ford took the extraordinary step of (voluntarily) testifying before a subcommittee of the House Judiciary Committee on 17 October 1974: see 10 *Weekly Compilation of Presidential Documents* 1301–16.

171.   H. A. Scarrow, 'Parliamentary and Presidential Government Compared' (1974) 66 *Current History* 264, 266 (June 1974).

172.   See Howard, *supra* note 126, chs 3 and 4, especially 90, 93–9, 138; C. Howard, 'Legal and Constitutional Implications', in *Republican Australia?* (G. Dutton ed., Melbourne, 1977), 60, 69; Walker, *supra* note 128 at 47–9. Some of the pros and cons are summarized by Dr Neal Blewett (1977), in McMillan, Evans and Storey, *supra* note 107 at 223–4.

173.   See, e.g., Evans, *supra* note 119 at 275–6; Evans, *supra* note 124 at 72–3; J. McClelland, 'Republican Australia — A Labor View', in *Republican Australia?* (G. Dutton ed., Melbourne, 1977), 132, 137–8, 141.

174.   See, e.g., G. Barwick, *The Monarchy in an Independent Australia* (Sir Robert Menzies Lecture Trust, Monash University, 1982), 19–20; Lord Hailsham of St Marylebone, *Hamlyn Revisited: The British Legal System Today* (London, 1983), 26–7.

175.   See, e.g., Hamer, *supra* note 146 at 64; Horne, *supra* note 110 at 20. See also McMillan, Evans and Storey, *supra* note 107 at 220 (noting the limited nature of criticism of Australian government).

176.   See Papua New Guinea, General Constitutional Commission, *Final*

Report (Port Moresby, 1983), 85, 93; Canadian Bar Association, Committee on the Constitution, *Towards a New Canada* (1978), 35.

177. *Sun Herald* (Sydney), 4 February 1979, p. 38.
178. See Livingston, *supra* note 14 at 894.
179. Cf. ibid., 882, 888.
180. F. A. Hermens, *The Representative Republic* (Notre Dame, Ind., 1958), 464 (emphasis added).
181. H. J. Laski, 'The Parliamentary and Presidential Systems' (1944) 4 *Public Admin. Rev.* 347.
182. Ibid., 358.
183. See J. A. Smith, *The Spirit of American Government* (C. Strout ed., Cambridge, Mass., 1965; orig. publ. 1907), 208–11, 226–9.
184. Cf. Scarrow, *supra* note 171 at 265.
185. See D. Solomon, *Elect the Governor-General!* (Melbourne, 1976), 76.
186. Burns, *supra* note 31 at 209.
187. Koenig, *supra* note 40 at 61–2 (emphasis added).

6   The States

1. See the Royal Style and Titles Act 1973 (C'th) section 2.
2. Cf. Malaysia, a federation with an elected monarch, in which nine of the thirteen States have their own hereditary ruler. Arguably, the oath of allegiance in Victoria and Queensland, whereby allegiance is sworn to the Queen 'as lawful Sovereign of the United Kingdom and of [the State]', already recognizes Victorian and Queensland monarchies: see the Constitution Act 1975 (Vic.) section 23 and Second Schedule; the Constitution Act 1867 (Qd.) section 4.
3. See P. W. Hogg, *Liability of the Crown* (Sydney, 1971), 198–9; P. J. Hanks, *Australian Constitutional Law* (3rd ed., Sydney, 1985), para. 5.063 (p. 352), and (2nd ed. 1980), para. 5.002 (p. 340) (not in 3rd ed.).
4. J. Bjelke-Petersen, 'Australian Federalism: A Queensland View', in *Australian Federalism: Future Tense* (A. Patience and J. Scott eds, Melbourne, 1983), 63, 71.
5. D. O'Connell, 'Monarchy or Republic?', in *Republican Australia?* (G. Dutton ed., Melbourne, 1977), 23, 38 (emphasis added); accord ibid., 31. Dr Eugene Forsey has similarly remarked that

   No Canadian province could become a republic without ceasing to be part of the one political nation, Canada. To propose, therefore, that any one province should be allowed to become a republic is to propose secession, separatism and total independence for that province.
   Freedom and Order (Toronto, 1974), 21.
6. See J. Wilson 'Lectures on Law' (1790–91), in 1 *The Works of James Wilson* (R. G. McCloskey ed., Cambridge, Mass., 1967), 264. (However, Justice Wilson appears to have contemplated only a combination of republics and 'arbitrary monarchies', not constitutional monarchies.)
7. G. Evans, 'God Save the Queen? — Australia as a Republic' (unpublished address to Counterpoint Forum, Murdoch University, 29 September 1982), 4. Accord J. McMillan, G. Evans and H. Storey, *Australia's Constitution: Time for Change?* (Sydney, 1983), 176; N.

Hunt, 'Legal and Constitutional Implications of Australia Becoming a Republic' (unpublished LL.B. thesis, University of New South Wales, 1978), 104: 'It may be theoretically possible to have an Australian Federal Republic in which one or more of the States retained their links with the Crown but . . . such an eventuality does not appear to be a practical possibility.'

8. See the United States Constitution article 4 section 4; Swiss Constitution article 6(2)(b); FRG Basic Law article 28; Indian Constitution article 355 (impliedly: see 1 H. M. Seervai, *Constitutional Law of India* (3rd ed., Bombay, 1983), para. 5.24 (pp. 157–8)); Constitution of Mexico article 115.1; Constitution of Argentina (1853) article 5; Constitution of Brazil (1969) articles 10 (VII)(a), 13(I). The Austrian Constitution prescribes the basic form of *Land* government: see Ch. IV Part A, especially article 101.

9. See *supra*, chapter 5, text accompanying note 148.

10. See the Swiss Constitution article 96. As examples of cantonal provisions, see the constitutions of Grisons article 25(1); Aargau article 88(1); and Jura article 93(2).

11. See the Constitution of India articles 52, 153, 155.

12. See the Austrian Constitution article 70.

13. See, e.g., the constitutions of Burgenland article 53; Carinthia articles 41, 43; Lower Austria articles 34, 35; Upper Austria article 34; Salzburg article 35; Styria articles 27, 28; and Vienna articles 31, 34.

14. See the Austrian Constitution article 74. For examples of *Land* provisions, see the constitutions of Burgenland article 56; Carinthia articles 46, 49; Lower Austria article 39; Upper Austria article 35; Salzburg article 42; Styria article 27; and Vienna article 37.

15. FRG Basic Law article 63(1).

16. See, e.g., the constitutions of Baden-Württemberg article 46; Bavaria article 44; Hesse article 101; Lower Saxony article 20; Saarland article 87; Schleswig-Holstein articles 21(2), 22.

17. FRG Basic Law article 64(1).

18. See, e.g. the constitutions of Baden-Württemberg article 46; Bavaria articles 45, 46; Hesse article 101; Lower Saxony article 20; Saarland article 87. See also J. Rydon and H. A. Wolfsohn, *Federalism in West Germany* (ACIR Information Paper No. 8, Canberra, 1980), 58.

19. See FRG Basic Law articles 67, 68. For examples of *Land* provisions, see the constitutions of Baden-Württemberg articles 54, 56; Bavaria article 44; Hesse article 114; Lower Saxony articles 23, 24; Saarland article 88; Schleswig-Holstein article 30.

20. FRG Basic Law article 63(4). See also ibid., article 68.

21. See, e.g., the constitutions of Baden-Württemberg article 47; Saarland articles 69, 87(4). Cf. the constitutions of Bavaria articles 18(2), 44(5) (dissolution by the *Landtag* President); Hamburg article 36(1) (dissolution by the *Land* government if it fails to secure a vote of confidence and a new government is not chosen); Lower Saxony article 21(1) (dissolution pursuant to a resolution of the *Landtag*); Schleswig-Holstein article 31(1) (dissolution by the chief minister if he fails to secure a vote of confidence and a new chief minister is not elected).

22. See, e.g., the constitutions of Baden-Württemberg article 43(1)

(dissolution by the *Land* government); Bavaria article 18(1); Hamburg article 11(1); Hesse article 80; Lower Saxony article 7(1); Saarland article 69; Schleswig-Holstein article 31(2) (on the motion of the chief minister).
23. See e.g., the constitutions of Bavaria article 44(5); Saarland article 87(5); Salzburg article 42(3).
24. The Indian Constitution article 153.
25. K. C. Wheare, *Federal Government* (4th ed., London, 1963), 46.
26. See Brandeis J., quoted *infra*, text accompanying note 28.
27. See *Truax* v. *Corrigan* (1921) 257 U.S. 312, 344 per Holmes J., dissenting.
28. *New State Ice Co.* v. *Liebmann* (1932) 285 U.S. 262, 311 per Brandeis J., dissenting. Accord G. Sawer, *Modern Federalism* (2nd ed., Melbourne, 1976), 111.

7 The President

1. D. Horne, 'What Kind of Head of State?', in *Change the Rules! Towards a Democratic Constitution* (S. Encel, D. Horne and E. Thompson eds, Ringwood, Vic., 1977), 66, 81.
2. E.g., President Kasavubu vs. Prime Minister Lumumba in Zaire, President Azikiwe vs. Prime Minister Sir Abubakar Tafawa Balewa in Nigeria, President Mutesa vs. Prime Minister Obote in Uganda, and King Moshoeshoe II vs. Prime Minister Leabua Jonathan in Lesotho. For details, see three books by B. O. Nwabueze: *Constitutionalism in the Emergent States* (London, 1973), 56–66; *Presidentialism in Commonwealth Africa* (London, 1974), 72–89; *A Constitutional History of Nigeria* (London, 1982), 256–66. Dr Nwabueze regards 'an arrangement whereby executive authority is vested in one person and exercised by another' as 'a wholly unnatural' one from which 'conflict is necessarily to be expected': *Constitutionalism, supra*, 56, repeated in *Constitutional History, supra*, 256–7.
3. C. J. Friedrich and R. H. Guttman, 'The Federal Executive', in *Studies in Federalism* (R. R. Bowie and C. J. Friedrich eds, Boston, 1954), 63, 74.
4. See 1 D. Pickles, *The Government and Politics of France* (London, 1972), 105, 356 note 12.
5. See *supra*, chapter 4, 'The French Presidency' (pp. 57–9).
6. V. Wright, *The Government and Politics of France* (2nd ed., London, 1983), 25.
7. Ibid.
8. B. Buckley, *Dawning of a Republic* (Sydney, 1979), 38.
9. G. Sawer, *Federation Under Strain* (Melbourne, 1977), 190.
10. The Finnish president's substantive role is centred on foreign affairs, especially relations with the Soviet Union: see, D. Arter, 'Government in Finland: A "Semi-Presidential" System' (1985) 38 *Parl. Affs.* 472, 476, 478, 481, 493; U. Kekkonen, *A President's View* (G. Coogan transl., London, 1982), 28–36.
11. See Papua New Guinea, General Constitutional Commission, *Final Report* (Port Moresby, 1983), pp. 88, 97–8; Canadian Bar Association, Committee on the Constitution, *Towards a New Canada* (1978), 34–5.
12. This form of electoral college has been proposed by Donald Horne in

Death of The Lucky Country (Ringwood, Vic., 1976), 54 and *Power From the People. A New Australian Constitution?* (Victorian Fabian Society Pamphlet No. 32, October 1977), 19.

13. See *Final Report, supra* note 11 at p. 99.

14. See D. McMahon, 'The Chief Justice and the Governor General Controversy in 1932' (1982) 17 *Irish Jurist* 145; F. Alexis, 'Key Issues in Commonwealth Caribbean Constitutional Law Arising from "Payne v. A.-G."' (1982) 6 *West Indian L.J.* 33, 77.

15. See C. Howard, *Australian Federal Constitutional Law* (3rd ed., Sydney, 1985), 121 note 8; Sir John Kerr, 'Kerr rejects 'ambush myth': "PM knew I could sack him"', *Bulletin*, 10 September 1985, 72, 78–9 (motives were to protect the Queen and, with very dubious justification, to prevent the appointment of a more compliant successor).

16. See Sawer, *supra* note 9 at 196; Z. Cowen, 'The Office of Governor-General' (1985) 114 *Daedalus*, No. 1, 127, 140; Kerr, *supra* note 15 at 79.

17. See A. R. Carnegie, 'Powers of Dissolution in Barbados, Jamaica, and Trinidad and Tobago: Relevance of Australian Constitutional Crisis' (1977) 58 *The Parliamentarian* 42, 44.

18. See the constitutions of India article 56(1)(b); Austria articles 60(6), 68 and 142(2)(a).

19. See the constitutions of France article 68; Finland article 47; Italy article 90; West Germany (FRG Basic Law) article 61; the United States article II section 4; Sri Lanka article 38(2)(a).

20. See the constitutions of Trinidad and Tobago section 35; Ireland article 12.10.7°; Israel, Basic Law on the President of the State section 20(a); Austria article 60(6); Iceland article 11.

21. Cf. 'misbehaviour' in section 72(ii) of the Commonwealth Constitution.

22. Accord the PNG General Constitutional Commission: see *Report, supra* note 11 at pp. 99–101.

23. *Att.-Gen. for Australia* v. *R.* [1957] A.C. 288 (P.C.).

24. See the Letters Patent Relating to the Office of Governor-General of the Commonwealth of Australia (21 August 1984) clause III, in Commonwealth of Australia *Gazette*, No. S 334 (24 August 1984); H. E. Renfree, *The Executive Power of the Commonwealth of Australia* (Sydney, 1984), 145–6.

25. See *supra*, chapter 3, text accompanying note 33.

26. Accord Horne, *supra* note 1 at 75, 78, 79; Horne, *Power From the People, supra* note 12 at 8.

27. See, e.g., D. Dunstan, 'The State, the Governors and the Crown', in *Republican Australia?* (G. Dutton ed., Melbourne, 1977), 202, 202–5; W. C. Wentworth, 'Australia and the Monarchy — A Liberal View', in ibid, 120, 123–4. Cf. PNG General Constitutional Commission, *Final Report, supra* note 11 at pp. 94–6.

28. See, e.g., R. J. L. Hawke, *The Resolution of Conflict* (1979 Boyer Lectures, Sydney, 1979), 22.

29. E. G. Whitlam, *The Truth of the Matter* (2nd ed., Ringwood, Vic., 1983), 184.

30. As was proposed recently for the Queen: J. Curran, 'Powers the Queen should renounce', *Times*, 31 July 1985, p. 12. Curran proposed that the

Queen's 'reserve powers' be transferred to the speaker — as in Sweden. Cf. P. J. Allott, 'Paradox of the Queen's Powers' (letter), *Times*, 18 September 1985, p. 13.

31. See *supra*, chapter 3 note 54.

32. However, the 'activist' non-executive president treads a fine line and must be careful not to overstep the proper boundary, as President Pertini probably did on one or two occasions, as when he publicly advocated withdrawal of Italian peace-keeping forces in Lebanon: see *Times*, 24 December 1983, p. 1; *International Herald Tribune*, 24–25 December 1983, p. 1. For the consequences, see *Financial Times* 29 December 1983, p. 2; *International Herald Tribune*, 2 January 1984, p. 2.

33. See G. Winterton, *Parliament, the Executive and the Governor-General* (Melbourne, 1983), chs 3, 6; Renfree, *supra* note 24, ch. 4.

34. These details are taken from Winterton, *supra* note 33 at 48.

35. A. Inglis Clark, *Studies in Australian Constitutional Law* (2nd ed., Melbourne, 1905), 191–2.

36. See the Irish Constitution article 49. (However, notwithstanding this provision, the Irish courts have held that some prerogatives were not inherited by the Irish Republic. The fiscal prerogative of prior payment of debts, for instance, was not, apparently because the Irish treasury is not a royal exchequer: see J. M. Kelly, *The Irish Constitution* (2nd ed., Dublin, 1984), 691–708.)

8   Constitutional Amendment

1. *Supra*, chapter 1, 'Formal Head of State without the Queen' (pp. 8–9).

2. R. D. Lumb, *Australian Constitutionalism* (Sydney, 1983), 131–2; R. D. Lumb, 'Fundamental Law and the Processes of Constitutional Change in Australia' (1978) 9 *F.L. Rev.* 148, 161; Z. Cowen, 'The Constitutional Aspects', in *Republican Australia?* (G. Dutton ed., Melbourne, 1977), 44, 59; Z. Cowen, 'The Constitution and the Monarchy', in *Australia and the Monarchy* (G. Dutton ed., Melbourne, 1966), 44, 60; *infra* note 24. But see C. Howard, *The Constitution, Power and Politics* (Melbourne, 1980), 107; W. A. Wynes, *Legislative, Executive and Judicial Powers in Australia* (5th ed., Sydney, 1976), 542; D. P. O'Connell, 'Monarchy or Republic?', in *Republican Australia?*, *supra*, 23, 37–8 (based upon a questionable view of parliamentary supremacy); D. P. O'Connell, 'Canada, Australia, Constitutional Reform and the Crown' (1979) 60 *The Parliamentarian* 5, 6.

3. See Lumb, *Australian Constitutionalism*, *supra* note 2 at 132; Lumb, 'Fundamental Law', *supra* note 2 at 161.

4. See G. J. Lindell, 'Conventions of the Constitution: Certain Powers of the Governor-General', in Australian Constitutional Convention 1984, Structure of Government Sub-Committee, *Report to Standing Committee* (August 1984), Appendix C, 44, 57 (para. 53(a)); W. S. Livingston, *Federalism and Constitutional Change* (Oxford, 1956), 112–13.

5. See *supra*, chapter 1, 'Executive Head of State under the Queen' (p. 8).

6. J. Quick and R. R. Garran, *The Annotated Constitution of the Australian Commonwealth* (Sydney, 1901, repr. Sydney, 1976), 989–90.

7. This power is expressly subject to sections 41 and 42 of the Constitution Act 1982 (U.K.).

8. See Quick and Garran, *supra* note 6 at 994 (but see ibid., 295–6); P. H. Lane, *An Introduction to the Australian Constitution* (3rd ed., Sydney, 1983), 3. See generally J. A. Thomson, 'Altering the Constitution: Some Aspects of Section 128' (1983) 13 *F.L. Rev.* 323, 331–5.
9. Emphasis added.
10. Wynes, *supra* note 2 at 542. Accord G. Sawer, 'Constitutional Law', in *The Commonwealth of Australia* (G. W. Paton ed., London, 1952), 38, 46; G. Sawer, '"Unamendable" parts of Constitution Act pose a patriation puzzle', *Canberra Times*, 21 July 1982, p. 2; Lumb, 'Fundamental Law', *supra* note 2 at 161 note 58. For the legal effect of the preamble, see G. Craven, 'The Constitutionality of the Unilateral Secession of an Australian State' (1985) 15 *F.L. Rev.* 123, 126–35.
11. Professor Sawer's comments in 'The British Connection' (1973) 47 *A.L.J.* 113, 114 note 3 and the *Canberra Times* (*supra* note 10) are too ambiguous to be regarded as a clear assertion to the contrary, especially in view of his comment on the 'indissoluble Federal Commonwealth' clause of the preamble: see 'Constitutional Law', *supra* note 10 at 46.
12. Accord (impliedly) C. Howard, *Australian Federal Constitutional Law* (3rd ed., Sydney, 1985), 110. The Melbourne (1975) and Hobart (1976) sessions of the Australian Constitutional Convention recommended that covering clause 2 be 'replaced by a provision referring to the Queen in the Sovereignty of Australia'.
13. See Quick and Garran, *supra* note 6 at 387–8, referring to chapter 1 clause 2 of the 1891 Commonwealth Bill — the predecessor of section 2 of the Constitution — which expressly authorized the Queen 'from time to time, [to] appoint a Governor-General'.
14. See the authorities cited in K. Booker and G. Winterton, 'The Act of Settlement and the Employment of Aliens' (1981) 12 *F.L. Rev.* 212, 215 note 22; Thomson, *supra* note 8 at 333 note 52; H. B. Higgins, 'The Convention Bill' (1898), in H. B. Higgins, *Essays and Addresses on The Australian Commonwealth Bill* (Melbourne, 1900), 69, 71; Livingston, *supra* note 4 at 155; G. J. Craven, 'The Lawfulness of the Secession of an Australian State' (unpublished LL.M. thesis, University of Melbourne, 1984), 287–9, 295–8, 300, 303, 310, 318, 327, 328, 340 (a book derived from this thesis, entitled *Secession: The Ultimate States Right*, is to be published by Melbourne University Press in 1986); J. McMillan, G. Evans and H. Storey, *Australia's Constitution: Time for Change?* (Sydney, 1983), 176, 359.
15. *Official Report of the National Australasian Convention Debates* (Sydney, 1891), 490.
16. See the authorities cited *supra*, note 14. The Commonwealth Parliament's power under section 51(xxxviii) would not extend to the amendment or repeal of the covering clauses: G. Winterton, 'Section 51(xxxviii) of the Constitution and Amendment of the "Covering Clauses"' (1982) 5 *U.N.S.W.L.J.* 327. But see *contra* Craven, *supra* note 14 at 317ff. (However, Craven's argument is unconvincing at a critical juncture: see ibid., 322–5.)
17. *Att.-Gen. for the Commonwealth* v. *Colonial Sugar Refining Co. Ltd.* [1914] A.C. 237, 256.
18. (1979) 145 C.L.R. 172, 236.
19. Lumb, 'Fundamental Law', *supra* note 2 at 160. See also Enid

Campbell's opinion, 'An Australian-Made Constitution for the Commonwealth of Australia', *Australian Constitutional Convention 1974*, Standing Committee D, *Report to Executive Committee* (1 August 1974), Appendix H, para. 21.

20. See the Statute of Westminster Adoption Act 1942 (C'th) section 3, adopting (*inter alia*) the Statute of Westminster 1931 (U.K.) section 2 which (*pace* Craven, *supra* note 14 at 292–3) applies to constitutional amendments pursuant to section 128. It is submitted that the term 'Parliament of a Dominion' in section 2 would include the legislature constituted by section 128, which comprises the Commonwealth parliament together with the electors of Australia. (Cf. *Sankey* v. *Whitlam* (1978) 142 C.L.R.1, 92–3, 105 per Mason and Aickin JJ. (a law amending the Constitution is a law made by the Commonwealth parliament).) It would indeed be ironic if the Commonwealth parliament acting alone could enact legislation repugnant to imperial legislation, but could not do so when joined by the electors of Australia. It would mean that, although the section 128 legislature could not itself amend or repeal imperial legislation applying in Australia by paramount force, it could authorize the Commonwealth parliament to do so by conferring upon it power to legislate on the relevant subject (whereupon section 2 of the Statute of Westminster 1931 would empower it to amend or repeal the imperial legislation). (Bearing in mind the different purposes of sections 2 and 9(3) of the Statute of Westminster, this interpretation of the term 'Parliament of a Dominion' in section 2 is not inconsistent with the interpretation of the term 'Parliament of the Commonwealth' in section 9(3) propounded *infra*, text accompanying notes 37–8.)

21. This proposition is not inconsistent with the Statute of Westminster 1931 (U.K.) section 8 (which provides that 'Nothing in this Act shall be deemed to confer any power to repeal or alter the Constitution or the Constitution Act of the Commonwealth of Australia . . . otherwise than in accordance with the law existing before the commencement of this Act.') provided, at any rate, that 'repeal or alter' therein be interpreted to mean *direct* repeal or alteration. Cf. Campbell, *supra* note 19 at para. 18, contradicted, however, by Craven, *supra* note 14 at 293–4, 304–8.

22. *Leges posteriores priores contrarias abrogant*: see D. C. Pearce, *Statutory Interpretation in Australia* (2nd ed., Sydney, 1981), paras 162 and 163.

23. Cf. M. J. Detmold, *The Australian Commonwealth* (Sydney, 1985), para. 11.10. But see *contra* Craven, *supra* note 14 at 299–308.

24. G. Evans, 'God Save the Queen? — Australia as a Republic' (unpublished address to Counterpoint Forum, Murdoch University, 29 September 1982), 4–5 (emphasis in original) essentially repeated in McMillan, Evans and Storey, *supra* note 14 at 176. See also the similar argument outlined (but neither accepted nor rejected) by Quick and Garran, *supra* note 6 at 295–6.

25. See Sawer, *supra* note 11 at 114 note 3; Sawer, *Canberra Times*, *supra* note 10; McMillan, Evans and Storey, *supra* note 14 at 177.

26. See the Statute of Westminster 1931 (U.K.) section 4.

27. On these concepts, see generally G. Winterton, 'The British Grundnorm: Parliamentary Supremacy Re-examined' (1976) 92 *L.Q.R.* 591.

28. See Sir Maurice Byers, former Commonwealth Solicitor-General, in 'Conventions Associated with the Commonwealth Constitution' (1982) 56 *A.L.J.* 316, 318 (letter), and 'Current Constitutional Problems', in *Current Constitutional Problems in Australia* (Canberra, 1982), 51, 55; *James* v. *Commonwealth* [1936] A.C. 578, 633 (P.C.): 'The Constitution . . . embodied the will of the people of Australia, and can *only* be altered by the will of the people of Australia expressed according to the provisions of s.128.' (emphasis added). But see *contra*, as to 'a certain period after 1900' during 'the first fifty years of federation', Lumb, 'Fundamental Law', *supra* note 2 at 154, quoted *infra*, text accompanying note 33.

29. See Quick and Garran, *supra* note 6 at 991.

30. *Kirmani* v. *Captain Cook Cruises Pty Ltd* (1985) 58 A.L.R. 29, 48–9. Accord *Bistricic* v. *Rokov* (1976) 135 C.L.R. 552, 565–7 per Murphy J.

31. See *Kirmani* v. *Captain Cook Cruises Pty Ltd* (1985) 58 A.L.R. 29, especially at 39 (Gibbs C. J.), 93 (Deane J.), 106 (Dawson J.); *China Ocean Shipping Co.* v. *South Australia* (1979) 145 C.L.R. 172; *Southern Centre of Theosophy Inc.* v. *South Australia* (1979) 145 C.L.R. 246; *Bistricic* v. *Rokov* (1976) 135 C.L.R. 552. See, likewise, *Ukley* v. *Ukley* [1977] V.R. 121 (F.C.).

32. Professor Lumb is, presumably, referring to an exercise of imperial legislative power against Australian wishes, because the Statute of Westminster 1931 (U.K.) was an exercise of Imperial legislative power which has affected 'the Australian federal system': see, e.g., *Kirmani* v. *Captain Cook Cruises Pty Ltd* (1985) 58 A.L.R. 29, especially per Mason, Brennan and Deane JJ.

33. Lumb, 'Fundamental Law', *supra* note 2 at 154–5 (emphasis added). Accord ibid., 157–8. But see *contra* Craven, *supra* note 14 at 249–53, 283, 310–11, 339.

34. Although his argument that the British parliament lacks power to amend the Commonwealth Constitution relies heavily on section 128, Professor Lumb is not prepared to date the extinction of British power from 1901: see Lumb, 'Fundamental Law', *supra* note 2 especially at 157–8.

35. Accord Craven, *supra* note 14 at 203–16.

36. See the Statute of Westminster Adoption Act 1942 (C'th) section 3, enacted pursuant to section 10 of the Statute of Westminster 1931.

37. G. Marshall, *Parliamentary Sovereignty and the Commonwealth* (Oxford, 1957), 116–17.

38. *Harris* v. *Minister of the Interior* 1952 (2) S.A. 428, cited by Dr Marshall (*supra* note 37 at 116 note 7), is distinguishable because the legislature constituted by the entrenched provisions of the South Africa Act 1909 (U.K.) comprised a joint sitting of both Houses of Parliament. Cf. the Commonwealth Constitution section 57.

39. 83 *Commonwealth Parliamentary Debates*, H. of R., 1490 (1 May 1973).

40. 923 *House of Commons Debates* 118 (Written Answer, Mr Crosland, 21 December 1976) (emphasis added), quoted in Foreign and Commonwealth Office Memorandum (11 November 1980), in United Kingdom Parliament, House of Commons, *First Report from the Foreign Affairs*

Committee, Session 1980–81: British North America Acts: The Role of Parliament. Vol. II: *Minutes of Evidence and Appendices* (HC 42 I and II), 61–2 (Q.7).

41. United Kingdom Parliament, *Report by the Joint Committee of the House of Lords and the House of Commons Appointed to Consider the Petition of the State of Western Australia in Relation to Secession* (H.L. 75, *H.C.* 88; 22 May 1935), para. 9 (emphasis added). (This report is reprinted in [1934–37] 3 *Commonwealth Parliamentary Papers* 2429 (No. 153).)

42. Memorandum by the Foreign and Commonwealth Office (28 November 1980), in *Minutes of Evidence, supra* note 40 at 135 (item 3(c)).

43. United Kingdom Parliament, House of Commons, *First Report from the Foreign Affairs Committee, Session 1980–81: British North America Acts: The Role of Parliament.* Vol. I: *Report* (HC 42), para. 111 (emphasis added).

44. Ibid (emphasis added).

45. C. Saunders and E. Smith, *A Paper . . . Identifying the Conventions Associated with the Commonwealth Constitution* (Australian Constitutional Convention, Standing Committee D, 1980), para. 2.6.2 (for further citation details, see *supra*, chapter 3 note 11).

46. *Supra*, text accompanying note 41.

47. See *Ukley* v. *Ukley* [1977] V.R. 121, 129–30 (F.C.).

48. Joint Committee *Report, supra* note 41 at para. 9.

49. Quoting Mr J. R. Freeland of the Foreign and Commonwealth Office in *Minutes of Evidence, supra* note 40 at 80 (Q.64).

50. *Report, supra* note 43 at para. 106 (emphasis added; the final sentence was italicized in the original).

51. Saunders and Smith, *supra* note 45 at para. 2.6.3; O'Connell, *supra* note 2 at 27. The debate which raged over Saunders and Smith's comments (see *supra*, chapter 1 note 40) focussed more on the correct interpretation of the events of 1973 (when two States unsuccessfully petitioned the Queen to seek an advisory opinion from the Judicial Committee of the Privy Council on the status of offshore areas — an issue strongly influenced, if not governed, by section 74 of the Commonwealth Constitution), rather than the accuracy of Saunders and Smith's general proposition.

52. Cf. Craven, *supra* note 14 at 277 who, while conceding the possibility that any amendment of the covering clauses automatically concerns the States 'because [the Constitution Act] binds all the States, and operates as part of their law', nevertheless appears impliedly to reach the opposite conclusion, i.e. that the mere fact that the covering clauses are amended is not sufficient to require State consent: see ibid., 277–82.

53. See the Australian Constitutions Act 1842 (U.K.) sections 30–33, 40; the Australian Constitutions Act 1850 (U.K.) section 12; the New South Wales Constitution Act 1855 (U.K.) section 3; the Victoria Constitution Act 1855 (U.K.) section 3; the Western Australia Constitution Act 1890 (U.K.) section 2; the Australian States Constitution Act 1907 (U.K.) section 1.

54. Justice Murphy is in a minority of one (at least among judges) in maintaining that the Colonial Laws Validity Act 1865 (U.K.) ceased to apply

to the States upon federation because they then ceased to be colonies: see *Western Australia* v. *Wilsmore* (1982) 149 C.L.R. 79, 86. Thirty years after federation, the Colonial Laws Validity Act 1865 was rendered inapplicable to the Commonwealth by the Statute of Westminster 1931 (U.K.) section 2, which also applied to the Canadian Provinces, but not, at their request, to the Australian States.

55. See *Re Scully* (1937) 32 Tas. L.R. 3, 42–5; *Clayton* v. *Heffron* (1960) 105 C.L.R. 214, 251 (*semble*); Lumb, 'Fundamental Law', *supra* note 2 at 176; R. D. Lumb, *The Constitutions of the Australian States* (4th ed., St Lucia, 1977), 111.

56. *Taylor* v *Att.-Gen. of Queensland* (1917) 23 C.L.R. 457, 473–4. Powers J. concurred: ibid., 481. Accord *Re Scully* (1937) 32 Tas. L.R. 3, 42–3; *Clayton* v. *Heffron* (1960) 105 C.L.R. 214, 251 (*semble*); *Att.-Gen. for New South Wales* v. *Trethowan* (1931) 44 C.L.R. 394, 429 per Dixon J.

57. Although the device of 'double entrenchment' may fall within the proviso to section 5 of the Colonial Laws Validity Act 1865 (U.K.) (because a law to which it applied would be one 'respecting the Constitution, Powers, and Procedure' of the legislature), simple (i.e. single) entrenchment of the office of governor would not, because a law to which it applied would not be one 'respecting the Constitution, Powers, and Procedure' of the legislature: see *supra*, text accompanying note 56. The simple entrenchment provisions would, nevertheless, probably bind the State legislature: see G. Winterton, 'Can the Commonwealth Parliament Enact "Manner and Form" Legislation?' (1980) 11 *F.L. Rev.* 167, 189–90. But see *contra West Lakes Ltd* v. *South Australia* (1980) 25 S.A.S.R. 389, 422 per Matheson J. (*obiter*).

58. See the Constitution Act 1975 (Vic.) section 18(2)(b); the Constitution Act 1867 (Qd.) sections 11A(2), 53; the Constitution Act 1889 (W.A.) sections 50(2), 73(2)(a) and (e). The unenacted Constitution (Reform) Bill 1983 (Vic.) clause 4, introduced by Liberal M.L.C. Haddon Storey, would have substituted a referendum for passage by absolute majorities in both houses.

59. See *McCawley* v. *R.* [1920] A.C. 691 (P.C.). For later cases, see Winterton, *supra* note 57 at 190 note 68.

60. Queensland Royal Instructions (1925) clause VII(5), reprinted in Lumb, *supra* note 55 at 131. The other State governors' royal Instructions are in similar terms.

61. See A. C. Castles, *An Australian Legal History* (Sydney, 1982), 451–2.

62. Lumb, *supra* note 55 at 72 note 48.

63. See A. C. Castles, 'Limitations on the Autonomy of the Australian States' [1962] *Public Law* 175, 195.

64. See Saunders and Smith, *supra* note 45 at para. 2.6.2; but see para. 2.6.3.

65. *Pace* Lumb, 'Fundamental Law', *supra* note 2 at 178–9 who strangely, and unwarrantably, equates 'representative government' with 'responsible government'. No one could deny that American government is 'representative', but it is, of course, not 'responsible'.

66. *Infra*, this chapter, '"Manner and Form" Provisions' — 'Section 128' (p. 141).

67. See *supra* note 20.

68. See *Kirmani* v. *Captain Cook Cruises Pty Ltd* (1985) 58 A.L.R. 29, 40 per Gibbs C. J.; K. Booker, 'Section 51(xxxviii) of the Constitution' (1981) 4 *U.N.S.W.L.J.* 91, 93, 100; G. Nettheim, 'The Power to Abolish Appeals to the Privy Council from Australian Courts' (1965) 39 *A.L.J.* 39, 45–6.
69. *Stuart-Robertson* v. *Lloyd* (1932) 47 C.L.R. 482, 491.
70. See O'Connell, *supra* note 2 at 38; R. D. Lumb and K. W. Ryan, *The Constitution of the Commonwealth of Australia Annotated* (3rd ed., Sydney, 1981), para. 687.
71. Commonwealth of Australia Parliament, Senate Standing Committee on Constitutional and Legal Affairs, *Commonwealth Law Making Power and the Privilege of Freedom of Speech in State Parliaments* (Canberra, 1985), para. 3.6 (Commonwealth Parliamentary Paper No. 235/1985).
72. See C. D. Gilbert, 'Federal Constitutional Guarantees of the States: Section 106 and Appeals to the Privy Council from State Supreme Courts' (1978) 9 *F.L. Rev.* 348, 357–66.
73. The majority gave precedence to section 106: *supra* note 71 at paras 3.17–3.42. Senators Tate (paras. 13–20, pp. 55–57) and Puplick (paras 30–31, pp. 70–1), who dissented, gave precedence to section 51.
74. *Kirmani* v. *Captain Cook Cruises Pty Ltd* (1985) 58 A.L.R. 29, 93–4 (emphasis added); see also ibid., 84 per Deane J. Accord Lumb and Ryan, *supra* note 70 at paras 686–687.
75. *Amalgamated Society of Engineers* v. *Adelaide Steamship Co. Ltd* (1920) 28 C.L.R. 129.
76. L. Zines, *The High Court and the Constitution* (Sydney, 1981), 243. Accord Senator Gareth Evans Q. C., A.-G. and Sir Maurice Byers Q. C., S.-G., Joint Opinion, *Re Royal Commission on Australian Security and Intelligence Agencies* (23 August 1983), para. 5 (published in 99 *Commonwealth Parliamentary Debates*, Senate, 12, 13 (23 August 1983); M. Crommelin, 'Offshore Mining and Petroleum: Constitutional Issues' (1981) 3 *Aust. Mining & Petroleum L.J.* 191, 203.
77. See *Melbourne Corporation* v. *Commonwealth* (1947) 74 C.L.R. 31, especially at 81, 83 per Dixon J.; *Commonwealth* v. *Tasmania* (1983) 46 A.L.R. 625, 694, 703 per Mason J.; *Queensland Electricity Commission* v. *Commonwealth* (1985) 61 A.L.R. 1.
78. See *Kirmani* v. *Captain Cook Cruises Pty Ltd* (1985) 58 A.L.R. 29, 47 (Mason J.), 50 (Murphy J.), 92–3 (Deane J.).
79. Ibid., 90 per Deane J.
80. Ibid., 90–1 per Deane J; accord ibid., 46–7 (Mason J.), 50 (Murphy J.).
81. See ibid., 93 per Deane J.
82. In contrast to United Kingdom legislation applying by 'reception': see ibid., 90 per Deane J. For an explanation of the difference between British legislation applying by 'reception' and such legislation applying by 'paramount force', see Booker and Winterton, *supra* note 14 at 212–13.
83. See *Kirmani* v. *Captain Cook Cruises Pty Ltd* (1985) 58 A.L.R. 29, 46–7. Equally glib, with respect, is Justice Dawson's atavistic single-subject characterization: 'A law which effects the repeal of another law is not a law with respect to repeal; its subject matter is the subject matter of the law which is repealed.' (ibid., 106).

84. Ibid., 39–40. Accord ibid., 59 (Wilson J.), 105–6 (Dawson J.).
85. See *supra*, this chapter, text accompanying notes 39 and 40.
86. See ibid., text accompanying notes 66 and 67.
87. See ibid., text accompanying notes 41–45.
88. *Report, supra* note 41 at para. 9.
89. Ibid.
90. *Ukley* v. *Ukley* [1977] V.R. 121, 129–30 (emphasis added).
91. This comment is, of course, misconceived: the head of state of the Australian States is the Queen of Australia, not the Queen of the United Kingdom. See *supra*, chapter 3, text accompanying note 1.
92. Memorandum, *supra* note 42 at 135 (item 3(d)).
93. Sir Maurice Byers, S.-G., 'Conventions Associated with the Commonwealth Constitution' (1982) 56 *A.L.J.* 316, 317; accord ibid., 318. See also Sawer, *supra* note 11 at 114–15.
94. Detmold, *supra* note 23 at 102.
95. Cf. J. M. Finnis, 'The Responsibilities of the United Kingdom Parliament and Government Under the Australian Constitution' (1983) 9 *Adel. L. Rev.* 91, 105.
96. Byers, *supra* note 93 at 318.
97. The structure of a State government might, for example, concern the Commonwealth if it contravened a civil liberties treaty implemented by the Commonwealth parliament pursuant to section 51(xxix) of the Constitution. However, with all respect, Cheryl Saunders and Ewart Smith may go too far in arguing that 'in all but the most obvious cases a Commonwealth interest in a matter affecting relations with the United Kingdom might be considered to exist if the Commonwealth Government makes representations with respect to it.': Saunders and Smith, *supra* note 45 at para. 2.6.3; see also para. 2.6.4.
98. *R.* v. *Governor of South Australia* (1907) 4 C.L.R. 1497, 1510.
99. Cf. *Clayton* v. *Heffron* (1960) 105 C.L.R. 214, 248–9 (even before amendment in 1977, section 15 of the Commonwealth Constitution did not require State parliaments to remain bicameral).
100. *Barwick C. J.*: *New South Wales* v. *Commonwealth* (1975) 135 C.L.R. 337, 372; G. Barwick, *The Monarchy in an Independent Australia* (Sir Robert Menzies Lecture Trust, Monash University, 1982), 6; G. Barwick, Book Review (1981) 4 *U.N.S.W.L.J.* 131, 134; *Murphy J.*: *Western Australia* v. *Wilsmore* (1982) 149 C.L.R. 79, 86; *Bistricic* v. *Rokov* (1976) 135 C.L.R. 552, 566; *Commonwealth* v. *Queensland* (1975) 134 C.L.R. 298, 337.
101. See *Western Australia* v. *Wilsmore* [1981] W.A.R. 179, 183.
102. Quick and Garran, *supra* note 6 at 930.
103. Ibid., 990 (emphasis added). Accord Sawer, *supra* note 11 at 113; G. Sawer, 'The Constitutional Crisis of Australian Federalism', in *Australian Federalism: Future Tense* (A. Patience and J. Scott eds., Melbourne, 1983), 94, 97; Lumb, 'Fundamental Law', *supra* note 2 at 182–3; A. P. Canaway, 'The Evolution of Section 128 of the Commonwealth Constitution' (1940) 14 *A.L.J.* 274, 276; A. P. Canaway, 'The Safety-Valve of the Commonwealth Constitution' (1938) 12 *A.L.J.* 108. But see *contra* Wynes, *supra* note 2 at 542 note 42. See, generally, Thomson, *supra* note 8 at 337–8.
104. Accord Evans, *supra* note 24 at 5; McMillan, Evans and Storey, *supra*

note 14 at 176. But see *contra* O'Connell, 'Constitutional Reform and the Crown', *supra* note 2 at 6; Cowen, *supra* note 2 at 61 (although he may be referring only to propriety, not power).

105. Sawer, *supra* note 11 at 114 (emphasis in original). Accord Lumb, 'Fundamental Law', *supra* note 2 at 183.

106. See the Constitution Act 1867 (Qd.) section 53(1); the Constitution Act 1889 (W.A.) section 73(2)(e) (emphasis added). But see *contra R. v. Minister for Justice, ex parte Skyring* (Qd. S.C., Connolly J., 17 February 1986, as yet unreported; appeal pending).

107. See Booker, *supra* note 68 at 110 note 43.

9 Arguments for Retaining Monarchy

1. Lord Hailsham of St Marylebone, Foreword, in J. Kerr, *Matters for Judgment* (London, 1979), xvii.

2. A point conceded by republicans: see, e.g., G. Evans, 'God Save the Queen? — Australia as a Republic' (unpublished address to Counterpoint Forum, Murdoch University, 29 September 1982), 1, 15.

3. See, e.g., Prime Minister Bob Hawke quoted in 'Australia will be republic, says PM', *Sydney Morning Herald*, 6 June 1983, p. 9, and answering questions at the National Press Club, Canberra, 29 November 1984.

4. F. Harrison, 'The Monarchy' (1872) 11 *Fortnightly Review* (N.S.) 613, 632.

5. G. Kirk, 'On Her Majesty's Diplomatic Service', in *The Monarchy and Its Future* (J. Murray-Brown ed., London, 1969), 125, 127.

6. See Justice Michael Kirby, 'Plenty of room for Constitution reform', *Weekend Australian Magazine*, 2–3 July 1983, p. 14.

7. D. O'Connell, 'Monarchy or Republic?', in *Republican Australia?* (G. Dutton ed., Melbourne, 1977), 23, 34.

8. Ibid., 33.

9. But exaggeration is not confined to one side of the debate. See, e.g., Thomas Jefferson's letter to Governor John Langdon (5 March 1810), in 4 *Memoirs, Correspondence, and Private Papers of Thomas Jefferson* (T. J. Randolph ed., London, 1829), 148, 150–1.

10. R. E. Ball, *The Crown, the Sages and Supreme Morality* (London, 1983), 136.

11. G. Barwick, *The Monarchy in an Independent Australia* (Sir Robert Menzies Lecture Trust, Monash University, 1982), 19.

12. See, e.g., C. Howard, *The Constitution, Power and Politics* (Melbourne, 1980), 117, 119.

13. See Evans, *supra* note 2 at 6–7.

14. Barwick, *supra* note 11 at 19 (emphasis added).

15. Hailsham, *supra* note 1 at xviii.

16. Memorandum of Prime Minister Asquith to King George V (September 1913), quoted in B. S. Markesinis, *The Theory and Practice of Dissolution of Parliament* (Cambridge, 1972), 69.

17. C. Macinnes, 'Our Own Kings', in *The Monarchy and Its Future* (J. Murray-Brown ed., London, 1969), 137, 145 (emphasis added).

18. Barwick, *supra* note 11 at 18.

19. R. G. Menzies, *Afternoon Light* (Melbourne, 1967), 236. See also D.

Dunstan, 'The State, the Governors and the Crown', in *Republican Australia?* (G. Dutton ed., Melbourne, 1977), 202, 209.

20. See, e.g., P. Worsthorne, 'The Case for the Monarchy', in *The Queen* (Harmondsworth, 1977), 165 ff. — admittedly an extreme instance of this genre.

21. W. Bagehot, *The English Constitution* (London and Glasgow, 1963; orig. publ. 1867), 86. Accord Lord Hailsham of St Marylebone, *Hamlyn Revisited: The British Legal System Today* (London, 1983), 27; 10 W. S. Holdsworth, *A History of English Law* (London, 1938), 364; Ball, *supra* note 10 at 91; A. V. Dicey, *Lectures on the Relation Between Law and Public Opinion in England During the Nineteenth Century* (2nd ed., London, 1914), 443.

22. See *The Complete Essays and other Writings of Ralph Waldo Emerson* (B. Atkinson ed., New York, 1940), 429. The quotation in the text refers to Ames's alleged remarks — supposedly made in a speech in the United States House of Representatives in 1795 — as reported in the *Oxford Dictionary of Quotations* and Bartlett's *Familiar Quotations*. However, their authenticity is doubtful. A perusal of the *Annals of the United States Congress* from 1791–97 both by the present writer and by the Library of Congress (at the request of the University of New South Wales Law Library) failed to find them. Nor could they be found in Seth Ames's collection of Fisher Ames's *Works* (2 vols., Boston, 1854, edited and enlarged by W. B. Allen, Indianapolis, 1983), or in secondary works, including Winfred E. A. Bernhard's biography, *Fisher Ames. Federalist and Statesman 1758–1808* (Chapel Hill, 1965). Moreover, the mystery is compounded by the quotation (unsourced) in 2 *The Annals of America, 1755–1783* (Chicago, 1968), 616 of a similar, but not identical, remark, attributed to Ames, which contrasts monarchy with democracy, not a republic.

23. Bagehot, *supra* note 21 at 100. Accord O'Connell, *supra* note 7 at 36 ('enshrined in mystery'); W. C. Wentworth, 'Australia and the Monarchy — A Liberal View', in *Republican Australia?* (G. Dutton ed., Melbourne, 1977), 120, 125 ('mystique').

24. R. Crossman, *Inside View* (London, 1972), 41. (Published in the United States as *The Myths of Cabinet Government* (Cambridge, Mass., 1972), 25.)

25. Ibid., 53. (*Myths of Cabinet Government*, 40.) It is well to recall that Mussolini came to power under a monarchy.

26. See M. Harris, 'Monarchy and the Australian Character', in *Australia and the Monarchy* (G. Dutton ed., Melbourne, 1966), 107, 117–18.

27. Quoted in J. McMillan, G. Evans and H. Storey, *Australia's Constitution: Time For Change?* (Sydney, 1983), 182.

Select Bibliography on Republicanism and Republican Government

Abbott, T., 'Needless Leap into the Dark', *Australian*, 11 August 1993, p.9.

Abbott, T., 'Political Impossibility of a Vision Not So Splendid', *Weekend Australian*, 9–10 October 1993, p.32.

Abbott, T., 'This Taxing Republic' (1993) 37 *Quadrant*, No.11, 16.

Abbott, T. and Turnbull, M., 'Debating Our Destiny: The Two Sides Shape Up', *Weekend Australian*, 9–10 October 1993, p.34.

Adams, J., *A Defence of the Constitutions of Government of the United States of America*, 3 vols (London, 1787–88, repr. New York, 1971).

Adams, J., *Novanglus: or, A History of the Dispute with America, From its Origin in 1754, to the Present Time* (Boston, 1774–75).

Adams, W. P., *The First American Constitutions* (R. and R. Kimber transl., Chapel Hill, 1980).

Adams, W. P., 'Republicanism in Political Rhetoric Before 1776' (1970) 85 *Pol. Sc. Q.* 397.

Alomes, S., 'Republican Flags Fly in the Land of Paradox', *Sunday Age*, 30 June 1991, News p.15.

Arena, F., 'Clinging to Britannia's Apron Strings', *Weekend Australian Magazine*, 25–26 June 1983, p. 14.

Arnold, J., Spearritt, P. and Walker, D. (eds.), *Out of Empire: The British Dominion of Australia* (Melbourne, 1993).

Atkinson, A., 'The Australian Monarchy: Imperfect But Important' (1993) 28 *Australian Journal of Political Science* 67.

Atkinson, A., *The Muddle-Headed Republic* (Melbourne, 1993).

Australians for Constitutional Monarchy, *Opinion* (unpublished, 8 September 1993).

Babb, J., *The Republican Debate: Implications for the States* (Victorian Parliamentary Library Background Paper no.4/93, Melbourne, July 1993).

Bagehot, W., *The English Constitution* (R. H. S. Crossman ed., London, 1963; orig. publ. 1867).

Bagwell, S., 'The Road to the Republic', *Australian Financial Review*, 2 April 1993, Weekend Review p.4.

Bailyn, B., *The Ideological Origins of the American Revolution* (Cambridge, Mass., 1967).

Ball, R. E., *The Crown, the Sages and Supreme Morality* (London, 1983).

Barker, G., 'Why Monarchists' Claims for Australia Lack Force', *Age*, 13 July 1991, p.11.

Barwick, G., *The Monarchy in an Independent Australia* (Sir Robert Menzies Lecture Trust, Monash University, 1982).

Bean, C., 'Politics and the Public: Mass Attitudes Towards the Australian Political System', in J. Kelley and C. Bean (eds.), *Australian Attitudes: Social and Political Analyses from the National Social Science Survey* (Sydney, 1988), 45.

Bean, C., 'Public Attitudes on the Monarchy — Republic Issue' (1993) 28 *Australian Journal of Political Science* 190.

Bean, C., 'Should Australia Become a Republic?' (1991) 2 *National Social Science Survey Report*, No.6, 20.

Beaumont, J., *Where to Now? Australia's Identity in the Nineties* (Sydney, 1993).

Blainey, G., 'Australia: A Bird's Eye View' (1985) 114 *Daedalus*, No. l, l.

Blainey, G. and Turnbull, M., 'The Great Republican Debate: Blainey v. Turnbull', *Age*, 25 June 1993, p.13.

Boehringer, K., 'Against Clayton's Republicanism' (1991) 16 *Legal Service Bulletin* 276.

Booker, M., *A Republic of Australia. What Would It Mean?* (Sydney, 1992).

Booker, M., 'Time to Discard Imperial Trappings of the Past', *Canberra Times*, 29 October 1992, p.11.

Bradley, G., 'The Constitution Needs an Overhaul' (1993) 28 *Australian Lawyer*, No.7, 16.

Bradley, G., 'Let's Throw Out the Constitution and Start Again', *Australian*, 7 July 1993, p.13.

Brunt, R., 'The Changing Face of Royalty' (1984) 28 *Marxism Today*, No. 7, 7.

Buckley, B., *Dawning of a Republic* (Sydney, 1979).

Bushman, R. L., *King and People in Provincial Massachusetts* (Chapel Hill, 1985).

Butler, D., "Republic Issue Lacks Passion', *Canberra Times*, 23 September 1993, p.13.

Canadian Bar Association, Committee on the Constitution, *Towards a New Canada* (1978).

Carter, D. and Hudson, W., 'Republicans Must Realise a President is Only the Start', *Australian*, 28 July 1993, p.18.

Carter, J., 'Republic Debate Puts Spotlight on Constitution' (1993) *Parliamentary Patter*, No.17, 6.

Carter, J., 'What Kind of Republic?' (1993) *Parliamentary Patter*, No.18, 6.

Caton, H., 'Farewell to Republics and Monarchies' (1992) 7 *Legislative Studies*, No.1, 39.

Clark, J., 'Altered States of Being Down Under', *Times* (London), 9 July 1991, p.14.

Cochrane, P., 'The 1990s: Daring Deeds or Mannered Meekness?', *Sydney Morning Herald*, 2 August 1993, p.15.

Cole-Adams, P., 'Monarchy *Will* Go, But Not For a While', *Canberra Times*, 17 September 1993, p.11.

Collins, H., 'Will Keating Be First to Fall in the Republican Revolution?', *Australian*, 13 May 1993, p.11.

Condren, C., 'The Australian Commonwealth, a Republic and Republican Virtue' (1992) 6 *Legislative Studies*, No.2, 31.

Constitutional Centenary Foundation Inc., *Heads of State: A Comparative Perspective. A Discussion Paper* (Melbourne, 1993).

Constitutional Centenary Foundation Inc., *Representing the People: The Role of Parliament in Australian Democracy. A Discussion Paper* (Melbourne, 1993).

Constitutional Commission, *Final Report* (2 vols., Canberra, 1988).

Constitutional Commission, *Report of the Executive Government Advisory Committee* (Canberra, June 1987).

Cowen, Z., 'Australia — Looking Ahead to the Twenty-first Century' (1993) 141 *Royal Society of Arts Journal* 296.

Cowen, Z., 'The Australian Head of State: A Legal Conundrum' (1992) 36 *Quadrant*, No.4, 63.

Cowen, Z., 'From Monarchy to Republic?' (1993) 2 *Constitutional Centenary*, No.3, 1.

Cowen, Z., 'The Office of Governor-General' (1985) 114 *Daedalus*. No.1, 127. (This issue was also published as a book: *Australia: The Daedalus Symposium* (S. R. Graubard ed., Sydney, 1985).)

Cowen, Z., *The Virginia Lectures* (University of Virginia, March-April 1983) (Sir Robert Menzies Memorial Trust, Canberra, 1984).

Craven, G., 'The Constitutional Minefield of Australian Republicanism', *Policy*, Spring 1992, 33.

Cristaudo, W., 'Republic of Australia? The Political Philosophy of Republicanism' (1993) 69 *Current Affairs Bull.*, No.11, 4.

Cunneen, C., *King's Men, Australia's Governors-General from Hopetoun to Isaacs* (Sydney, 1983).

Dawson, D., 'The Constitution — Major Overhaul or Simple Tune-up?' (1984) 14 *M.U.L.R.* 353.

Derriman, P., 'Australia a Republic by the Year 2089?', *Sydney Morning Herald*, 13 January 1989, p.9.

Derriman, P., 'Royalty: the Equal Opportunity Argument', *Sydney Morning Herald*, 19 November 1992, p.14.

Derriman, P., 'Why the Queen Can Marry Hindu, Jew or Jane, But Never a Papist', *Sydney Morning Herald*, 9 September 1988, p.17.

Devine, F., 'Model Ways of Yanking Free of the Past ...', *Australian*, 7 October 1991, p.11.

Devine, F., 'Never Mind the Olympics, the Republic Can't Be Rushed', *Australian*, 11 October 1993, p.11.

Doyle, T., 'The Conservative Mythology of Monarchy: Impacts Upon Australian Republicanism' (1993) 28 *Australian Journal of Political Science* 121.

Dunstan, K., *Knockers* (Melbourne, 1972).

Dutton, G. (ed.), *Australia and the Monarchy* (Melbourne, 1966).

Dutton, G. (ed.), *Republican Australia?* (Melbourne, 1977).

Elazar, D. J. (ed.), *Republicanism, Representation, and Consent: Views of the Founding Era* (New Brunswick, N. J., 1979). (Also published as 9 *Publius* No.2.)

Evans, G., 'God Save the Queen? — Australia as a Republic' (unpublished address to Counterpoint Forum, Murdoch University, 29 September 1982).

Evans, H., 'The Agenda of the True Republicans', in Walker, G. de Q., *et al.*, *Restoring the True Republic, infra*, 3.

Evans, H., 'Crowning Irony: Reformers Wear Monarchist Hat', *Australian*, 17 May 1993, p.9.

Evans, H., 'A Note on the Meaning of "Republic"' (1992) 6 *Legislative Studies*, No.2, 21.

Evans, H., 'Republicanism and the Australian Constitution' (1993) 12 *House Magazine*, No.2.

Evans, H., 'Republicanism, Continued: A Brief Rejoinder to Graham Maddox' (1993) 7 *Legislative Studies*, No.2, 65.

Everdell, W. R., *The End of Kings: A History of Republics and Republicans* (New York, 1983).

Fahey, J., 'A Train of Thought Labor Mustn't Hijack', *Weekend Australian*, 3–4 April 1993, p.17.

The Federalist (J. E. Cooke ed., Middletown, Conn., 1961; orig. publ. 1787–88).

Field, P.A., *Union Under the Crown: The Legal Possibilities of an Australian Republic* (unpublished LL.B. (Hons.) thesis, Monash University, September 1984).

Forell, C., 'Between Our Gracious Queen and a Republic', *Age*, 19 February 1992, p.13.

Forell, C., 'A Republic Needs a Whole New System', *Age*, 10 July 1991, p.13.

Fraser, A.W., *The Spirit of the Laws: Republicanism and the Unfinished Project of Modernity* (Toronto, 1990).

Fraser, M., 'Complex Task Goes to Heart of Government', *Weekend Australian*, 9–10 October 1993, p.33.

Friedrich, C. J. and R. H. Guttman, 'The Federal Executive', in *Studies in Federalism* (R. R. Bowie and C. J. Friedrich eds, Boston, 1954), 63.

Fullilove, M., 'We Must Re-imagine and Re-dream Australia' (1992) *Australian Republican Movement Newsletter*, No.3, 2.

Galligan, B., 'Regularising the Australian Republic' (1993) 28 *Australian Journal of Political Science* 56.

Geise, J. P., 'Republican Ideals and Contemporary Realities' (1984) 46 *Rev. of Politics* 23.

Gibbs, H., 'Changes Would Bring Country No Material Benefit', *Weekend Australian*, 9–10 October 1993, p.34.

Gibbs, H., 'Remove the Queen, and the Whole Structure Could Fall', *Australian*, 7 June 1993, p.11.

Gibbs, H., 'Republic: Difficult and Dangerous', *Canberra Times*, 28 June 1993, p.11.

Gibbs, H., *The States and a Republic* (unpublished opinion, endorsed by the Legal Committee of Australians for Constitutional Monarchy, undated, released 3 November 1993).

Goot, M., 'Monarchy or Republic? An Analysis of the Questions and Answers in Surveys of Australian Public Opinion, 1953–1986', in Constitutional Commission, *Report of the Executive Government Advisory Committee* (Canberra, June 1987), 85.

Grant, B., *The Australian Dilemma* (Sydney, 1983).

Grassby, A.J., *The Australian Republic* (Sydney, 1993).

Greiner, N., 'A New Era in Australian Politics: A Win in 96, Stupid', *Weekend Australian*, 20–21 March 1993, p.16.

Lord Hailsham of St Marylebone, Foreword, in J. Kerr, *Matters for Judgment* (London, 1979).

Harrison, F., 'The Monarchy' (1872) 11 *Fortnightly Review* (N.S.) 613.

Hasluck, P., *The Office of Governor-General* (Melbourne, 1979).

Hawke, R. J. L., *The Resolution of Conflict* (1979 Boyer Lectures, Sydney, 1979).

Headon, D., 'God's Aristocracy: Daniel Henry Deniehy's Vision of a Great Australian Republic' (1993) 28 *Australian Journal of Political Science* 136.

Headon, D., Warden, J. and Gammage, W., *Crown or Country: Essays on the Australian Republic* (Sydney, 1994).

Henderson, G., 'The Role of Religion in a Republic', *Age*, 21 September 1993, p.14. (Also in *Sydney Morning Herald*, 21 September 1993, p.11.)

Hermens, F. A., *The Representative Republic* (Notre Dame, Ind., 1958).

Hill, R., 'Breaking Up is Hard to Do', *Bulletin* (Sydney), 20 April 1993, p.22.

Hirst, J., 'Australian History and European Civilisation' (1993) 37 *Quadrant*, No.5, 28.

Hirst, J., 'The Conservative Case for an Australian Republic' (1991) 35 *Quadrant*, No.9, 9.

Hirst, J., 'Must the Baby Go Out With the Bathwater?', *Sydney Morning Herald*, 23 April 1992, p.15.

Hirst, J., *A Republican Manifesto* (Melbourne, 1994).

Hirst, J., 'The Time Has Come to Manage On Our Own', *Weekend Australian*, 9–10 October 1993, p.34.

Hirst, J., 'Wanted: One Republican Role Model', *Australian*, 28 December 1992, p.9.

Horne, D. (et al.), *The Coming Republic* (Sydney, 1992).

Horne, D., *Death of the Lucky Country* (Ringwood, Vic., 1976).

Horne, D., *His Excellency's Pleasure* (Melbourne, 1977).

Horne, D., 'The One-Third Monarchy' (1993) 37 *Quadrant*, Nos.7–8, 32.

Horne, D., 'Out of Empire, Into What?', *Sydney Morning Herald*, 8 July 1993, p.11

Horne, D., *Power from the People. A New Australian Constitution?* (Victorian Fabian Society Pamphlet No. 32, October 1977).

Horne, D., 'What Kind of Head of State?' in *Change the Rules! Towards a Democratic Constitution* (S. Encel, D. Horne and E. Thompson eds, Ringwood, Vic., 1977), 66.

Howard, C., *The Constitution, Power and Politics* (Melbourne, 1980).

Howard, C., 'Minimal Approach to Republicanism', *Australian Financial Review*, 13 May 1993, p.19.

Howard, C., 'Republic Talk Lacks Design', *Australian Financial Review*, 7 April 1993, p.13.

Howard, J., 'Howard Defends the Crown', *Australian Business Monthly*, July 1993, p.82.

Howard, J., 'Some Arguments Against An Australian Republic' (unpublished paper, September 1991).

Hudson, W., 'An Australian Federal Republic?' (1992) 64 *A.Q.* 229.

Hudson, W. and Carter, D. (eds.), *The Republicanism Debate* (Sydney, 1993).

Hunt, N., 'Legal and Constitutional Implications of Australia Becoming a Republic' (unpublished LL.B. thesis, University of New South Wales, July 1978).

Hull, C., 'The Path to a Republic is Frought with Pitfalls', *Canberra Times*, 1 April 1993, p.9.

Hull, C., 'The Poser of Where Power Will Reside', *Canberra Times*, 4 May 1993, p.9.

Ireland, I., *Monarchy or Republic? A Comparative Outline of Major Presidential Powers* (Parliamentary Research Service, Canberra, Background Paper No.18, 1993).

Jarvis, W. C., *The Republican; or, A Series of Essays on the Principles and Policy of Free States* (Pittsfield. Mass., 1820, repr. New York, 1974).

Kakathas, C., 'Whether the Australian Government Inclines More to Monarchy, or to a Republic' (1992) 6 *Legislative Studies*, No.2, 43.

Kavanagh, P., 'A Republican Meeting at Manly-by-the-Sea' (1993) 18 *Alternative Law Journal* 216.

Kelly, P., 'The Case for the Republic' (1993) 37 *Quadrant*, No.11, 10.

Kemp, R., 'Australia's Crowning Glory', *Australian*, 7 October 1991, p.11.

Kemp, R., 'Australia's Future: Constitutional Monarchy or Constitutional Chaos' (unpublished paper, 1991).

Kemp, R., 'The Case Against [a Republic]', *Australian*, 1 April 1992, Constitution Special p.2.

Keneally, T., *Our Republic* (Melbourne, 1993).

Kirby, M., 'A Defence of the Constitutional Monarchy' (1993) 37 *Quadrant*, No.9, 30. (Also in Hudson, W. and Carter, D. (eds.), *supra*, 61; (1993) *Reform*, No.65, 26; [1993] *New Zealand Law Journal* 201.)

Kirby, M., 'Plenty of room for constitutional reform', *Weekend Australian Magazine*, 2–3 July 1983, p. 14.

Knox, B.A., 'Fantasies and Furphies: The Australian Republican Agenda', in *Upholding the Australian Constitution: Proceedings of the Inaugural Conference of the Samuel Griffith Society* (Melbourne, 1992), 209.

Lake, M., 'Sexing the Republic: What Do Women Want?', *Age*, 2 December 1993, p.13.

Lang, J. D., *The Coming Event! or Freedom and Independence for the Seven United Provinces of Australia* (Sydney, 1870).

Lang, J. D., *Freedom and Independence for the Golden Lands of Australia* (London, 1852).

Lawson, S. and Maddox, G., 'Introduction' (1993) 28 *Australian Journal of Political Science* 4.

Leaver, R., 'Biting the Dust: The Imperial Conventions Within Republican Pretences' (1993) 28 *Australian Journal of Political Science* 146.

Lee, H.P., 'Minimal Change Best', *Herald Sun* (Melbourne), 7 May 1993, p.54.

Lindell, G.J., 'The Arrangements for Self-government for the Australian Capital Territory: A Partial Road to Republicanism in the Seat of Government?' (1992) 3 *Public Law Review* 5.

Lumb, R.D., 'The Australian States and Australia's Head of State System' (unpublished paper presented at Australians for Constitutional Monarchy Seminar, Sydney, 4 June 1993).

MacDonagh, M., *The English King* (London, 1929, repr. Port Washington, N.Y., 1971).

Mabbett, I., 'Not Plato's' (1993) 37 *Quadrant*, Nos. 7–8, 28.

Mackay, H., 'Minimalists Could Lose Out', *Australian Financial Review*, 11 May 1993, p.15.

Maddox, G., 'The Origins of Republicanism' (1992) 7 *Legislative Studies*, No.1, 35.

Maddox, G., 'Republic or Democracy?' (1993) 28 *Australian Journal of Political Science* 9.

Mandle, B., 'Tinkering Will Not a Republic Make', *Canberra Times*, 10 October 1993, p.9.

Manne, R., 'Why I am Not a Republican', *Age,* 4 May 1993, p.15.

Mansfield, B., 'The Background to Radical Republicanism in New South Wales in the Eighteen-Eighties' (1953) 5 *Hist. Stud.* 338.

Markwell, D.J., *The Crown and Australia* (Trevor Reese Memorial Lecture, University of London Australian Studies Centre, 1987).

Marsh, Y., *Monarchy or Republic? Reserve Powers of the Head of State. The Gordian Knot* (Parliamentary Research Service, Canberra, Background Paper No.17, 1993).

Martin, K., *Britain in the Sixties: The Crown and the Establishment* (London, 1962).

Mathie, L., *Republican Australia: A Bibliography* (Lionel Murphy Library, Attorney-General's Department, Canberra, 1993).

Mautner, T., 'Some Thoughts on Our Monarchy' (1992) 6 *Legislative Studies*, No.2, 39.

McGarvie, R.E., 'Governorship in Australia Today' (unpublished Address to Senior Executive Chapter Luncheon of the Australian Institute of Management, Melbourne, 8 September 1993).

McGuinness, P.P., 'Constitutionally, a Republic is Just the Easy Way Out', *Australian*, 3 March 1992, p.11.

McGuinness, P.P., 'Polity Demands a Political President', *Australian*, 7 October 1993, p.9.

McGuinness, P.P., 'Power and Glory Real Issues in Republic', *Australian,* 6 October 1993, p.13.

McGuinness, P.P., 'President Needs Proper Powers', *Australian*, 14 May 1993, p.13.

McGuinness, P.P., 'Putting the Republic to the Vote', *Australian*, 21 July 1993, p.9.

McGuinness, P.P., 'States in Constitutional Confusion', *Australian*, 31 July 1991, p.11.

McKenna, M., 'Brave New World of You's and Me's', *Sydney Morning Herald,* 16 September 1993, p.15.

McKenna, M., '1788 to 1993: Tracking the Australian Republic' (1993) *Australian Republican Movement Newsletter*, No.4, 3.

McMillan, J., G. Evans, and H. Storey, *Australia's Constitution: Time for Change?* (Sydney, 1983).

McMullan, B., 'It's Time for Us to Choose our Head of State', *Canberra Times*, 20 December 1992, p.9.

Milne, G., 'The Battle Begins', *Weekend Australian*, 1–2 May 1993, p.15.

Milne, G., 'Republicanism: Will it Split the Liberals?', *Weekend Australian*, 3–4 April 1993, p.17.

Murray-Brown, J. (ed.), *The Monarchy and Its Future* (London, 1969).

Nwabueze B. O., *Presidentialism in Commonwealth Africa* (London, 1974).

O'Brien, P., 'From Westminster Man to Democratic Man' (1993) 37 *Quadrant*, Nos.7–8, 38.

O'Brien, P., 'The Importance of "The Public Thing"', *Time* (Australia), 26 April 1993, p.64.

O'Brien, P., 'We the People', *Independent Monthly*, June 1993, 20.

O'Connell, D. P., 'Canada, Australia, Constitutional Reform and the Crown' (1979) 60 *The Parliamentarian* 5.

O'Farrell, E., 'Democracy's Crowning Achievement', *Mercury* (Hobart), 9 March 1993, p.20.

Omar, I., 'Inaugurating an Australian Republic Through Constitutional Change' (unpublished paper presented to Australasian Law Teachers' Association Conference, Government Law Interest Group, 1993).

Paine, T., *Common Sense* (I. Kramnick ed., Harmondsworth, 1976; orig. publ. 1776).

Paine, T., *Rights of Man* (H. Collins ed., Harmondsworth, 1969; orig. publ. 1791).

Papua New Guinea, General Constitutional Commission, *Final Report* (Port Moresby, 1983).

Parris, M., 'This Royal Fiction', *Times* (London), 13 February 1993, p.14.

Paul, J.B., 'An Australian Republic? But Why?' (1991) 35 *Quadrant*, No.9, 11.

Paul, J., 'The Head of State in Australia', in *Upholding the Australian Constitution: Proceedings of the Inaugural Conference of the Samuel Griffith Society* (Melbourne, 1992), 177.

Paul, J., 'Republicans Don't Realise What a State They're In', *Australian*, 28 June 1991, p.13.

Peterson, P., 'The Meaning of Republicanism in *The Federalist*' (1979) 9 *Publius*, No. 2, 43.

Pettit, P., 'The Ideal of the Republic' (1993) 3 *Eureka Street*, No.7, 15.

Pettit, P., 'Liberalism and Republicanism' (1993) 28 *Australian Journal of Political Science* 162.

Pettit, P., 'Republican Themes' (1992) 6 *Legislative Studies*, No.2, 29.

Pincus, C.W., *An Australian Republic* (unpublished paper presented at Constitutional Centenary Conference, Sydney, 1991).

Pincus, C.W., 'An Australian Republic? Legal Aspects' (unpublished paper presented at Labor Lawyers National Conference, Brisbane, 22 September 1990).

Pocock, J. G. A., *The Machiavellian Moment: Florentine Political Thought and the Atlantic Republican Tradition* (Princeton, 1975).

Power, J., 'Building the Republic' (1993) 72 *Australian Municipal Journal*, No.1071, 3.

Preston, Y., 'Royalty — still the "best of British"', *Sydney Morning Herald*, 11 July 1985, p.11.

Pryles, M., 'Nuts and Bolts for a Republic', *Time* (Australia), 3 May 1993, p.72.

Pryles, M., 'The Options Are Out; Let the People Decide', *Age*, 6 October 1993, p.15.

Pryles, M., 'Uniformity Essential to Republic', *Age*, 7 May 1993, p.13.

The Queen (Harmondsworth, 1977).

Reid, G. S., 'Executive-parliamentary relationships', in *Small is Beautiful:*

Parliament in the Northern Territory (Australasian Study of Parliament Group and North Australia Research Unit, Australian National University, Canberra, 1981, Working Paper No. 3), 5.

Republic Advisory Committee, *An Australian Republic: The Options* (2 vols., Canberra, 1993).

Republic Advisory Committee, *An Australian Republic: The Options — An Overview* (Canberra, 1993).

Republic Advisory Committee, *Issues Paper* (Canberra, May 1993).

'Republicanism and the States' (1993) 6 *Intergovernmental News*, No.1, 1.

Reynolds, H., 'Signs of a Thaw in the Monarchical Ice Age?', *Australian Society*, November 1990, p.22.

Robbins, C., 'Introduction', in *Two English Republican Tracts* (C. Robbins ed., Cambridge, 1969).

Ryan, S., 'Trinidad and Tobago: The Transition from Monarchy to Republic' (1977) 58 *The Parliamentarian* 153.

Saunders, C., 'An Australian Republic: Minimalist or Otherwise' (1993) 3 *Australian Corporate Lawyer*, No.2, 26.

Saunders, C., 'Can Less Be More for Constitutional Reform?', *Australian*, 30 April 1993, p.19.

Saunders, C., 'Constitutional Considerations for a Republic', *Age*, 29 March 1993, p.13.

Sawer, G., 'Constitutional Problems in Achieving a Republic', *Canberra Times*, 17 September 1991, p.9.

Sawer, G., *Federation Under Strain* (Melbourne, 1977).

Sexton, M., 'Hurdles on the Road to a Republic', *Sydney Morning Herald*, 17 August 1993, p.13.

Sexton, M., 'Republican Debate Needs the Shrouds of Mythology Stripped Away', *Sydney Morning Herald*, 3 May 1993, p.11.

Shalhope, R. E., 'Toward a Republican Synthesis: The Emergence of an Understanding of Republicanism in American Historiography' (1972) 29 *William & Mary Quarterly* (3rd ser.) 49.

Sharman, C., 'Executive Privileges' (1992) 6 *Legislative Studies*, No.2, 27.

Sheridan, G., 'No Knighthoods, No Curtsies, Just Bowing to Reality', *Australian*, 4 March 1992, p.9.

Sheridan, G., 'Our Inevitable Republic', *Weekend Australian*, 14–15 March 1992, p.18.

Shoemaker, R. W., '"Democracy" and "Republic" as Understood in Late Eighteenth Century America' (1966) 41 *American Speech* 83.

Smith, D.I., 'A Republic — Who Needs It?' (1992) 6 *Legislative Studies*, No.2, 35.

Smith, D., 'Some Thoughts on the Monarchy/Republic Debate', in *Upholding the Australian Constitution: Proceedings of the Inaugural Conference of the Samuel Griffith Society* (Melbourne, 1992), 159.

Smith, D., 'A Toast to Australia' (1991) 35 *Quadrant*, No.5, 11.

Snedden, B. M., 'Contemporary Westminster', in *Liberals Face the Future* (G. Brandis, T. Harley and D. Markwell eds, Melbourne, 1984), 213.

Solomon, D., *Elect the Governor-General!* (Melbourne, 1976).

Souter, G., *Lion and Kangaroo: The Initiation of Australia* (Sydney, 2d ed. 1992).

Stephens, T., 'Spirit of Kerr Hovers over Republic Debate', *Sydney Morning Herald*, 22 July 1993, p.15.

Stephenson, M.A. and Turner, C. (eds), *Australia — Republic or Monarchy* (Brisbane, 1994).

Stickney, A., *A True Republic* (New York, 1879).

Tanner, L., ' "The People First" Should Be the Rallying Cry', *Canberra Times*, 6 July 1993, p.9.

Turnbull, M., 'The Case For [a Republic]', *Australian*, 1 April 1992, Constitution Special, p.2.

Turnbull, M., 'A Day in the Life of an Australian President' (1993) 1 *Evatt Papers*, No.2, 128.

Turnbull, M., 'Off With Her Head' (1993) 3 *Polemic* 164.

Turnbull, M., 'The Queen is British' (1993) 28 *Australian Lawyer*, No.5, 16.

Turnbull, M., 'Real Substance of Constitution is Unwritten', *Australian*, 9 June 1993, p.11.

Turnbull, M., *The Reluctant Republic* (Melbourne, 1993).

Turnbull, M., 'Why We Need the Republic' (National Press Club Speech) (1992) 1 *Verbatim Report* 103.

Twomey, A., *Methods of Choosing a Head of State* (Parliamentary Research Service, Canberra, Background Paper No.12, 1993).

Twomey, A., *Monarchy or Republic? A Collection of Arguments For and Against* (Parliamentary Research Service, Canberra, Background Paper No.26, 1993).

Twomey, A., *Monarchy or Republic? The Constitutional Options of the States* (Parliamentary Research Service, Canberra, Background Paper No.7, 1993).

Uhr, J., 'Instituting Republicanism: Parliamentary Vices, Republican Virtues?' (1993) 28 *Australian Journal of Political Science* 27.

Usher, R., 'Goodbye to All That', *Time* (Australia), 12 April 1993, p.26.

Waddy, L., 'Inevitable? Not At All' (1993) 28 *Australian Lawyer*, No.5, 16.

Waddy, L., 'Time to Put the Genie Back in the Bottle', *Canberra Times*, 6 October 1993, p.15.

Walker, G. de Q., Ratnapala, S. and Kasper, W., *Restoring the True Republic* (Sydney, 1993).

Walsh, C. M., *The Political Science of John Adams* (New York, 1915, repr. Freeport, N.Y., 1969).

Warden, J., 'The Fettered Republic: The Anglo-American Commonwealth and the Traditions of Australian Political Thought' (1993) 28 *Australian Journal of Political Science* 83.

Warhurst, J., 'The Future of Australia's Political Relationship to Britain' (1986) 24 *Journal of Commonwealth and Comparative Politics* 35.

Warhurst, J., 'Nationalism and Republicanism in Australia: The Evolution of Institutions, Citizenship and Symbols' (1993) 28 *Australian Journal of Political Science* 100.

Warhurst, J., 'Political Studies and the Monarchy' (1988) 23 *Politics* 1.

Warhurst, J., 'Prospects for a Republic in 2001: Reflections on 1988' (1993) 6 *Policy Organisation and Society* 66.

Watson, G., 'An Age of Monarchs?' (1993) 37 *Quadrant*, Nos.7–8, 35.

Whyte, J.D., 'The Australian Republican Movement and Its Implications for Canada' (1993) 4 *Constitutional Forum* 88.

Winterton, G., 'An Australian Republic' (1988) 16 *M.U.L.R.* 467.

Winterton, G., 'Binding a Republic and its Constitution', *Age*, 1 May 1993, p.15 (and Letter, *Age*, 12 May 1993, p.12).

Winterton, G., 'Change Must be Slow, Gradual', *Weekend Australian*, 9–10 October 1993, p.32.

Winterton, G., 'Choosing a President', *Herald-Sun* (Melbourne), 7 April 1992, p.13.

Winterton, G., 'A Constitution For An Australian Republic', *Independent Monthly*, March 1992, reprinted *Independent Monthly*, June 1993.

Winterton, G., 'The Constitutional Implications of a Republic', in Stephenson, M.A. and Turner, C., *supra.*

Winterton, G., 'The Evolution of a Separate Australian Crown" (1993) 19 *Monash University Law Review* 1.

Winterton, G., 'Formula For a Presidency', *Independent Monthly*, March 1992, 18.

Winterton, G., 'How to Create the Republic of Australia', *Australian*, 26 February 1993, p.13.

Winterton, G., 'Modern Republicanism' (1992) 6 *Legislative Studies*, No.2, 24.

Winterton, G., *Monarchy to Republic: Australian Republican Government* (Melbourne, 1986).

Winterton, G., 'No Hereditary Barriers to Coming of Age in the Pacific', *Australian*, 23 September 1991, p.11.

Winterton, G., 'On the Road to the Republic' (1993) 1 *Evatt Papers,* No.2, 45.

Winterton, G., *Parliament, the Executive and the Governor-General* (Melbourne, 1983).

Winterton, G., 'President — and a Question of Power', *Herald-Sun* (Melbourne), 8 April 1992, p.12.

Winterton, G., 'Presidential Power in Republican Australia' (1993) 28 *Australian Journal of Political Science* 40.

Winterton, G., 'Removing the Crown with Light Fingers', *Australian*, 11 August 1993, p.9.

Winterton, G., 'Reserve Powers in an Australian Republic' (1993) 12 *University of Tasmania Law Review* 249.

Winterton, G.(ed.), *We, the People: Australian Republican Government* (Sydney, 1994).

Wood, G. S., *The Creation of the American Republic, 1776–1787* (Chapel Hill, 1969).

Ziegler, P., *Crown and People* (London, 1978).

Zifcak, S. M., 'A Modest Proposal for a Democratic Republic' (1993) 67 *Law Institute Journal* 1159.

Index

A
Republican
MANIFESTO

John Hirst

'Australia was born in chains and is not yet fully free. We are an old dependency of the British Crown which has not stirred itself to claim complete independence. But surely, you will say, we are a sovereign independent State? Not quite. We depend on Britain to provide us with our head of state. The Queen may be called the Queen of Australia, but she is not Made in Australia. If for any reason there ceased to be a monarch in Britain, our Constitution would seize up. Australia does not have a self-sufficient Constitution.'

In this timely and cogent republican manifesto — which is partly a response to Alan Atkinson's *A Muddle-headed Republic* — John Hirst sets out his reasons for believing that until Australia becomes a republic, until it provides its own head of state rather than importing one, its constitutional arrangements will be inadequate and its sense of nationhood imperfect.

John Hirst is Reader in History at La Trobe University. He is the author of several books, including *Convict Society and Its Enemies* and *The Strange Birth of Colonial Democracy*. He was a member of the Prime Minister's Republic Advisory Committee.

0 19 553649 5   Paperback

THE

Muddle-Headed

REPUBLIC

Alan Atkinson

Is the Australian Republic really as inevitable as Paul Keating would have us believe? Has monarchy been rejected as foreign and outmoded by the majority of Australians? During two years of intense debate support for the republic has swung backwards and forwards. Australians have begun to make up their minds as to where they stand, and it is clear that they are thinking, not just about the promised virtues of the republic, but also about the traditional virtues of the status quo.

Succinct and provocative, *The Muddle-Headed Republic* is the most eloquent defence of the monarchy to be published in this country. Written by one of our leading historians, it shows what the monarchy meant in the past for Australians, and what it means still. It also shows where the new vision of a republic has come from. Alan Atkinson argues that the vision is muddle-headed, full of tension and contradictions.

0 19 553638 X   Paperback